The BORZOI SERIES in Eighteenth-Century Literature

POLITICAL WRITERS OF EIGHTEENTH-
CENTURY ENGLAND,
edited by
Jeffrey Hart,
COLUMBIA UNIVERSITY

ENGLISH POETRY OF THE MID AND LATE
EIGHTEENTH CENTURY,
edited by
Ricardo Quintana and Alvin Whitley,
BOTH OF THE UNIVERSITY OF WISCONSIN

In Preparation
ENGLISH POETRY OF THE RESTORATION AND
EARLY EIGHTEENTH CENTURY,
edited by
H. T. Swedenberg, Jr.,
UNIVERSITY OF CALIFORNIA AT LOS ANGELES

LITERARY CRITICISM IN ENGLAND, 1660-1800.
edited by
Gerald Webster Chapman,
UNIVERSITY OF DENVER

ENGLISH POETRY
*of the Mid and Late
Eighteenth Century*

ENGLISH POETRY

OF THE *Mid* AND *Late*

Eighteenth Century

AN HISTORICAL ANTHOLOGY

Edited by
RICARDO QUINTANA
&
ALVIN WHITLEY

NEW YORK *Alfred A. Knopf* 1967

L. C. catalog card number: 63-14613

THIS IS A BORZOI BOOK,
PUBLISHED BY ALFRED A. KNOFF, INC.

Copyright © 1963 by Alfred A. Knopf, Inc. All rights reserved. No part of this book may be reproduced, except by a reviewer, who may quote brief passages in a review to be printed in a magazine or newspaper. Manufactured in the United States of America, and distributed by Random House, Inc. Published simultaneously in Toronto, Canada, by Random House of Canada, Limited.

PUBLISHED OCTOBER 1963
SECOND PRINTING, MAY 1967

Preface

We trust that we have taken into account most of the major English and Scottish poets whose creative work was done between 1740 and 1800 and who are generally recognized as taking an important part in eighteenth-century letters. In consideration of length, we have reluctantly omitted the political and literary satirist, Charles Churchill.

Our selections are based on the best available texts, occasionally modernized in respect of typography, spelling, and punctuation, though never at the expense of meter or sense. (The most frequent, and now the most common, editorial alteration has been that of the participial ending *'d* to *ed* or, in the rare instances where the scansion requires it, to *èd*.)

The treatment of the biographical and bibliographical facts of the individual authors varies according to the accessibility of the material. The details of Collins's life and Goldsmith's literary career, for example, are not so readily come by.

The bibliographies are selective, including those books and essays which illuminate an important side of the writer as poet.

Dr. Johnson approved of anthologies, or at least that kind of book "at which . . . a man will often look and be tempted to go on, when he would have been frightened at books of a larger size and of more erudite appearance."

R. Q.
A. W.

Contents

INTRODUCTION   3

    Eighteenth-Century Poetry: Some Historical Considerations

EDWARD YOUNG (1683-1765)   18
    Night I FROM The Complaint, or Night Thoughts   24

ROBERT BLAIR (1699/1700-1746)   36
    FROM The Grave   38

SAMUEL JOHNSON (1709-1784)   42
    London: A Poem   45
    The Vanity of Human Wishes   54

WILLIAM SHENSTONE (1714-1763)   66
    The Schoolmistress   69

THOMAS GRAY (1716-1771)   79
    Ode on a Distant Prospect of Eton College   84
    Sonnet: On the Death of Richard West   88
    Elegy Written in a Country Church-yard   89
    The Progress of Poesy   94
    The Bard   101
    The Fatal Sisters   108

MARK AKENSIDE (1721-1770)   112
    FROM Book I OF The Pleasures of Imagination   115

WILLIAM COLLINS (1721-1759) — 121
- Ode to Pity — 126
- Ode to Fear — 128
- Ode on the Poetical Character — 131
- Ode: Written in the Beginning of the Year 1746 — 134
- Ode to Evening — 135
- An Ode on the Popular Superstitions of the Highlands of Scotland — 138

CHRISTOPHER SMART (1722-1771) — 145
- A Song to David — 148

JOSEPH WARTON (1722-1800) — 167
- The Enthusiast — 172
- Ode to Fancy — 180

OLIVER GOLDSMITH (1730?-1774) — 184
- The Traveller, or A Prospect of Society — 191
- The Deserted Village — 208

WILLIAM COWPER (1731-1800) — 223
- FROM Olney Hymns — 229
  - Walking with God — 229
  - Light Shining out of Darkness — 230
- Book III: The Garden FROM The Task — 231
- On the Receipt of My Mother's Picture Out of Norfolk — 254
- The Castaway — 258

JAMES BEATTIE (1735-1803) — 261
- FROM Book I OF The Minstrel, or The Progress of Genius — 264

JAMES MACPHERSON (1736-1796) — 273
- FROM Carthon — 278

THOMAS CHATTERTON (1752-1770) — 280
- An Excelente Balade of Charitie — 284
- GLOSSARY — 287

GEORGE CRABBE (1754-1832) — 288
FROM *Book I* OF *The Village* — 291
FROM *Part III: Burials* OF *The Parish Register* — 293
Peter Grimes, Letter XXII FROM *The Borough* — 296

WILLIAM BLAKE (1757-1827) — 307
FROM *Songs of Innocence* — 311
    Introduction — 311
    The Lamb — 312
    The Little Black Boy — 312
    The Chimney Sweeper — 313
    Holy Thursday — 314
    The Divine Image — 315
FROM *Songs of Experience* — 317
    Introduction — 317
    Earth's Answer — 318
    Holy Thursday — 319
    The Chimney Sweeper — 319
    The Tiger — 320
    London — 321

ROBERT BURNS (1759-1796) — 322
Address to the Deil — 329
Epistle to John Lapraik — 334
Holy Willie's Prayer — 339
Address to the Unco Guid — 343
Green Grow the Rashes — 345
John Anderson My Jo — 346
Auld Lang Syne — 347
A Man's a Man for A' That — 348
Scots Wha Hae — 350
O, Wert Thou in the Cauld Blast — 352
    GLOSSARY — 353

SELECTED BIBLIOGRAPHIES — 355
INDEX OF AUTHORS
INDEX OF TITLES AND FIRST LINES   } follow page 368

ENGLISH POETRY
of the Mid and Late
Eighteenth Century

Introduction

EIGHTEENTH-CENTURY POETRY: SOME HISTORICAL CONSIDERATIONS

THE PRESENT anthology reflects in a number of ways the conviction that English poetry from 1740 to 1800 constitutes what is properly to be regarded as a definite era. Like all other eras it was of course transitional. Too often in the past, however, the transitional aspect of the mid and late eighteenth century in English letters has received an unfortunately distorting emphasis. Today there are those who see the matter in a somewhat different light, having become aware of the presence, in the art and culture of these five or six decades, of qualities of thought, sensibility, and style that are distinctive. To regard this period merely as a bridge between an earlier neoclassicism and a later romanticism, or to label it as has so often been done the period of pre-romanticism—this is to miss entirely the fact that it possesses an identity of its own and can be approached for what it reveals of its own proper nature. There is more at issue here than might at first appear. If it is of some importance that we understand the age of Collins, Gray, Johnson, Goldsmith, and Crabbe for its own sake, it is equally important that we do so in order to clarify our understanding both of neoclassicism and romanticism as concepts and as styles.

• 2 •

It seems scarcely necessary to point out that the poetry of these years is not the greatest in the language. Nevertheless, our informed judgments regarding it are not so harsh as they once tended to be. Some though not all of this verse is assuredly second-rate, but even when it is undeniably inferior it has been shown to embody in various ways more of the elements of genuine art than was once perceived. Enjoyment of it does, however, lay certain demands on the reader—more demands, perhaps, than the representative verse of most other periods. Because it does not, save in rare instances, rise clear of the idioms—linguistic and otherwise—of its own period, a sympathetic approach requires some historical understanding. Even if the absolute value of poetry is ultimately an aesthetic matter and not an historical one, all art is mediated by its particular time and place in human culture and is interesting for this reason as well.

One of the notable features of the latter half of the eighteenth century is the presence side by side of several different poetic styles. These have certain features in common, all related, however differently, to that manner which had come to be firmly established after the Restoration and which Dryden, Pope, and the earlier Augustans practiced. Johnson's poems conform most closely to this older style, which is also present clearly enough in Goldsmith and Crabbe. Lately we have enhanced our appreciation of this more traditional neoclassical line, running into and through the later eighteenth century, by our ready acknowledgment of Dryden and Pope as poets of a very high order. Johnson the poet has risen immeasurably in our esteem, and *The Vanity of Human Wishes*, somber in theme and working through a magnificently controlled language and imagery, now takes its place among the greatest English poems. Goldsmith never suffered as badly as some others from that nineteenth-century shift of taste which left several generations of readers unable to enjoy much of the poetry written between Milton's time and Wordsworth's, but that was doubtless because Goldsmith's *The Deserted Village* was better known than his *The Traveller* and seemed to speak an emotional language which was assumed to be incompatible with anything neoclassical. Today many would place *The Traveller*, with its brilliant, sharply etched verse "characters" of Italy, Switzerland, France, and England almost as high as *The Deserted Village*. Crabbe, whose manner and matter are so closely linked, has come to have general appeal for modern readers.

Along with this willingness to accede to a poetic art which operates in a recognizably neoclassical manner, there has been a reconsideration of certain of its distinctive stylistic elements, such as its poetic diction, its rhetorical and structural parallelism and antithesis, and its generalizations of concept and statement. Here modern critical reappraisal has pretty well disposed of the older charge that the neoclassical style is a compound of clichés and stereotypes employed almost mechanically. The poets not only knew what they were doing, but they did it with a tough wit that becomes apparent when we realize the effects they secured by playing off their own variants against the long-familiar. All this does not of itself validate this order of verse, but in convincing us of the knowingness of the writers, it prepares us to find in them some degree of imaginative awareness as well.

But our period, more especially the 1740s and 1750s of the century, saw the appearance of another style. Actually the aesthetic school, the Wartons, the later Young, Gray, and Collins, were not in long or deep revolt against the tradition represented by Pope, and it is in reference to that tradition, not to romantic art, that they are best understood. Yet while their poetry represents no revolutionary break with the traditional line, least of all in its use of the eighteenth-century poetic diction, it does spring out of a somewhat different ordering of intentions. We cannot ask from it what the poetry of the Johnsonian kind gives, nor apply to it exactly the same criteria. It has often been repudiated—exceptions being made of Gray's *Elegy* and Collins's *Ode to Evening*—on the grounds that it is basically trivial. While it cannot be said to have undergone the kind of revaluation that has taken place in the case of poetry of the more traditional order, it does stand today in a substantially different light, for we are impressed with the important rôle which aesthetics assumed not only in eighteenth-century philosophy, but in the realm of taste generally and in the approach to all the arts, including literature. The aesthetic movement strongly influenced the poets we associate with this other style. They were striving consciously, theoretically, after certain special effects. We may not always like what they produced, but it engages our interest as any experimental art generally does today.

· 3 ·

Besides the two styles just referred to, there are other modes carrying stylistic peculiarities that can readily be distinguished, the number depending upon how fine we choose to make our distinctions. There is a large group of blank-verse poems showing the direct influence of *Paradise Lost*; there are poems specializing in the emotional and moral effects of death and graveyards; there are imitations of Milton's octosyllabic verses; there are odes, Horatian and Pindaric, allegorical and descriptive; there are poems variously descriptive of nature and of places—the listing could be extended. In the face of such diversity, how can we say that the age exhibits in its poetry anything other than a plurality of intentions and resulting effects? To find the common element, it is necessary to bear in mind the broad context within which eighteenth-century poetry took place, the context of presuppositions and stated theories concerning the nature and function of the poetic art. The theory of imitation, central in the entire European tradition from the time of Greece and Rome onwards into the eighteenth century, conceived a very definite sort of relationship between poet and reader. The poet was always in touch with the reader through the created poem. The poem could be thought of in different ways: (1), as something complete in itself, to be admired for its own perfection; (2), as an achievement of style; or (3), as a *communiqué* bearing some kind of message, usually moral or philosophic. If one never altogether lost sight of the poem as a finished work of art, it was the stylistic and moralistic aspects that took on major importance. The poet combined in himself genius, inspiration, and extraordinary skill. These attributes were thought of as realizing themselves as they worked through the poem upon the reader. The poet's concern was with normal, typical, human experience, even when it was self-experience. He and his reader inhabited the same world, shared the same problems, were emotionally moved in the same way. It was our common humanity that was being held up before us—imitated—in the mirror of art. Our enjoyment of this representation and our profit from it went hand in hand, "pleasure" and "instruction," poetry's official *raison d'être*, presenting no dichotomy.

The rhetorical element in this poetic of imitation has sometimes been overlooked. The poet, like the orator, commanded the means of moving his audience. It is simply not true that neoclassicism as found in English poetry precluded all emotionalism. The poet was the master of our emotions. Observe how purposefully Dryden plays upon his readers' feelings in a poem like *Absalom and Achitophel*, how Pope arouses hatred and contempt in the *Satires* and engages sympathy in *The Epistle to Dr. Arbuthnot*. When we find emotionalism later on in eighteenth-century poetry, as in Young's *The Complaint, or Night Thoughts*, let us not put it down as a matter of course to the spirit of a new romanticism in revolt against an astringent neoclassic art. Such emotionalism is more closely related to the rhetorical element implicit in the theory of imitation than to anything revolutionary in spirit.

A somewhat different kind of emotionalism was also present in the traditional theory and literary practice, an emotionalism less obviously rhetorical, arising out of our natural sympathy with human endeavors and tribulations. English criticism was wont to make much of the moving qualities of tragedy and linked Shakespeare and Otway as masters of pathos. Pope's *Elegy to the Memory of An Unfortunate Lady* employs a non-dramatic version of pathos. Eighteenth-century drama developed, it is true, a most unpleasant form of emotionalism which came to be labelled sentimentalism and which we rightly contemn as did Goldsmith and others of his time for its exploitation in stereotyped situations of shallow, insincere feeling. Yet the repertoire of plays will be found to include a great many which are not sentimental in this restricted sense but which are nevertheless highly emotional in their representation of men's common experience. Everywhere in the century we find, in fact, a background of accepted emotionalism of this humanistic sort. Johnson's *Vanity of Human Wishes* surely implies it; Cowper's *Task* preaches it; Goldsmith's distrust of the artificial in life and letters, his insistence upon what he called the natural stem from it; the effectiveness of Crabbe's realism and irony depends upon it, however restrained it is.

For these varieties of emotionalism we look chiefly to the poetry associated with the traditional line, that is, the poetry most closely answering to the time-honored principles of imitation. The poetry of the aesthetic school implies a variant theory. Hobbes and Locke —and Addison in his critical rôle—are usually regarded as the fathers of English aesthetic theory, the development of which is such an important episode in the course of the eighteenth century. The basic ideas which eventually influenced the point of view of certain poets and gave their work a different slant rested upon a simple form of empiricism. The individual was seen as responding to the messages conveyed to him by his senses from the outside world; the artist embodied this sense data in the imagery of the work of art; the reader of the poem or the viewer of the painting or sculpture experienced the work sensationalistically as he would any other object outside himself.

This kind of psychologizing was taken up with avidity, not only because it was easy but because it made a direct and strong appeal to a large and growing group. With increasing wealth, leisure, and refinement, men were turning to the arts with new enthusiasm and occupying themselves earnestly with matters of what now came to be called "taste." In fact, the Age of Taste may be the most appropriate name for the eighteenth century in England. How did one judge a work of art? How, to go back to first things, did a work of art produce its effect, and what spectrum of effects was revealed by a closer examination of our responses?

The theory of poetry associated with such interests shows a difference but—and this is the significant fact—it marks no serious break with the tenets of neoclassicism. As the effect of the poem upon the reader, upon the man of taste, assumed a new and enhanced significance in the light of popular psychologizing, the poet was seen as more of an experimental artificer, the poem more as an object both of aesthetic appreciation and analysis, and the strictly moralistic importance of the *communiqué* diminished as the significance of its emotional effect was stressed. This emphasis on effect is the outstanding characteristic of the aesthetic school flourishing in the middle decades: how the poet can produce effects with his verbal images, how the reader responds to them.

The English romantics inherited something of the empirical psychology of the century, along with something of the contrived aestheticism of Collins and those we associate with him and, by virtue of this fact, are in some ways to be regarded as prolongers of the eighteenth century. The writers we are concerned with here did not significantly anticipate romanticism, which lay not in any readjustment of the doctrine of imitation, but rather in a totally different set of conceptions. Only Blake—though the eighteenth-century accent is still strong in him—rejected the poetic theories which had long served. In doing so he moved into a different universe where reality, experience, and art all took on a new, strange meaning. Blake takes us from a poetry of common sense to one of symbolic prophecy. The shift was drastic, and more sudden than we used to think.

• 4 •

The reading public of the eighteenth century was not large by modern standards, and it was smaller for poetry than for most of the forms of prose—especially the new fiction—and for printed plays. The poets scarcely felt this as a disadvantage. They had the highest place accorded writers in the accepted scheme of values, and they could enjoy their privileged position in security. And there was real gain in the way of a small, compact, educated audience, decidedly aristocratic and upper-middle-class. In the course of the century, the general reading public grew larger, and we gather from the records of the later years that those to whom poetry was of genuine interest were becoming less a group apart.

But though eighteenth-century poetry did not have a wide appeal numerically, we must not think of it as cut off from its time, failing through inability or unwillingness to engage the themes and the spirit of English life. There have been few periods in the history of our literature when the poet understood so clearly who constituted his audience and when he spoke so directly to it about subjects of common interest and in a common language. Indeed, it was this very *rapport* which is often responsible for the low tension that we find in much eighteenth-century verse. To the writers of unquestionable genius there was, as always, no problem. The color and excitement of Pope's *Satires* comes through to us not in spite of but because of the middle style and colloquial tone; Goldsmith's natural manner never results in a slackness in thought or emotion. It was the writers of lesser talent who suffered most.

The poetry of the century remained in touch with its age in several notable ways, not, to be sure, through any marked intuitive sense of what lay as yet unexpressed in the consciousness of the time, but in a spirit of compliance with the everyday forms of thought and behavior. It was, in other words, limited in sensibility. This does not mean, however, that it went its own way without regard for the common concerns and interests.

Consider, in this respect, the poetry of the aesthetic variety. There have always been those who have reacted strongly against it, and we may recall that some of its severest critics lived not in the twentieth century but the eighteenth. Johnson had no use at all for it; and in an amusing passage in his *London Journal*, Boswell has recorded how Goldsmith, at their first meeting, made fun of Gray's Pindaric manner (though, in justice, Goldsmith thought well of Collins's work). Everything that has been said about the excessive artificiality of this poetry—the finer examples excepted—is perhaps justified.

But are we right in regarding it as no more than an episode in trivial aestheticism? After all it represented one of the strongest interests of the English Enlightenment, making direct appeal to men of taste in much the same way that an estate newly terraced and planted in accordance with the latest theories pleased those properly grounded in the art of landscaping. Aestheticism was not yet the highly self-conscious affair, one may almost say the organized movement, it was to become in the late nineteenth century. As in Gray's *Odes*, it sometimes spoke only to the few, but in an age when there were no democrats in the modern sense among the educated, it can scarcely be called anti-democratic. Besides, the man of taste was not a rare and isolated genus. He was surely present part of the time in most readers. Ordinarily his literary taste was satisfied with the settled, traditionalist manner, but he was not impervious to the charm and novelty of what the school of the Wartons and Collins called "the poetry of the imagination," poetry abounding in verbal images and therefore appealing to him more sensuously and less dogmatically.

Now to turn from aestheticism and taste, which were generally confined to one group, to the more general experience of the entire class of educated men. The middle class had now come into its own. The fierce issues of the previous century had resolved themselves. The new spirit of tolerance and of goodwill founded in reasonableness had spoken in the terms of the Revolution Settlement of 1689, and before many more years had passed it was speaking, delightfully and persuasively, through the pages of the *Spectator*. But long before James II had departed, at least as early as the Restoration, the anti-dogmatic spirit had begun to show itself, turning men's minds from the narrower political and religious dogmas towards such ideas as toleration and benevolence.

Benevolence was understood as a condition of the mind and the heart, and also a way of life which directed the more fortunate members of society to extend practical charity to the poor. Humanitarianism was firmly established by the eighteenth century. It had already been responsible for the founding of numerous charitable societies and charity schools, and it was to put constant pressure on men's consciences through the century. It would have been strange if nothing of this spirit had appeared in literature.

Some Historical Considerations

Leaving the drama and prose fiction aside and confining ourselves to eighteenth-century poetry, we find expression of humanitarianism from Thomson's *Seasons* onwards, most notably in Goldsmith, Cowper, Burns, and Blake (whose sense of social injustice came straight out of the Enlightenment).

It is regrettable if we hesitate to respond to this particular strain because of a suspicion that this is one of the forms taken by eighteenth-century sentimentalism, and hence open to the familiar charges of softness, blindness to the facts of life, emotional hypertrophy, and overwriting of a singularly objectionable sort. Sentimental drama and the melodramas of later decades are included in this bill of indictment, along with much sentimental fiction. Perhaps we can look to Oliver Goldsmith for the wisest guidance in these matters. Goldsmith thoroughly shared our contempt for the sentimentalizing fashion in vogue on the English stage. Likewise, he saw in a great deal of social behavior purportedly motivated by benevolence an impractical idealism and an easy selfishness that took no account of consequences. Yet he was deeply sensitive to social evils and in his verse as well as his prose he did not hesitate to touch the emotions of his readers in many episodes involving insensitivity and injustice. Among the poets, this social consciousness and refinement of feeling were not confined to Goldsmith, as witness William Cowper. To be sure, the satiric verse of the century came to grips with evil in a different spirit; it is hard and ironic, even when, as in Crabbe, it presents many situations which imply a humanitarian approach. And the poetry of aestheticism was generally preoccupied with other things, though Collins—and this is his distinction—and sometimes Gray recognized compassion. But the note of sympathy and concern that we find in Goldsmith's *The Deserted Village* occurs repeatedly in other verse of the century, and it is not to be dismissed out of hand as a sign of sentimental posturing. In many cases it is a genuine expression of the deepening sense of obligation towards one's fellow men which the entire age was experiencing.

The spirit of the English Enlightenment—of the period, roughly speaking, between the mid-seventeenth century and the close of the eighteenth—also manifested itself in the new sense of history that was now developing and which became increasingly strong. The historical perspectives that had served since the Renaissance had not yet been seriously called in question, but there was a greater interest in areas that had formerly been passed over, particularly the medieval period, a growing curiosity about them, and an increasing awareness of the profound differences in culture separating different eras. The old assumptions concerning the uniformity of human nature and of our historical experience had begun to give way before that preoccupation with individuality, change, and substantial differences which has characterized Western thought ever since. We are not concerned here with historiography but only with eighteenth-century poetry as it registered this new attitude.

There is a certain kind of history in Johnson's *Vanity of Human Wishes* (and his Preface to the *Dictionary* shows that he was not blind to the factors of linguistic and cultural change). But verse such as this is not what we mean when we speak of response to the new historical spirit. Nor does Goldsmith's *Traveller* come to mind, though actually it can be shown to derive from Goldsmith's keen sense of the differences, rather than the similarities, which as a young man he had noted in European societies. The strict neoclassical temperament was not so open to this new frame of mind. But it is dangerous to generalize here. The fact that Christopher Smart was a thoroughgoing Horatian in certain of his verses did not prevent him from giving notable imaginative expression, in the *Song to David*, to the Hebraic spirit, with which certain eighteenth-century scholars and literary critics had already been concerned. It is, however, to the poets of the aesthetic school —the Wartons, Gray, Collins—and then to Shenstone, Macpherson, and Chatterton that we look for the clearest signs of the new spirit. The Warton brothers exhibit less of it in their poetry, where it is present, than in their criticism. Collins's orientalism in his early *Persian Eclogues* is scarcely significant, nor was he ever much of a medievalist; his sensitiveness to modes of experience separated by time and culture from the eighteenth-century seems to have been awakened largely by the supernatural elements in Shakespeare's plays, and it is Shakespeare that he has chiefly in mind in the *Popular Superstitions* as he writes of the wealth of imaginative material which Scottish folklore holds for the poet. Gray, as much scholar as he was poet, was led to medievalism by his interest both in history and philology, and the *Bard* and his Old Norse translations or imitations testify to his learning, as well as to his poetic genius. The enthusiasm aroused in certain quarters by Macpherson's publications can be attributed only in part to any growing interest in history, for it was in the so-called sublime style of *Ossian* that its chief appeal seems to have lain. But as a phenomenon of taste it cannot, of course, be separated from such things as the increasing interest in the ballad, in medieval Scandinavian poetry, and in pre-Renaissance English literature. Chatterton is the supreme, the amazing example of an absorption with the past so complete as to amount to identification with it.

It has been customary to see in the increasing historical sophistication of eighteenth-century poetry a spirit which, if not positively at odds with the Enlightenment, was anticipatory of the coming romantic revolution. It can be viewed in such a light. It is possible, however, to take it as an integral part of the eighteenth-century syndrome; and the poetry, simply as poetry, suffers less distortion in our minds when approached in this latter way.

• 5 •

Gradually the history of eighteenth-century poetic style in England is being rewritten. Walter Bate has studied the changes taking place during the period with particular reference to the underlying critical and aesthetic views, Geoffrey Tillotson has thrown new light on poetic diction, Wallace Brown has emphasized the artistic mastery of the later practitioners of the heroic couplet, C. V. Deane and John Arthos have made us aware of aspects of eighteenth-century nature poetry which we might otherwise have passed over, and Marjorie Nicolson has revealed the manner in which the new science affected descriptive poetry. There are studies like B. H. Bronson's, Earl Wasserman's and C. F. Chapin's concerning personification and Jean Hagstrum's on pictorialism which add to our understanding of certain of the symbolic conventions peculiar to these years. Josephine Miles, in her *Eras and Modes in English Poetry*, has arrived through her own method of stylistic analysis at a number of significant conclusions concerning the dominant poetic styles between Dryden and Wordsworth. There are many other recent studies—too many, regrettably, to cite individually at this point—which have similarly increased our understanding and our sensitiveness.

There are obvious stylistic differences between the two orders of eighteenth-century poetry, the poetry of the more traditional kind and that of the aesthetic group. Behind differences of meter, rhyme, imagery, and verbal convention lie deeper differences in respect of subject matter, point of view, and general intuition. Modern criticism is highly conscious of both the stylistic and thematic elements in all art and sees them as coördinate. Eighteenth-century literary criticism as a rule made less of what we think of as stylistic details than of the nature of the poet's material and his general treatment of it; but sometimes, when this criticism seems to be preoccupied with questions of subject matter and approach, it is actually addressing itself to matters of style.

In his *Letters on Chivalry and Romance*, which appeared in 1762, Bishop Richard Hurd protests against a certain kind of criticism which refuses to acknowledge that there can be such a thing as "poetical truth" distinct from philosophic truth: such criticism, he says, insists that poetry must stay within Nature and that Nature can mean only the known and the experienced. Rejecting such dogma, Hurd insists that the poet has a world of his own, where experience has less to do than "consistent imagination." He then goes on, in one of the most helpful and revealing passages in mid-century criticism, to mark off three kinds of poetry which he regards as distinct from one another because of their different intentions. To stay within nature, to follow nature, Hurd says, is a doctrine that can legitimately be observed by the kind of poetry that has men and manners for its theme. It may also be observed by another kind, which is aimed at the heart and would obtain its end through the passions. "But," he proceeds,

> the case is different with the more sublime and creative poetry. This species, addressing itself solely or principally to the Imagination; a young and credulous faculty, which loves to admire and to be deceived; has no need to observe those cautious rules of credibility so necessary to be followed by him, who would touch the affections and interest the heart.

Poetry of imitation, poetry of passion, poetry of the "imagination" —the categories are sharply drawn. We recognize the first of these as poetry of the traditional neoclassical line. Poetry addressed to the heart and the passions also falls within the first category. Poetry of the imagination is that produced by the aesthetic school; it is "sublime," "creative," it works principally through the faculty of the Imagination. Nothing is directly implied about the stylistic properties of the first two categories, but the terms Hurd uses in describing the third do carry such reference, for here he is asking us to think of a kind of poetry which abounds in word images of

Some Historical Considerations

a descriptive sort, and which by means of these images, these products of our image-making faculty, produces an effect upon the reader different from that of poetry having men, morals, and the human passions for its themes. This poetry of the imagination is not intended to imitate Nature; it seeks to create its own realm out of its own kind of imagery.

What are we especially aware of today as we analyze the traditional neoclassical style? The balance and antithesis, the personification, the generalizing terms are accepted as reflecting the intellectual temper of a period in European culture characterized by a desire for a rational ordering of experience. But the obvious stylistic patterns and the generalizing disposition behind them do not seem so interesting or so significant as the wit and irony which inform this style at its best. The greater poets of this tradition were men deeply committed, drawn before everything else to the exploration of human experience. In their wit, they were assenting to the universal terms imposed on us all with human life; in their irony, they were protesting our short-sightedness and our hypocrisies. It is the dry, intellectual passion of their approach to the human scene that, for us today, confers on this literary art an impressiveness formerly denied it.

The humanistic mode, with its established forms, suffered a decline during the middle period, when Collins, Gray, and others of similar views and practice took over, but it was again to dominate in the work of Johnson, Goldsmith, Cowper, and Crabbe, and its vitality is apparent in its later modulations. Goldsmith's version, if not more interesting than Crabbe's, is perhaps harder to follow. The humanistic quality of Goldsmith's poems is never in doubt, but he may seem to have substituted simplicity and sweetness for wit and irony. Yet his language lies quite within the tradition, there is a crispness about his characterizations of national and human types, and simplicity is a quality of thought and expression prized in classical art. Subtlety, not naïveté, lies behind his poetry, and in his placid words there is often irony.

The recognizably different style associated with the aesthetic movement has recently been analyzed by Josephine Miles, who regards it as peculiar to this period and an intrusion into English poetry, which otherwise discloses a fairly regular alternation between a curt, abrupt, highly verbal style (Skelton, Donne, the ballad style adopted by Wordsworth and Coleridge) and a style in balance between its grammatical subjects and its predicates

(Shakespeare's sonnets, Dryden, Johnson and Goldsmith, Matthew Arnold). The anomalous style appearing in the eighteenth century, the "sublime style," is one in which descriptive words, especially adjectives, verbs turned into adjectives, and long periodic passages of description predominate; action is at a minimum; wit and irony disappear. Any searching discussion of what lies behind this style leads one straight into the most complex regions of eighteenth-century aesthetic theory and practice, of which there is more to say than we can summarize briefly here.

Of the poets represented in the present volume, Akenside and Joseph Warton are the earliest of the mid-century group to concern themselves directly with poetics. Akenside's discussion of the "pleasures of the imagination" looks both forwards and backwards; forwards in respect of the theory of imagery resting upon empiricism; backwards to Shaftesbury and Thomson in its celebration of beauty in the natural world and the benevolence of the Creator. By the time we come to Collins and Gray, this Shaftesburian note has disappeared. What, if anything, has replaced it? Is the aesthetic experience, induced through imagery, significant beyond itself? When this poetry works to create an effect of sublimity as the eighteenth century, interpreting Longinus, understood it, it places man, to his wonderment, against some background suggestive of vast, cosmic forces. Gray achieves such an effect in *The Bard*, Collins in the *Ode on the Poetical Character*.

But they did not always aim at sublimity, as the pastoral odes of Collins remind us. The *Ode to Evening* is the evocation, through its controlled imagery and tone, of a mood which seems to need no further interpretation. Norman MacLean, in an essay entitled "From Action to Image: Theories of the Lyric in the Eighteenth Century" (in *Critics and Criticism*), shows how, in the allegorical and descriptive odes and the odes of terror in the middle and later century, the material of the poet, traditionally assumed to be external to him and in the nature of plots to be unfolded and action to be described, is here being replaced by his own power to create images. Further implications have recently been taken up by E. L. Tuveson in several chapters of his book, *The Imagination As a Means of Grace*.

· 6 ·

The preceding sections are intended to place a certain body of poetry in its historical setting and to establish the broader context within which it was written. The actual quality of this poetry is a different matter, demanding another approach. Surely, however, informed appreciation can not be wholly divorced from historical knowledge.

Edward Young

1683: born in June at Upham near Winchester, the son of a clergyman who was later Dean of Salisbury
1695-1702: at Winchester College
1702: to Oxford: first at New College, then Corpus Christi, then All Souls (law fellowship: B.C.L. 1714, D.C.L. 1719); resided at Oxford until 1730
1712: *Epistle to . . . Lord Lansdowne*, first published poem
1713: began to make frequent trips to London; a member of Addison's circle; *The Last Day*
1714: *The Force of Religion, or Vanquished Love*
1715: acquaintance with Pope
1719: *A Paraphrase on Part of the Book of Job; Busiris, King of Egypt*, a blank-verse tragedy, performed at Drury Lane
1721: *The Revenge* performed at Drury Lane; the tragedy had a long popularity
1724: acquaintance with Lady Mary Wortley Montagu
1725-28: *Love of Fame, the Universal Passion: In Seven Characteristical Satires*
1726: met Voltaire
1727: took holy orders (the actual date is uncertain); preached and published *A Vindication of Providence*, the first of a group of widely known sermons
1728: appointed chaplain to George II; *Ocean: An Ode, Occasioned by His Majesty's Royal Encouragement of the Sea Service*, one of several occasional odes and poems

1730: *Two Epistles to Mr. Pope* (part of *The Dunciad* warfare); left Oxford on receiving the living (£300) at Welwyn, Hertfordshire, where he lived the rest of his life
1731: married Lady Elizabeth Lee, daughter of the Earl of Litchfield, widow of Col. F. H. Lee
1740: death of Lady Elizabeth Young
1742-46: *The Complaint, or Night Thoughts* published anonymously in nine parts; immediate and long popularity
  I. *On Life, Death, and Immortality,* 1742
  II. *On Time, Death, and Friendship,* 1742
  III. *Narcissa,* 1742
  IV. *The Christian Triumph,* 1743
  V. *The Relapse,* 1743
  VI. *The Infidel Reclaimed,* part i, 1744
  VII. *The Infidel Reclaimed,* part ii, 1744
  VIII. *Virtue's Apology, or The Man of the World Answered,* 1745
  IX. *The Consolation,* 1746
1744: beginning of friendship and correspondence with Samuel Richardson
1753: *The Brothers* (written much earlier) performed at Drury Lane with Garrick
1754: *The Centaur Not Fabulous* (prose satire)
1759: *Conjectures on Original Composition in a Letter to the Author of Sir Charles Grandison*
1762: *Resignation*
1765: died 5 April

THE FACTS of Young's life and the titles and kinds of his works seem to show that he was a conforming citizen of his historical world, so much so that his enormous contemporary reputation in England and on the continent has scarcely survived it. Yet for an author once famous but now officially dead, there has been a surprising amount of recent scholarship devoted to the investigation of his romantic qualities—his subjectivity, his deathwish, his championship of original genius. Those who take this slant must minimize the greater part of Young's life and works—the correct Anglican sermons, the formal occasional poems, the rhetorical tragedies, the epistles, and the satires (a vein in which he was so ingeniously successful that his "characteristical" satires of 1725-28, in which he adopted the manner of La Bruyère, impressed Pope and are thought to have influenced his *Moral Essays*).

Young's romantic tenets, or at least the romantic image of the poet as original, inspired genius, are often detected in the *Conjectures on Original Composition*, which he wrote in his mid-seventies. Young did think that he was being original about originality; certain passages have the ring of a manifesto. But by "original" Young largely meant "modern," in opposition to translation or imitation of the classics. M. W. Steinke has shown that the *Conjectures* were not the first salvo in the battle for romanticism but one of the last in the battle of the ancients and moderns, begun by Temple almost seventy years before. Dr. Johnson "was surprised to find Young receive as novelties, what he thought very common maxims," and he added, rightly, that he believed "Young was not a great scholar, nor had studied regularly the art of writing." The *Conjectures* made little stir in England not because they were ahead of their time, but because they were very nearly behind it.

The *Night Thoughts*, however, had been enthusiastically welcomed. They were not, of course, revolutionary. The elegiac tradition, secular or religious, lyric or philosophic, is a long one in literature. That particular eighteenth-century manifestation of it—the melancholy meditation with Gothic settings which Young, for all practical historical purposes, inaugurated as a popular literary form—had been dimly foreshadowed by Thomas Parnell (*A Night-Piece on Death*, 1721) and Lady Winchelsea (*A Nocturnal Reverie*, 1713) and is said to be descended from Milton's *Penseroso*. Young knew his Milton, as his blank verse tries to show, but he also knew his Bible and had, early in his career as a writer, written two Biblical adaptations, *The Last Day* (1713) and *A Paraphrase on Part of the Book of Job* (1719), which, if not pre-studies of the *Night Thoughts*, were an unconscious preparation for them. In matter the *Night Thoughts* were as ancient as Ecclesiastes and as modern as the anti-deistic and anti-atheistic apologetics of contemporary Anglican theology. Young himself feared that the poem might be too heavily argumentative and moralistic: "It differs from the common mode of poetry, which is, from long narrations to draw short morals. Here, on the contrary, the narrative is short, and the morality arising from it makes the bulk of the poem."

But it was the manner of the *Night Thoughts* that made them famous and that spawned so many "graveyard" imitations. (Warburton was to complain of the *Conjectures:* "had he known that original composition consisted in the manner, and not in the matter, he had wrote with common-sense.") They hit perfectly the growing taste, perceptible in the 1740s, for a more "feeling" poetry which had a personal center, or the illusion of a personal center, but which did not violate the basic concept of poetry as the rising "to general and transcendental truths." They were one man's lament for his own losses, one man's night thoughts, to be sure, but also and primarily his complaint for all men and his general and transcendental answers to the questions of life which death and the elegy always pose. The epigraph from Virgil was no mere polite tag: "Sunt lacrimae rerum, et mentem mortalia tangunt." Young was paying to the world its "much-indebted tear."

The *Night Thoughts* purport to arise out of a personal occasion, the details of which have teased all of Young's readers from first to last. "As the occasion of this poem was real, not fictitious," he wrote in the Preface, "so the method pursued in it was rather imposed, by what spontaneously arose in the author's mind on that occasion, than meditated or designed." In the course of the poem he alludes to three deaths within three months (i. 198-213) —those of Lucia (vi. 1-39), Narcissa (iii. 58-282), and Philander (ii. 592-712), often somewhat tenuously identified as Young's wife, his stepdaughter, and her husband, although they died within forty-seven months not three. Henry Pettit and others have suspected that "in their different kinds"—gradual, early, and sudden —"the three deaths afford an over-neat framework for a three-dimensional complaint."

Whether the facts are true or fictitious or something in between is undeterminable and unimportant; what matters is how they are given and shaped in the poem. Young has achieved the desired balance between the particular and the generic both in the expression of individual grief and in the statement of the moral discipline of grief. The "Insatiate archer" has attacked him thrice, "and thrice my peace was slain." But "why complain for one? . . . I mourn for millions; 'tis the common lot." Very little of any one book of the *Night Thoughts* is devoted to personal circumstances as such, a great deal to the lessons of mortality which are developed in great detail and stated in concentrated proverbial wisdom ("Procrastination is the thief of time").

Young made his readers conscious of feeling the emotional and imaginative implications of his themes. He accomplished this by a kind of rhetoric of passion which belongs more to the drama than to the lyric. Many sequences of lines sound much like a soliloquy from a contemporary declamatory tragedy—Young himself wrote three—and we should remember that the eighteenth century did thrill to the grandeur of *Cato* and the plays of Rowe as well as to the dramatic pathos of *Eloisa to Abelard* and *Verses to the Memory of an Unfortunate Lady*. In his *Epistle to Lord Lansdowne* Young, in comparing English with French drama, had caught the English admiration for dramatic rhetoric:

> Our genius more affects the grand, than fine. . . .
> We rouse th'affections, and that hero show
> Gasping beneath some formidable blow;
> They sigh; we weep; the Gallic doubt and care
> We heighten into terror and despair;
> Strike home, the strongest passions boldly touch. . . .

Young admired the dramatic qualities and language of certain books of the Bible: "The book of Job is well known to be dramatic, and, like the tragedies of old Greece, is fiction built on truth."

In the *Night Thoughts* there is theatrical sensationalism, what was to become the fashionable Gothic shudder, in the nocturnal setting with its funereal appurtenances which Young, unlike his imitators, exploits in an organic way. Night is symbolic of both faces of death: " 'Tis as the general pulse/Of life stood still, and Nature made a pause . . . prophetic of her end," yet "Even silent night proclaims eternal day." Young attempted "sublimity," a quality he also found in the dramatic books of the Bible, in the richness and grandeur of the imagery and in the awe-inspiring question ("Longinus has a chapter on interrogations, which shows that they contribute much to the sublime").

The *Night Thoughts* noticeably extended the emotional and imaginative scope of the poetry of its time. Young wrote for and helped to create an audience that cared increasingly for taste and sensibility. The 1740s witnessed an aestheticism which delighted in its own response to a work of art that stressed sensibility and delineated the process of it. But to delineate sensibility, even to a small degree, requires length, looseness, and fluidity, qualities the modern reader is impatient with in a poem. Johnson, however, was acute in defending the *Night Thoughts* against the charges of imprecision and diffuseness: "The excellence of this work is not exactness, but copiousness; particular lines are not to be regarded; the power is in the whole, and in the whole there is a magnificence like that ascribed to Chinese Plantation, the magnificence of vast extent and endless diversity."

THE COMPLAINT,
OR NIGHT THOUGHTS ON LIFE,
DEATH AND IMMORTALITY

NIGHT I

Tired Nature's sweet restorer, balmy Sleep!
He, like the world, his ready visit pays
Where Fortune smiles; the wretched he forsakes;
Swift on his downy pinion flies from woe,
And lights on lids unsullied with a tear.
 From short (as usual) and disturbed repose,
I wake; how happy they who wake no more!
Yet that were vain, if dreams infest the grave.
I wake, emerging from a sea of dreams
Tumultuous; where my wrecked desponding thought   10
From wave to wave of fancied misery
At random drove, her helm of reason lost.
Though now restored, 'tis only change of pain,
(A bitter change!) severer for severe.
The day too short for my distress; and Night,
Even in the zenith of her dark domain,
Is sunshine to the colour of my fate.
 Night, sable goddess! from her ebon throne,
In rayless majesty now stretches forth
Her leaden scepter o'er a slumbering world.   20
Silence, how dead! and darkness, how profound!
Nor eye nor listening ear an object finds;

The Complaint . . . : For the titles of the other eight *Nights*, see the biographical table. Young was tempted by the vogue of the poem to write more parts than he had originally intended. The general didactic theme of the whole poem is immortality; one of his motives for writing was to supply Pope's omission in the *Essay on Man:* "Man too he sung; immortal man I sing" (l. 452). The last four *Nights* are even stronger exercises in Christian apologetics than the first five.

Creation sleeps. 'Tis as the general pulse
Of life stood still, and Nature made a pause;
An awful pause! prophetic of her end.
And let her prophecy be soon fulfilled;
Fate! drop the curtain; I can lose no more.
    Silence and Darkness! solemn sisters! twins
From ancient Night, who nurse the tender thought
To reason, and on reason build resolve,   30
(That column of true majesty in man),
Assist me; I will thank you in the grave;
The grave, your kingdom; there this frame shall fall
A victim sacred to your dreary shrine.
But what are ye?—Thou who didst put to flight
Primeval silence, when the morning stars,
Exulted, shouted o'er the rising ball;
O Thou, whose word from solid darkness struck
That spark, the sun; strike wisdom from my soul;
My soul, which flies to Thee, her trust, her treasure,   40
As misers to their gold, while others rest.
    Through this opaque of nature and of soul,
This double night, transmit one pitying ray,
To lighten and to cheer. Oh, lead my mind,
(A mind that fain would wander from its woe),
Lead it through various scenes of life and death;
And from each scene, the noblest truths inspire.
Nor less inspire my conduct than my song;
Teach my best reason, reason; my best will
Teach rectitude; and fix my firm resolve   50
Wisdom to wed, and pay her long arrear;
Nor let the phial of thy vengeance, poured
On this devoted head, be poured in vain.
    The bell strikes one. We take no note of time
But from its loss. To give it then a tongue
Is wise in man. As if an angel spoke,
I feel the solemn sound. If heard aright,
It is the knell of my departed hours;
Where are they? With the years beyond the flood.
It is the signal that demands dispatch;   60
How much is to be done? My hopes and fears
Start up alarmed, and o'er life's narrow verge
Look down—on what? a fathomless abyss;

A dread eternity! how surely mine!
And can eternity belong to me,
Poor pensioner on the bounties of an hour?
　How poor, how rich, how abject, how august,
How complicate, how wonderful is man!
How passing wonder He who made him such!
Who centered in our make such strange extremes!　　70
From different natures marvellously mixed,
Connection exquisite of distant worlds!
Distinguished link in being's endless chain!
Midway from nothing to the Deity!
A beam ethereal, sullied and absorpt!
Though sullied and dishonoured, still divine!
Dim miniature of greatness absolute!
An heir of glory! a frail child of dust!
Helpless immortal! insect infinite!
A worm! a god!—I tremble at myself,　　80
And in myself am lost! At home a stranger,
Thought wanders up and down, surprised, aghast,
And wondering at her own; how reason reels!
Oh, what a miracle to man is man,
Triumphantly distressed! what joy, what dread!
Alternately transported and alarmed!
What can preserve my life? or what destroy?
An angel's arm can't snatch me from the grave;
Legions of angels can't confine me there.
'Tis past conjecture; all things rise in proof;　　90
While o'er my limbs sleep's soft dominion spread,
What though my soul fantastic measures trod
O'er fairy fields; or mourned along the gloom
Of pathless woods; or down the craggy steep
Hurled headlong, swam with pain the mantled pool;
Or scaled the cliff, or danced on hollow winds,
With antic shapes, wild natives of the brain?
Her ceaseless flight, though devious, speaks her nature
Of subtler essence than the trodden clod;
Active, aerial, towering, unconfined,　　100
Unfettered with her gross companion's fall.
Even silent night proclaims my soul immortal;
Even silent night proclaims eternal day.
For human weal, Heaven husbands all events;

Dull sleep instructs, nor sport vain dreams in vain.
Why then their loss deplore, that are not lost?
Why wanders wretched thought their tombs around,
In infidel distress? Are angels there?
Slumbers, raked up in dust, ethereal fire?
   They live! they greatly live a life on earth   110
Unkindled, unconceived; and from an eye
Of tenderness let heavenly pity fall
On me, more justly numbered with the dead.
This is the desert, this the solitude;
How populous, how vital, is the grave!
This is creation's melancholy vault,
The vale funereal, the sad cypress gloom;
The land of apparitions, empty shades!
All, all on earth is shadow, all beyond
Is substance; the reverse is Folly's creed;   120
How solid all, where change shall be no more!
   This is the bud of being, the dim dawn,
The twilight of our day, the vestibule.
Life's theatre as yet is shut, and Death,
Strong Death, alone can heave the massy bar,
This gross impediment of clay remove,
And makes us embryos of existence free.
From real life, but little more remote
Is he, not yet a candidate for light,
The future embryo, slumbering in his sire.   130
Embryos we must be, till we burst the shell,
Yon ambient azure shell, and spring to life,
The life of gods, oh transport! and of man.
   Yet man, fool man! here buries all his thoughts;
Inters celestial hopes without one sigh.
Prisoner of earth, and pent beneath the moon,
Here pinions all his wishes; winged by Heaven
To fly at infinite; and reach it there,
Where seraphs gather immortality,
On life's fair tree, fast by the throne of God.   140
What golden joys ambrosial clustering glow
In His full beam, and ripen for the just,
Where momentary ages are no more!
Where time, and pain, and chance, and death expire!
And is it in the flight of threescore years,

To push eternity from human thought,
And smother souls immortal in the dust?
A soul immortal, spending all her fires,
Wasting her strength in strenuous idleness,
Thrown into tumult, raptured or alarmed   150
At aught this scene can threaten or indulge,
Resembles ocean into tempest wrought,
To waft a feather or to drown a fly.
   Where falls this censure? It o'erwhelms myself;
How was my heart encrusted by the world!
Oh, how self-fettered was my groveling soul!
How, like a worm, was I wrapped round and round
In silken thought, which reptile Fancy spun,
Till darkened Reason lay quite clouded o'er
With soft conceit of endless comfort here,   160
Nor yet put forth her wings to reach the skies!
   Night-visions may befriend (as sung above);
Our waking dreams are fatal. How I dreamt
Of things impossible! (Could sleep do more?)
Of joys perpetual in perpetual change!
Of stable pleasures on the tossing wave!
Eternal sunshine in the storms of life!
How richly were my noontide trances hung
With gorgeous tapestries of pictured joys!
Joy behind joy, in endless perspective!   170
Till at Death's toll, whose restless iron tongue
Calls daily for his millions at a meal,
Starting I woke, and found myself undone.
Where now my frenzy's pompous furniture?
The cobwebbed cottage, with its ragged wall
Of mouldering mud, is royalty to me!
The spider's most attenuated thread
Is cord, is cable, to man's tender tie
On earthly bliss; it breaks at every breeze.
   Oh, ye blest scenes of permanent delight!   180
Full above measure! lasting beyond bound!
A perpetuity of bliss is bliss.
Could you, so rich in rapture, fear an end,
That ghastly thought would drink up all your joy,
And quite unparadise the realms of light.
Safe are you lodged above these rolling spheres,

The baleful influence of whose giddy dance
Sheds sad vicissitude on all beneath.
Here teems with revolutions every hour;
And rarely for the better; or the best,   190
More mortal than the common births of Fate.
Each Moment has its sickle, emulous
Of Time's enormous scythe, whose ample sweep
Strikes empires from the root; each Moment plays
His little weapon in the narrower sphere
Of sweet domestic comfort, and cuts down
The fairest bloom of sublunary bliss.
　　Bliss! sublunary bliss!—proud words, and vain!
Implicit treason to divine decree!
A bold invasion of the rights of Heaven!   200
I clasped the phantoms, and I found them air.
Oh, had I weighed it ere my fond embrace!
What darts of agony had missed my heart!
　　Death! great proprietor of all! 'tis thine
To tread out empire and to quench the stars.
The sun himself by thy permission shines,
And one day thou shalt pluck him from his sphere.
Amid such mighty plunder, why exhaust
Thy partial quiver on a mark so mean?
Why thy peculiar rancour wreaked on me?   210
Insatiate archer! could not one suffice?
Thy shaft flew thrice; and thrice my peace was slain;
And thrice, ere thrice yon moon had filled her horn.
O Cynthia! why so pale? dost thou lament
Thy wretched neighbour? Grieve to see thy wheel
Of ceaseless change outwhirled in human life?
How wanes my borrowed bliss! from Fortune's smile
Precarious courtesy! not virtue's sure,
Self-given, solar ray of sound delight.
　　In every varied posture, place, and hour,   220
How widowed every thought of every joy!
Thought, busy thought! too busy for my peace!
Through the dark postern of time long elapsed
Led softly, by the stillness of the night—
Led like a murderer (and such it proves!)
Strays (wretched rover!) o'er the pleasing past;
In quest of wretchedness perversely strays;

And finds all desert now; and meets the ghosts
Of my departed joys; a numerous train!
I rue the riches of my former fate;   230
Sweet comfort's blasted clusters I lament;
I tremble at the blessings once so dear;
And every pleasure pains me to the heart.
    Yet why complain? or why complain for one?
Hangs out the sun his lustre but for me,
The single man? Are angels all beside?
I mourn for millions: 'tis the common lot;
In this shape or in that has fate entailed
The mother's throes on all of woman born,
Not more the children, than sure heirs, of pain.   240
    War, famine, pest, volcano, storm, and fire,
Intestine broils, Oppression with her heart
Wrapped up in triple brass, besiege mankind.
God's image disinherited of day,
Here, plunged in mines, forgets a sun was made.
There, beings deathless as their haughty lord,
Are hammered to the galling oar for life;
And plough the winter's wave, and reap despair.
Some, for hard masters, broken under arms,
In battle lopped away, with half their limbs,   250
Beg bitter bread through realms their valour saved,
If so the tyrant, or his minion, doom.
Want and incurable disease (fell pair!)
On hopeless multitudes remorseless seize
At once; and make a refuge of the grave.
How groaning hospitals eject their dead!
What numbers groan for sad admission there!
What numbers, once in Fortune's lap high-fed,
Solicit the cold hand of Charity!
To shock us more, solicit it in vain!   260
Ye silken sons of Pleasure! since in pains
You rue more modish visits, visit here,
And breathe from your debauch: give, and reduce
Surfeit's dominion o'er you; but, so great
Your impudence, you blush at what is right.
    Happy! did sorrow seize on such alone.
Not prudence can defend or virtue save;
Disease invades the chastest temperance;

And punishment the guiltless; and alarm
Through thickest shades pursues the fond of peace.   270
Man's caution often into danger turns,
And, his guard falling, crushes him to death.
Not Happiness itself makes good her name!
Our very wishes give us not our wish.
How distant oft the thing we dote on most,
From that for which we dote, felicity!
The smoothest course of nature has its pains;
And truest friends, through error, wound our rest.
Without misfortune, what calamities!
And what hostilities, without a foe!   280
Nor are foes wanting to the best on earth.
But endless is the list of human ills,
And sighs might sooner fail, than cause to sigh.
  A part how small of the terraqueous globe
Is tenanted by man! the rest a waste,
Rocks, deserts, frozen seas, and burning sands:
Wild haunts of monsters, poisons, stings, and death.
Such is earth's melancholy map! But, far
More sad! this earth is a true map of man.
So bounded are its haughty lord's delights   290
To woe's wide empire; where deep troubles toss,
Loud sorrows howl, envenomed passions bite,
Ravenous calamities our vitals seize,
And threatening Fate wide opens to devour.
  What then am I, who sorrow for myself?
In age, in infancy, from others' aid
Is all our hope; to teach us to be kind.
That, Nature's first, last lesson to mankind;
The selfish heart deserves the pain it feels;
More generous sorrow, while it sinks, exalts;   300
And conscious virtue mitigates the pang.
Nor virtue, more than prudence, bids me give
Swoln thought a second channel; who divide,
They weaken too, the torrent of their grief.
Take then, O world! thy much-indebted tear;
How sad a sight is human happiness,
To those whose thought can pierce beyond an hour!
O thou! whate'er thou art, whose heart exults!
Wouldst thou I should congratulate thy fate?

I know thou wouldst; thy pride demands it from me.
Let thy pride pardon what thy nature needs,
The salutary censure of a friend.
Thou happy wretch! by blindness art thou blessed;
By dotage dandled to perpetual smiles.
Know, smiler! at thy peril art thou pleased;
Thy pleasure is the promise of thy pain.
Misfortune, like a creditor severe,
But rises in demand for her delay;
She makes a scourge of past prosperity,
To sting thee more and double thy distress.
    Lorenzo, Fortune makes her court to thee;
Thy fond heart dances, while the siren sings.
Dear is thy welfare; think me not unkind;
I would not damp, but to secure thy joys.
Think not that fear is sacred to the storm;
Stand on thy guard against the smiles of Fate.
Is Heaven tremendous in its frowns? Most sure;
And in its favours formidable too;
Its favours here are trials, not rewards;
A call to duty, not discharge from care;
And should alarm us, full as much as woes;
Awake us to their cause and consequence;
And make us tremble, weighed with our desert;
Awe Nature's tumult and chastise her joys,
Lest while we clasp, we kill them; nay, invert
To worse than simple misery, their charms.
Revolted joys, like foes in civil war,
Like bosom friendships to resentments soured,
With rage envenomed rise against our peace.
Beware what earth calls happiness; beware
All joys, but joys that never can expire.
Who builds on less than an immortal base,
Fond as he seems, condemns his joys to death.
    Mine died with thee, Philander! thy last sight
Dissolved the charm; the disenchanted earth
Lost all her lustre. Where her glittering towers?
Her golden mountains, where? all darkened down
To naked waste; a dreary vale of tears;
The great magician's dead! Thou poor, pale piece
Of outcast earth, in darkness! what a change

The Complaint, or Night Thoughts

From yesterday! Thy darling hope so near
(Long-laboured prize!), oh, how ambition flushed
Thy glowing cheek! ambition truly great,
Of virtuous praise. Death's subtle seed within,
(Sly, treacherous miner!) working in the dark,
Smiled at thy well-concerted scheme, and beckoned
The worm to riot on that rose so red,
Unfaded ere it fell—one moment's prey!
   Man's foresight is conditionally wise;
Lorenzo, wisdom into folly turns   360
Oft, the first instant its idea fair
To labouring thought is born. How dim our eye!
The present moment terminates our sight;
Clouds, thick as those on doomsday, drown the next;
We penetrate, we prophesy in vain.
Time is dealt out by particles; and each,
Ere mingled with the streaming sands of life,
By fate's inviolable oath is sworn
Deep silence, "Where eternity begins."
   By Nature's law, what may be, may be now;   370
There's no prerogative in human hours.
In human hearts what bolder thought can rise
Than man's presumption on tomorrow's dawn?
Where is tomorrow? In another world.
For numbers this is certain; the reverse
Is sure to none; and yet on this perhaps,
This peradventure, infamous for lies,
As on a rock of adamant, we build
Our mountain hopes; spin our eternal schemes,
As we the fatal sisters could outspin,   380
And, big with life's futurities, expire.
   Not even Philander had bespoke his shroud.
Nor had he cause; a warning was denied;
How many fall as sudden, not as safe!
As sudden, though for years admonished home.
Of human ills the last extreme beware—
Beware, Lorenzo! a slow-sudden death.
How dreadful that deliberate surprise!
Be wise to-day; 'tis madness to defer;
Next day the fatal precedent will plead;   390
Thus on, till wisdom is pushed out of life.

Procrastination is the thief of time;
Year after year it steals, till all are fled,
And to the mercies of a moment leaves
The vast concerns of an eternal scene.
If not so frequent, would not this be strange?
That 'tis so frequent, this is stranger still.
   Of man's miraculous mistakes, this bears
The palm, "That all men are about to live,"
Forever on the brink of being born.   400
All pay themselves the compliment to think
They one day shall not drivel; and their pride
On this reversion takes up ready praise;
At least, their own; their future selves applauds;
How excellent that life they ne'er will lead!
Time lodged in their own hands is Folly's vails;
That lodged in Fate's, to wisdom they consign;
The thing they can't but purpose, they postpone;
'Tis not in folly, not to scorn a fool;
And scarce in human wisdom to do more.   410
All promise is poor dilatory man,
And that through every stage: when young, indeed,
In full content we sometimes nobly rest,
Unanxious for ourselves; and only wish,
As duteous sons, our fathers were more wise.
At thirty man suspects himself a fool;
Knows it at forty, and reforms his plan;
At fifty chides his infamous delay,
Pushes his prudent purpose to resolve;
In all the magnanimity of thought   420
Resolves; and re-resolves; then dies the same.
   And why? Because he thinks himself immortal.
All men think all men mortal, but themselves;
Themselves, when some alarming shock of Fate
Strikes through their wounded hearts the sudden dread;
But their hearts wounded, like the wounded air,
Soon close; where passed the shaft, no trace is found.
As from the wing no scar the sky retains,
The parted wave no furrow from the keel;
So dies in human hearts the thought of death.   430

---

l.406. vails: tip, gratuity.

Even with the tender tear which Nature sheds
O'er those we love, we drop it in their grave.
Can I forget Philander? That were strange!
Oh, my full heart—but should I give it vent,
The longest night, though longer far, would fail,
And the lark listen to my midnight song.
    The sprightly lark's shrill matin wakes the morn;
Grief's sharpest thorn hard-pressing on my breast,
I strive, with wakeful melody, to cheer
The sullen gloom, sweet Philomel! like thee,   440
And call the stars to listen; every star
Is deaf to mine, enamoured of thy lay.
Yet be not vain; there are, who thine excel,
And charm through distant ages; wrapped in shade,
Prisoner of darkness! to the silent hours,
How often I repeat their rage divine,
To lull my griefs, and steal my heart from woe!
I roll their raptures, but not catch their fire.
Dark, though not blind, like thee, Maeonides!
Or, Milton! thee; ah, could I reach your strain!   450
Or his, who made Maeonides our own,
Man too he sung; immortal man I sing;
Oft bursts my song beyond the bounds of life;
What now but immortality can please?
Oh, had he pressed his theme, pursued the track,
Which opens out of darkness into day!
Oh, had he, mounted on his wing of fire,
Soared where I sink, and sung immortal man!
How had it blessed mankind, and rescued me!

---

l.449. Maeonides: Homer.
l.451. who made Maeonides our own:
Pope, who translated Homer.

Robert Blair

1699-1700: born in Edinburgh, son of a minister of the Scottish church; educated at the University of Edinburgh and in Holland
c. 1718-30: lived in Edinburgh as an unemployed probationer; received license to preach 15 August 1729
1728: *Poem Dedicated to the Memory of William Law,* professor of philosophy at Edinburgh
1731: appointed to the living of Athelstaneford, East Lothian, where he spent the rest of his life
1738: married Isabella, daughter of William Law
1743: *The Grave*
1746: died 4 February

BLAIR IS A "Scottish Augustan," one of those Scotsmen of the eighteenth century who wrote in English with an eye toward pleasing London. When Blair was trying to persuade them to publish *The Grave*, he complained that the London booksellers "can scarce think (considering how critical an age we live in . . .) that a person living three hundred miles from London, could write so as to be acceptable to the fashionable and polite."

The Grave was published in 1743 when the first *Night Thoughts* had already appeared, but the poem was apparently not written to capitalize on Young's success. Blair maintained that it was complete some time before February 1742 and that the greater part of it had been written before 1731. The *Night Thoughts* and *The Grave* are a remarkable literary coincidence, and they entered into a century of fame together.

Allowing for natural differences of voice and style, nearly everything said of the *Night Thoughts* applies to *The Grave*. Blair's poem was as moral as Young's. It was written, he hoped, "in a way not unbecoming my profession as a minister of the gospel," although he confessed that

> in order to make it more generally liked, I was obliged sometimes to go cross to my own inclination, well knowing, that whatever poem is written upon a serious argument, must, upon that very account, be under peculiar disadvantages; and, therefore, proper arts must be used to make such a piece go down with a licentious age, which cares for none of those things.

Like Young, too, Blair draws on dramatic devices for his effects; he must have known the Jacobean and Restoration tragedians.

Dr. Robert Anderson, to whom we owe what little we know of Blair, has perfectly described *The Grave* and its intended effect in eighteenth-century terms:

> It is composed of a succession of unconnected descriptions, and of reflections that seem independent of one another, interwoven with striking allusions, and digressive sallies of imagination. It is a series of pathetic representations, without unity of design, variegated with imagery and allusion; which exhibit a wide display of original poetry The poet's eye is awake on the objects of creation, and on the scenes of human misery; and he is alive to every feeling of compassion and benevolence. Through a shade of melancholy, which peculiar impressions of religion throw over the scenes he describes, we always perceive an amiable and generous principle struggling to overcome the degeneracy which it deplores. Whatever subject is either discussed or aimed at, he always endeavours to melt the heart, and alarm the conscience, by pathetic description and serious remonstrances; and his sentiments are always delivered in a novel and energetic manner, that impresses them strongly on the mind. He is always moral, yet never dull . . . copious without being tiresome.

from THE GRAVE

The house appointed for all living.
JOB, XXX. 23

Whilst some affect the sun and some the shade,
Some flee the city, some the hermitage,
Their aims as various as the roads they take
In journeying through life—the task be mine
To paint the gloomy horrors of the tomb,
The appointed place of rendezvous, where all
These travellers meet. Thy succours I implore,
Eternal King! whose potent arm sustains
The keys of hell and death. The Grave, dread thing!
Men shiver when thou'rt named; Nature, appalled,   10
Shakes off her wonted firmness. Ah! how dark
Thy long-extended realms and rueful wastes,
Where naught but silence reigns, and night, dark night,
Dark as was chaos ere the infant sun
Was rolled together, or had tried his beams
Athwart the gloom profound! The sickly taper
By glimmering through thy low-browed misty vaults
(Furred round with mouldy damps and ropy slime)
Lets fall a supernumerary horror,
And only serves to make thy night more irksome.   20
Well do I know thee by thy trusty yew,
Cheerless, unsocial plant! that loves to dwell
Midst skulls and coffins, epitaphs and worms;
Where light-heeled ghosts and visionary shades,

The Grave: The poem (767 ll.) loosely falls into three parts: i (ll. 1-110) setting and opening reflections; ii (111-368) homily on the vanity of human wishes, with copious illustrations; iii (369-767) the terror of death and the grave and the consolation of the Resurrection. The first section, poetically the best, is given here.

The Grave

Beneath the wan cold moon (as fame reports)
Embodied thick, perform their mystic rounds.
No other merriment, dull tree! is thine.
   See yonder hallowed fane—the pious work
Of names once famed, now dubious or forgot,
And buried midst the wreck of things which were;   30
There lie interred the more illustrious dead.
The wind is up—hark! how it howls! Methinks
Till now I never heard a sound so dreary.
Doors creak, and windows clap, and night's foul bird,
Rooked in the spire, screams loud; the gloomy aisles,
Black-plastered, and hung round with shreds of 'scutcheons
And tattered coats of arms, send back the sound
Laden with heavier airs, from the low vaults,
The mansions of the dead. Roused from their slumbers,
In grim array the grisly spectres rise,   40
Grin horrible, and obstinately sullen
Pass and repass, hushed as the foot of night.
Again the screech-owl shrieks—ungracious sound!
I'll hear no more; it makes one's blood run chill.
   Quite round the pile, a row of reverend elms
(Coeval near with that) all ragged show,
Long lashed by the rude winds; some rift half down
Their branchless trunks, others so thin at top
That scarce two crows could lodge in the same tree.
Strange things, the neighbours say, have happened here: 50
Wild shrieks have issued from the hollow tombs;
Dead men have come again, and walked about;
And the great bell has tolled, unrung, untouched.
(Such tales their cheer, at wake or gossiping,
When it draws near to witching time of night.)
   Oft in the lone churchyard at night I've seen,
By glimpse of moonshine checkering through the trees,
The schoolboy, with his satchel in his hand,
Whistling aloud to bear his courage up,
And lightly tripping o'er the long flat stones   60
(With nettles skirted and with moss o'ergrown)
That tell in homely phrase who lie below.
Sudden he starts, and hears, or thinks he hears,

---

l.59. Cf. Dryden, *Amphitryon*, III, i: afraid."
"Whistling to keep myself from being

The sound of something purring at his heels;
Full fast he flies, and dares not look behind him,
Till out of breath he overtakes his fellows;
Who gather round, and wonder at the tale
Of horrid apparition, tall and ghastly,
That walks at dead of night, or takes his stand
O'er some new-opened grave, and (strange to tell!) 70
Evanishes at crowing of the cock.
    The new-made widow too I've sometimes spied,
Sad sight! slow moving o'er the prostrate dead;
Listless she crawls along in doleful black,
Whilst bursts of sorrow gush from either eye,
Fast falling down her now untasted cheek.
Prone on the lowly grave of the dear man
She drops; whilst busy-meddling memory
In barbarous succession musters up
The past endearments of their softer hours, 80
Tenacious of its theme. Still, still she thinks
She sees him, and indulging the fond thought
Clings yet more closely to the senseless turf,
Nor heeds the passenger who looks that way.
    Invidious Grave—how dost thou rend in sunder
Whom love has knit, and sympathy made one!
A tie more stubborn far than nature's band.
Friendship! mysterious cement of the soul!
Sweetener of life, and solder of society!
I owe thee much. Thou hast deserved from me 90
Far, far beyond what I can ever pay.
Oft have I proved the labours of thy love,
And the warm efforts of the gentle heart,
Anxious to please. Oh, when my friend and I
In some thick wood have wandered heedless on,
Hid from the vulgar eye, and sat us down
Upon the sloping cowslip-covered bank,
Where the pure limpid stream has slid along
In grateful errors through the underwood,
Sweet-murmuring—methought the shrill-tongued thrush 100
Mended his song of love; the sooty blackbird
Mellowed his pipe and softened every note;
The eglantine smelled sweeter, and the rose
Assumed a dye more deep; whilst every flower

The Grave

    Vied with its fellow plant in luxury
Of dress. Oh, then the longest summer's day
Seemed too, too much in haste; still the full heart
Had not imparted half; 'twas happiness
Too exquisite to last! Of joys departed,
Not to return, how painful the remembrance!   110

                    *   *   *

Samuel Johnson

1709: 18 September, born at Lichfield; later went to school at Lichfield and Stourbridge
1728-31: Pembroke College, Oxford, leaving upon death of his father
1735: marriage to Mrs. Elizabeth Porter; opened a school near Lichfield
1737: to London
1738: *London; A Poem*
1747: issued his Plan for a *Dictionary*
1749: *The Vanity of Human Wishes; Irene* produced by Garrick at Drury Lane
1750-52: *The Rambler*
1755: *Dictionary of the English Language* printed
1758-60: *The Idler*
1763: 16 May, met Boswell
1764: founding of The Club
1769-81: The *Lives* in *Works of the English Poets*
1784: died 13 December

No OTHER literary figure of the eighteenth century has been treated so extensively as Samuel Johnson, and modern editions, biographies, and criticisms provide ample evidence of our sustained interest in him. Here we are only concerned with Johnson as poet. He wrote verse from the time he was a schoolboy: formal verse, prologues, occasional verse, a play in blank verse; he wrote in English, in Latin, and in a few instances in Greek. Some of it appeared only after his death, but a good deal was published during his lifetime, though often anonymously. His contemporary reputation as a poet, deservedly great, rested largely upon the few pieces which appeared as separate publications. These included *London* in 1738, the *Prologue* for the opening of Drury Lane Theatre in 1747, and *The Vanity of Human Wishes* in 1749. The *Vanity* had Johnson's name on the title page for the first time, but his authorship of the two earlier poems was known. The first collected edition of his poems appeared the year after his death, but it has remained for modern editorship to reveal the full range and variety of his verse.

Johnson's *London* appeared on 13 May 1738. The "imitation" of one or another of the satires of Juvenal and Horace was a well established tradition going back to Oldham and Dryden in the post-Restoration era and achieving the most striking effects at the hands of Swift and Pope in their Horatian adaptations. It did not call for a faithful line-by-line rendering of the original so much as an adjustment of the scene and sentiments of the Latin verse to modern scenes and instances, and in this respect *London* was a signal triumph. Indeed, it seems to have suffered little by comparison with Pope's *One Thousand Seven Hundred and Thirty Eight. A Dialogue Something like Horace*, which appeared three days later, and the numerous editions through which Johnson's poems quickly went (a second and a third in 1738, a fourth in 1739) prove its popular appeal. In 1738 Johnson himself had only recently arrived in London, and the hardships he endured are undoubtedly reflected in the rancor of the poem. But the rancor was more than personal. It had been Juvenal's toward corruptions in Rome; it was now England's in the face of Spanish hostility and the reluctance of Walpole's administration to respond to this challenge. As Mr. John Butt has wittily observed, Pope had, in his satires, enrolled Horace in the Tory Party, and Johnson now demonstrated that Juvenal was likewise a Tory champion. However, the topicality has by this time lost something of its force, and consequently *London* seems a good deal less striking than it did to Johnson's contemporaries.

It is *The Vanity of Human Wishes* with its grave tone and universal theme that finds full response today and in so doing reveals to us Johnson's true strength as a poet. In the later imitation Johnson was still following Juvenal, but at a greater distance than in *London*. He replaced the original portraits of Sejanus and Hannibal with his own unforgettable ones of Wolsey and Charles XII of Sweden. Above all, Juvenal's tone—that of the civilized Roman accepting as inevitable the bitter jokes life can play—disappeared entirely, and in its stead Johnson voiced his own sense of the tragedy of life, tragedy relieved by Christian resignation and hope.

But more than theme makes *The Vanity of Human Wishes* one of the great poems in the language. Johnson's "wit," admirably described by F. R. Leavis as "a conscious neatness and precision of critical intelligence," is everywhere present in it, giving to the eighteenth-century generalizing terms all the weight of actual experience. Beneath the surface we find wit and intelligence at work, pointing the language and the images, contriving the dramatic tension, and enforcing the emotion that runs through the entire poem.

LONDON: A POEM

IN IMITATION OF THE THIRD SATIRE OF JUVENAL

*Quis ineptae
tam patiens urbis, tam ferrens ut
teneat se?*
JUV.

Though grief and fondness in my breast rebel,
When injured THALES bids the town farewell,
Yet still my calmer thoughts his choice commend,
I praise the hermit, but regret the friend,
Resolved at length, from vice and LONDON far,
To breathe in distant fields a purer air,
And, fixed on Cambria's solitary shore,
Give to St. David one true Briton more.
   For who would leave, unbribed, Hibernia's land,
Or change the rocks of Scotland for the Strand?   10
There none are swept by sudden fate away,
But all whom hunger spares, with age decay:
Here malice, rapine, accident, conspire,
And now a rabble rages, now a fire;
Their ambush here relentless ruffians lay,

Juvenal: From ll. 30 and 31 of Juvenal's Third Satire. Juvenal has not "Quis ineptae" but "Quis iniquae," the passage being translated as "Who is so resigned, who so hardened to the inequalities of our city as to hold his rage?" Johnson's version: "Who . . . so resigned . . . so hardened to the absurdities of our city . . . ?"

l.2. THALES: said to refer to J's friend Richard Savage, but J himself once declared he had no particular person in mind.
l.7. Cambria: medieval name for Wales.
l.8. St. David: patron Saint of Wales.
l.9. Hibernia's land: Ireland.

And here the fell attorney prowls for prey;
Here falling houses thunder on your head,
And here a female atheist talks you dead.
   While THALES waits the wherry that contains
Of dissipated wealth the small remains,   20
On Thames's banks, in silent thought we stood,
Where Greenwich smiles upon the silver flood:
Struck with the seat that gave Eliza birth,
We kneel, and kiss the consecrated earth;
In pleasing dreams the blissful age renew,
And call Britannia's glories back to view;
Behold her cross triumphant on the main,
The guard of commerce, and the dread of Spain,
Ere masquerades debauched, excise oppressed,
Or English honour grew a standing jest.   30
   A transient calm the happy scenes bestow,
And for a moment lull the sense of woe.
At length awaking, with contemptuous frown,
Indignant THALES eyes the neighb'ring town.
   Since worth, he cries, in these degen'rate days,
Wants ev'n the cheap reward of empty praise;
In those curst walls, devote to vice and gain,
Since unrewarded science toils in vain;
Since hope but soothes to double my distress,
And ev'ry moment leaves my little less;   40
While yet my steady steps no staff sustains,
And life still vig'rous revels in my veins;
Grant me, kind heaven, to find some happier place,
Where honesty and sense are no disgrace;
Some pleasing bank where verdant osiers play,
Some peaceful vale with nature's paintings gay;
Where once the harassed Briton found repose,
And safe in poverty defied his foes;

---

l.23. J's note: "Queen Elizabeth born at Greenwich."
l.29. excise: in 1738 the hatred of this form of taxation had not subsided since Walpole's unsuccessful attempt in 1733 to extend it to wine and tobacco. (Cf. J's definition of *excise* in his *Dictionary*.)
l.30. The feeling against Spain, England's rival in the growing trans-Atlantic trade, was at the boiling point. England went to war with Spain in October of 1739.
l.35. From this point on Thales is speaking.
l.47. Briton: refers to the Anglo-Saxon invasion of ancient Britain.

London: A Poem

Some secret cell, ye pow'rs, indulgent give.
Let ——— live here, for ——— has learned to live. 50
Here let those reign, whom pensions can incite
To vote a patriot black, a courtier white;
Explain their country's dear-bought rights away,
And plead for pirates in the face of day;
With slavish tenets taint our poisoned youth,
And lend a lie the confidence of truth.
  Let such raise palaces, and manors buy,
Collect a tax, or farm a lottery,
With warbling eunuchs fill a licensed stage,
And lull to servitude a thoughtless age. 60
  Heroes, proceed! what bounds your pride shall hold?
What check restrain your thirst of pow'r and gold?
Behold rebellious virtue quite o'erthrown,
Behold our fame, our wealth, our lives your own.
  To such, a groaning nation's spoils are giv'n,
When public crimes inflame the wrath of heav'n:
But what, my friend, what hope remains for me,
Who start at theft, and blush at perjury?
Who scarce forbear, though BRITAIN'S Court he sing,
To pluck a titled Poet's borrowed wing; 70
A Stateman's logic unconvinced can hear,
And dare to slumber o'er the Gazetteer;
Despise a fool in half his pension dressed,
And strive in vain to laugh at H———y's jest.
  Others with softer smiles, and subtler art,
Can sap the principles, or taint the heart;
With more address a lover's note convey,

---

l.50. It is not known whether J had any particular person in mind.
l.52. These lines were of course recalled when, in 1762, J was given a pension of £300 a year by Bute's government.
l.54. J's note: "The invasion of the Spaniards was defended in the houses of Parliament." J is referring to Walpole's attempt to prevent war in the face of English indignation over the manner in which Spain, under certain treaty rights, was searching English vessels.

l.56. These are standard Tory references to the bribery and corruption under Walpole.
l.59. The Licensing Act of 1737 had given Walpole a certain control over the stage.
l.70. a titled poet: Colly Cibber, Poet Laureate.
l.72. *The Daily Gazetteer* was the newspaper of the Walpole administration.
l.74. H ———y: Lord Hervey, the "Sporus" of Pope's *Epistle to Arbuthnot.*

Or bribe a virgin's innocence away.
Well may they rise, while I, whose rustic tongue
Ne'er knew to puzzle right, or varnish wrong, 80
Spurned as a begger, dreaded as a spy,
Live unregarded, unlamented die.
　For what but social guilt the friend endears?
Who shares Orgilio's crimes, his fortune shares.
But thou, should tempting villainy present
All Marlb'rough hoarded, or all Villiers spent,
Turn from the glitt'ring bribe thy scornful eye,
Nor sell for gold, what gold could never buy,
The peaceful slumber, self-approving day,
Unsullied fame, and conscience ever gay. 90
　The cheated nation's happy fav'rites, see!
Mark whom the great caress, who frown on me!
LONDON! the needy villain's gen'ral home,
The common shore of Paris and of Rome;
With eager thirst, by folly or by fate,
Sucks in the dregs of each corrupted state.
Forgive my transports on a theme like this,
I cannot bear a French metropolis.
　Illustrious EDWARD! from the realms of day,
The land of heroes and of saints survey; 100
Nor hope the British lineaments to trace,
The rustic grandeur, or the surly grace,
But lost in thoughtless ease, and empty show,
Behold the warrior dwindled to a beau;
Sense, freedom, piety, refined away,
Of France the mimic, and of Spain the prey.
　All that at home no more can beg or steal,
Or like a gibbet better than a wheel;
Hissed from the stage, or hooted from the court,
Their air, their dress, their politics, import; 110
Obsequious, artful, voluble and gay,

1.86. The Duke of Marlborough had, according to his enemies, prolonged the War of the Spanish Succession for his personal profit.
1.86. George Villiers, second Duke of Buckingham, was the "Zimri" of Dryden's *Absalom and Achitophel*.
1.99. Edward III, victorious at Crécy in 1346.
1.108. Capital punishment in England was administered by the gibbet, in France by the wheel.

On Britain's fond credulity they prey.
No gainful trade their industry can 'scape,
They sing, they dance, clean shoes, or cure a clap:
All sciences a fasting Monsieur knows,
And bid him go to hell, to hell he goes.
   Ah! what avails it, that, from slav'ry far,
I drew the breath of life in English air;
Was early taught a Briton's right to prize,
And lisp the tale of HENRY'S victories; 120
If the gulled conqueror receives the chain,
And flattery prevails when arms are vain?
   Studious to please, and ready to submit,
The supple Gaul was born a parasite:
Still to his int'rest true, where'er he goes,
Wit, brav'ry, worth, his lavish tongue bestows;
In ev'ry face a thousand graces shine,
From ev'ry tongue flows harmony divine.
These arts in vain our rugged natives try,
Strain out with falt'ring diffidence a lie, 130
And gain a kick for awkward flattery.
   Besides, with justice, this discerning age
Admires their wond'rous talents for the stage:
Well may they venture on the mimic's art,
Who play from morn to night a borrowed part;
Practised their master's notions to embrace,
Repeat his maxims, and reflect his face;
With ev'ry wild absurdity comply,
And view each object with another's eye;
To shake with laughter ere the jest they hear, 140
To pour at will the counterfeited tear,
And as their patron hints the cold or heat,
To shake in dog-days, in December sweat.
   How, when competitors like these contend,
Can surely virtue hope to fix a friend?
Slaves that with serious impudence beguile,
And lie without a blush, without a smile;
Exalt each trifle, ev'ry vice adore,
Your taste in snuff, your judgment in a whore;

---

l.120. Henry V, victorious at Agincourt in 1415.

 Can Balbo's eloquence applaud, and swear   150
He gropes his breeches with a monarch's air.
 For arts like these preferred, admired, caressed,
They first invade your table, then your breast;
Explore your secrets with insidious art,
Watch the weak hour, and ransack all the heart;
Then soon your ill-placed confidence repay,
Commence your lords, and govern or betray.
 By numbers here from shame or censure free,
All crimes are safe, but hated poverty.
This, only this, the rigid law pursues,   160
This, only this, provokes the snarling muse.
The sober trader at a tattered cloak,
Wakes from his dream, and labours for a joke;
With brisker air the silken courtiers gaze,
And turn the varied taunt a thousand ways.
Of all the griefs that harass the distressed,
Sure the most bitter is a scornful jest;
Fate never wounds more deep the gen'rous heart,
Than when a blockhead's insult points the dart.
 Has heaven reserved, in pity to the poor,   170
No pathless waste, or undiscovered shore;
No secret island in the boundless main?
No peaceful desert yet unclaimed by SPAIN?
Quick let us rise, the happy seats explore,
And bear oppression's insolence no more.
This mournful truth is ev'ry where confessed,
SLOW RISES WORTH, BY POVERTY DEPRESSED:
But here more slow, where all are slaves to gold,
Where looks are merchandise, and smiles are sold;
Where won by bribes, by flatteries implored,   180
The groom retails the favors of his lord.
 But hark! th' affrighted crowd's tumultuous cries
Roll through the streets, and thunder to the skies;
Raised from some pleasing dream of wealth and pow'r,
Some pompous palace, or some blissful bow'r,
Aghast you start, and scarce with aching sight

---

l.151. gropes: *O.E.D.* gives as an obsolete meaning "to take hold of, grasp, seize."

l.173. J's note: "The Spaniards at this time were said to make claim to some of our American provinces."

London: A Poem

    Sustain th' approaching fire's tremendous light;
Swift from pursuing horrors take your way,
And leave your little ALL to flames a prey;
Then through the world a wretched vagrant roam,   190
For where can starving merit find a home?
In vain your mournful narrative disclose,
While all neglect, and most insult your woes.
Should heav'n's just bolts Orgilio's wealth confound,
And spread his flaming palace on the ground,
Swift o'er the land the dismal rumor flies,
And public mournings pacify the skies;
The laureat tribe in servile verse relate,
How virtue wars with persecuting fate;
With well-feigned gratitude the pensioned band   200
Refund the plunder of the beggared land.
See! while he builds, the gaudy vassals come,
And crowd with sudden wealth the rising dome;
The price of boroughs and of souls restore,
And raise his treasures higher than before:
Now blessed with all the baubles of the great,
The polished marble, and the shining plate,
Orgilio sees the golden pile aspire,
And hopes from angry heav'n another fire.
    Could'st thou resign the park and play content,   210
For the fair banks of Severn or of Trent;
There might'st thou find some elegant retreat,
Some hireling senator's deserted seat;
And stretch thy prospects o'er the smiling land,
For less than rent the dungeons of the Strand;
There prune thy walks, support thy drooping flow'rs,
Direct thy rivulets, and twine thy bow'rs;
And, while thy grounds a cheap repast afford,
Despise the dainties of a venal lord:
There ev'ry bush with nature's magic rings,   220
There ev'ry breeze bears health upon its wings;
On all thy hours security shall smile,
And bless thine evening walk and morning toil.

---

l.194. J's note: "This was by Hitch a Bookseller justly remarked to be no picture of modern manners, though it might be true at Rome."
l.215. dungeons: probably refers to certain dilapidated houses.

Prepare for death, if here at night you roam,
And sign your will before you sup from home.
Some fiery top, with new commission vain,
Who sleeps on brambles till he kills his man;
Some frolic drunkard, reeling from a feast,
Provokes a broil, and stabs you for a jest.
Yet ev'n these heroes, mischievously gay,　　　　　　　230
Lords of the street, and terrors of the way;
Flushed as they are with folly, youth and wine,
Their prudent insults to the poor confine;
Afar they mark the flambeau's bright approach,
And shun the shining train, and golden coach.
　　　In vain, these dangers past, your doors you close,
And hope the balmy blessings of repose;
Cruel with guilt, and daring with despair,
The midnight murd'rer bursts the faithless bar;
Invades the sacred hour of silent rest,　　　　　　　240
And leaves, unseen, a dagger in your breast.
　　　Scarce can our fields, such crowds at Tyburn die,
With hemp the gallows and the fleet supply.
Propose your schemes, ye Senatorian band,
Whose Ways and Means support the sinking land;
Lest ropes be wanting in the tempting spring,
To rig another convoy for the k——g.
　　　A single jail, in ALFRED'S golden reign,
Could half the nation's criminals contain;
Fair Justice then, without constraint adored,　　　　250
Held high the steady scale, but deeped the sword;
No spies were paid, no special juries known,
Blest age! but ah! how diff'rent from our own!
　　　Much could I add,—but see the boat at hand,
The tide retiring, calls me from the land:
Farewell!—When youth, and health, and fortune spent,
Thou fly'st for refuge to the wilds of Kent;
And tired like me with follies and with crimes,
In angry numbers warn'st succeeding times;

---

l.242. Tyburn: the place of execution until the 1780s.
l.245. Ways and Means: J's note: "A cant term in the House of Commons for methods of raising money."
l.247. References to George II's unpopular visits to Hanover.
l.251. deeped: held the sword point down.

Then shall thy friend, nor thou refuse his aid, 260
Still foe to vice, forsake his Cambrian shade;
In virtue's cause once more exert his rage,
Thy satire point, and animate thy page.

THE VANITY OF HUMAN WISHES

IN IMITATION OF THE TENTH SATIRE OF JUVENAL

    Let observation with extensive view
Survey mankind, from China to Peru;
Remark each anxious toil, each eager strife,
And watch the busy scenes of crowded life;
Then say how hope and fear, desire and hate,
O'erspread with snares the clouded maze of fate,
Where wav'ring man, betrayed by vent'rous pride,
To tread the dreary paths without a guide,
As treach'rous phantoms in the mist delude,
Shuns fancied ills, or chases airy good;   10
How rarely reason guides the stubborn choice,
Rules the bold hand, or prompts the suppliant voice;
How nations sink, by darling schemes oppressed,
When vengeance listens to the fool's request.
Fate wings with ev'ry wish th' afflictive dart,
Each gift of nature, and each grace of art,
With fatal heat impetuous courage glows,
With fatal sweetness elocution flows,
Impeachment stops the speaker's pow'rful breath,
And restless fire precipitates on death.   20
    But scarce observed, the knowing and the bold
Fall in the gen'ral massacre of gold;
Wide-wasting pest! that rages unconfined,
And crowds with crimes the records of mankind;
For gold his sword the hireling ruffian draws,
For gold the hireling judge distorts the laws;
Wealth heaped on wealth, nor truth nor safety buys,

---

l.10. airy: defined by J in his *Dictionary* as "without reality."
l.16. Taste provides the dart with wings in the form of wishes, gifts, arts.
l.22. fall from a plague of materialism.

The dangers gather as the treasures rise.
  Let hist'ry tell where rival kings command,
And dubious title shakes the madded land, 30
When statutes glean the refuse of the sword,
How much more safe the vassal than the lord:
Low skulks the hind beneath the rage of power,
And leaves the wealthy traitor in the Tower,
Untouched his cottage, and his slumbers sound,
Though confiscation's vultures hover round.
  The needy traveller, serene and gay,
Walks the wild heath, and sings his toil away.
Does envy seize thee? crush th' unbraiding joy,
Increase his riches and his peace destroy; 40
Now fears in dire vicissitude invade,
The rustling brake alarms, and quiv'ring shade,
Nor light nor darkness bring his pain relief,
One shows the plunder, and one hides the thief.
  Yet still one gen'ral cry the skies assails,
And gain and grandeur load the tainted gales:
Few know the toiling statesman's fear or care,
Th' insidious rival and the gaping heir.
  Once more, Democritus, arise on earth,
With cheerful wisdom and instructive mirth, 50
See motley life in modern trappings dressed,
And feed with varied fools th' eternal jest:
Thou who couldst laugh where want enchained caprice,
Toil crushed conceit, and man was of a piece;
Where wealth unloved without a mourner died;
And scarce a sycophant was fed by pride;
Where ne'er was known the form of mock debate,
Or seen a new-made mayor's unwieldy state;
Where change of fav'rites made no change of laws,
And senates heard before they judged a cause; 60
How wouldst thou shake at Britain's modish tribe,
Dart the quick taunt, and edge the piercing gibe?

---

l.31. J has remembered a line in Addison's *Campaign*, "Refuse of swords, and gleanings of a fight."
l.34. wealthy traitor: the original reading had been "bonny traitor," which in 1749 was an unmistakable, sympathetic reference to the Scottish supporters of the Young Pretender in the 1745 rebellion.
l.46. their strong scent is in the wind.
l.48. gaping: gaping after, eager to obtain. It has been suggested that the reference is to George II's recalcitrant heir, Frederick Prince of Wales.

Attentive truth and nature to descry,
And pierce each scene with philosophic eye.
To thee were solemn toys, or empty show,
The robes of pleasure and the veils of woe:
All aid the farce, and all thy mirth maintain,
Whose joys are causeless, or whose griefs are vain.
  Such was the scorn that filled the sage's mind,
Renewed at ev'ry glance of humankind;   70
How just that scorn ere yet thy voice declare,
Search ev'ry state, and canvass ev'ry pray'r.
  Unnumbered suppliants crowd Preferment's gate,
Athirst for wealth and burning to be great;
Delusive Fortune hears th' incessant call,
They mount, they shine, evaporate, and fall.
On ev'ry stage the foes of peace attend,
Hate dogs their flight, and insult mocks their end.
Love ends with hope, the sinking stateman's door
Pours in the morning worshipper no more;   80
For growing names the weekly scribbler lies,
To growing wealth the dedicator flies,
From ev'ry room descends the painted face,
That hung the bright Palladium of the place,
And smoked in kitchens, or in auctions sold,
To better features yields the frame of gold;
For now no more we trace in ev'ry line
Heroic worth, benevolence divine:
The form distorted justifies the fall,
And detestation rids th' indignant wall.   90
  But will not Britain hear the last appeal,
Sign her foes' doom, or guard her fav'rites' zeal?
Through Freedom's sons no more remonstrance rings,
Degrading nobles and controlling kings;
Our supple tribes repress their patriot throats,
And ask no questions but the price of votes;
With weekly libels and septennial ale,
Their wish is full to riot and to rail.

---

l.84. Palladium: the statue of Pallas at Troy, thought to insure the safety of the city.

l.93. remonstrance: Parliament's Grand Remonstrance of 1641.

l.97. septennial ale: In 1716 the Whigs had passed the Septennial Act, extending the life of parliaments from three to seven years; much ale was dispensed at election time.

In full-blown dignity, see Wolsey stand,
Law in his voice, and fortune in his hand; 100
To him the church, the realm, their pow'rs consign,
Through him the rays of regal bounty shine,
Turned by his nod the stream of honor flows,
His smile alone security bestows:
Still to new heights his restless wishes tow'r,
Claim leads to claim, and pow'r advances pow'r;
Till conquest unresisted ceased to please,
And rights submitted, left him none to seize.
At length his sov'reign frowns—the train of state
Mark the keen glance, and watch the sign to hate. 110
Where'er he turns he meets a stranger's eye,
His suppliants scorn him, and his followers fly;
At once is lost the pride of awful state,
The golden canopy, the glitt'ring plate,
The regal palace, the luxurious board,
The liv'ried army, and the menial lord.
With age, with cares, with maladies oppressed,
He seeks the refuge of monastic rest.
Grief aids disease, remembered folly stings,
And his last sighs reproach the faith of kings. 120
    Speak thou, whose thoughts at humble peace repine,
Shall Wolsey's wealth, with Wolsey's end be thine?
Or liv'st thou now, with safer pride content,
The wisest justice on the banks of Trent?
For why did Wolsey near the steeps of fate,
On weak foundations raise th' enormous weight?
Why but to sink beneath misfortune's blow,
With louder ruin to the gulfs below?
    What gave great Villiers to th' assassin's knife,
And fixed disease on Harley's closing life? 130

---

l.99. Cardinal Wolsey (c. 1475-1530) rose to great secular and ecclesiastical power under Henry VIII, only to be charged with treason shortly before his death. His pride and his fall were traditional themes. J obviously had in mind Shakespeare's treatment of Wolsey in *Henry VIII*.
l.124. Lichfield, J's birthplace, was not far from the River Trent.
l.129. George Villiers, first Duke of Buckingham and father of the Villiers of *London*, l. 86; killed by an assassin in 1628.
l.130. Robert Harley, first Earl of Oxford (1661-1724); with Bolingbroke he led the Tory ministry during the last four years of Anne (1710-1714); after his fall from power in 1714 an unsuccessful attempt was made to impeach him.

What murdered Wentworth, and what exiled Hyde,
By kings protected, and to kings allied?
What but their wish indulged in courts to shine,
And pow'r too great to keep, or to resign?
When first the college rolls receive his name,
The young enthusiast quits his ease for fame;
Through all his veins the fever of renown
Burns from the strong contagion of the gown;
O'er Bodley's dome his future labours spread,
And Bacon's mansion trembles o'er his head.   140
Are these thy views? Proceed, illustrious youth,
And virtue guard thee to the throne of Truth!
Yet should thy soul indulge the gen'rous heat
Till captive Science yields her last retreat;
Should Reason guide thee with her brightest ray,
And pour on misty Doubt resistless day;
Should no false Kindness lure to loose delight,
Nor Praise relax, nor Difficulty fright;
Should tempting Novelty thy cell refrain,
And Sloth effuse her opiate fumes in vain;   150
Should Beauty blunt on fops her fatal dart,
Nor claim the triumph of a lettered heart;
Should no Disease thy torpid veins invade,
Nor Melancholy's phantoms haunt thy shade;
Yet hope not life from grief or danger free,
Nor think the doom of man reversed for thee:
Deign on the passing world to turn thine eyes,
And pause awhile from letters, to be wise;
There mark what ills the scholar's life assail,

---

l.131. Thomas Wentworth, Earl of Strafford, Charles I's advisor, was impeached and executed in 1641.
l.131. Edward Hyde, Earl of Clarendon (1609-1674), was Charles II's chief advisor before the Restoration; in 1660 he became the most powerful figure in the administration, but fell in 1667 and fled to France, dying there. In 1660 his daughter married the Duke of York, afterwards James II, making him the grandfather of both Queen Mary and Queen Anne.
l.135. J's friend, Mrs. Thrale, has made it clear that in this passage J had his own youthful experiences in mind.
l.139. Bodley: the Bodleian Library, Oxford; dome: a building (according to J's *Dictionary*).
l.140. Bacon's mansion: the gatehouse on Folley Bridge (demolished later in the century) over the Thames near Oxford. J's note: "There is a tradition, that the study of friar Bacon, built on an arch over the bridge, will fall when a man greater than Bacon shall pass under it."

The Vanity of Human Wishes

Toil, envy, want, the patron, and the jail. 160
See nations slowly wise, and meanly just,
To buried merit raise the tardy bust.
If dreams yet flatter, once again attend;
Here Lydiat's life, and Galileo's end.
  Nor deam, when learning her last prize bestows,
The glitt'ring eminence exempt from foes;
See when the vulgar 'scape, despised or awed,
Rebellion's vengeful talons seize on Laud.
From meaner minds, though smaller fines content,
The plundered palace or sequestered rent; 170
Marked out by dangerous parts he meets the shock,
And fatal Learning leads him to the block:
Around his tomb let Art and Genius weep,
But hear his death, ye blockheads, hear and sleep.
  The festal blazes, the triumphal show,
The ravished standard, and the captive foe,
The senate's thanks, the gazette's pompous tale,
With force resistless o'er the brave prevail.
Such bribes the rapid Greek o'er Asia whirled,
For such the steady Romans shook the world; 180
For such in distant lands the Britons shine,
And stain with blood the Danube or the Rhine;
This pow'r has praise, that virtue scarce can warm,
Till fame supplies the universal charm.
Yet Reason frowns on War's unequal game,
Where wasted nations raise a single name,
And mortgaged states their grandshires' wreaths regret,
From age to age in everlasting debt;
Wreaths which at last the dear-bought right convey
To rust on medals, or on stones decay. 190

---

l.160. patron: J had Lord Chesterfield in mind, since it was not until the 1755 edition of the poem that J, having on 7 February 1755 written his famous letter to C, substituted *patron* for the original *garret*.
l.164. Thomas Lydiat (1572-1646), famous scholar and mathematician; he was always poor.
l.164. Galileo (1564-1642) was blind during his last years.
l.168. William Laud (1573-1645), Archbishop of Canterbury, impeached by the Long Parliament in 1642 and finally executed early in 1645.
l.172. It was scarcely "Learning" that brought about Laud's impeachment, trial, and death. Here J allows his Toryism free expression.
l.179. the rapid Greek: Alexander the Great.
l.183. praise possesses this power, virtue scarcely does. . . .

  On what foundation stands the warrior's pride,
How just his hopes, let Swedish Charles decide;
A frame of adamant, a soul of fire,
No dangers fright him, and no labors tire;
O'er love, o'er fear, extends his wide domain,
Unconquered lord of pleasure and of pain;
No joys to him pacific sceptres yield,
War sounds the trump, he rushes to the field;
Behold surrounding kings their pow'rs combine,
And one capitulate, and one resign;   200
Peace courts his hand, but spreads her charms in vain;
'Think nothing gained,' he cries, 'till nought remain,
'On Moscow's walls till Gothic standards fly,
'And all be mine beneath the polar sky.'
The march begins in military state,
And nations on his eye suspended wait;
Stern Famine guards the solitary coast,
And Winter barricades the realms of Frost;
He comes, nor want nor cold his course delay;—
Hide, blushing Glory, hide Pultowa's day: 210
The vanquished hero leaves his broken bands,
And shows his miseries in distant lands;
Condemned a needy supplicant to wait,
While ladies interpose, and slaves debate.
But did not Chance at length the error mend?
Did no subverted empire mark his end?
Did rival monarchs give the fatal wound?
Or hostile millions press him to the ground?
His fall was destined to a barren strand,
A petty fortress, and a dubious hand;   220

---

l.192. Charles XII of Sweden (1682-1718). Voltaire's *History of Charles XII* (1732) was well known. J had once proposed writing a play about him.
l.200. one capitulate: Frederick IV of Denmark; one resign: August II of Poland.
l.203. Gothic: Swedish (i.e., Teutonic).
l.210. Charles tried to march to Moscow but was defeated (1709) by Peter the Great at Pultowa and took refuge in Turkey.
l.214. possibly refers to the part played by Peter the Great's Empress, Catherine I, in events subsequent to Pultowa.
l.219. Charles died while besieging Fredrikshald on the Norwegian coast.
l.220. There was a question whether Charles fell by a cannon-ball or was shot by Siker, one of his own officers.

The Vanity of Human Wishes

He left the name, at which the world grew pale,
To point a moral, or adorn a tale.
All times their scenes of pompous woes afford,
From Persia's tyrant to Bavaria's lord.
In gay hostility and barb'rous pride,
With half mankind embattled at his side,
Great Xerxes comes to seize the certain prey,
And starves exhausted regions in his way;
Attendant Flatt'ry counts his myriads o'er,
Till counted myriads soothe his pride no more;   230
Fresh praise is tried till madness fires his mind,
The waves he lashes, and enchains the wind;
New pow'rs are claimed, new pow'rs are still bestowed,
Till rude resistance lops the spreading god;
The daring Greeks deride the martial show,
And heap their valleys with the gaudy foe;
Th' insulted sea with humbler thought he gains,
A single skiff to speed his flight remains;
Th' incumbered oar scarce leaves the dreaded coast
Through purple billows and a floating host.   240
    The bold Bavarian, in a luckless hour,
Tries the dread summits of a Caesarean pow'r,
With unexpected legions bursts away,
And sees defenseless realms receive his sway;
Short sway! fair Austria spreads her mournful charms,
The queen, the beauty, sets the world in arms;
From hill to hill the beacon's rousing blaze
Spreads wide the hope of plunder and of praise;
The fierce Croatian, and the wild Hussar,
With all the sons of ravage crowd the war;   250
The baffled prince, in honour's flatt'ring bloom
Of hasty greatness finds the fatal doom,
His foes' derision, and his subjects' blame,
And steals to death from anguish and from shame.
    Enlarge my life with multitude of days,

---

l.224. Persia's tyrant: Xerxes; Bavaria's lord: the hapless Charles Albert (1697-1745), Elector of Bavaria.
l.241. During the War of the Austrian Succession (1740-48), Charles Albert was crowned Emperor Charles VII in 1742, but Maria Theresa overran Bavaria and he soon sank under misfortunes.
l.249. Hussar: a Hungarian light cavalryman.

In health, in sickness, thus the suppliant prays;
Hides from himself his state, and shuns to know,
That life protracted is protracted woe.
Time hovers o'er, impatient to destroy,
And shuts up all the passages of joy: 260
In vain their gifts the bounteous seasons pour,
The fruit autumnal, and the vernal flow'r,
With listless eyes the dotard views the store,
He views, and wonders that they please no more;
Now pall the tasteless meats, and joyless wines,
And Luxury with sighs her slave resigns.
Approach, ye minstrels, try the soothing strain,
Diffuse the tuneful lenitives of pain:
No sounds alas would teach th' impervious ear,
Though dancing mountains witnessed Orpheus near; 270
Nor lute nor lyre his feeble pow'rs attend,
Nor sweeter music of a virtuous friend;
But everlasting dictates crowd his tongue,
Perversely grave, or positively wrong.
The still returning tale, and ling'ring jest,
Perplex the fawning niece and pampered guest,
While growing hopes scarce awe the gath'ring sneer,
And scarce a legacy can bribe to hear;
The watchful guests still hint the last offense,
The daughter's petulance, the son's expense, 280
Improve his heady rage with treach'rous skill,
And mould his passions till they make his will.
   Unnumbered maladies his joints invade,
Lay siege to life and press the dire blockade;
But unextinguished Avarice still remains,
And dreaded losses aggravate his pains;
He turns, with anxious heart and crippled hands,
His bonds of debt, and mortgages of lands;
Or views his coffers with suspicious eyes,
Unlocks his gold, and counts it till he dies. 290
   But grant, the virtues of a temp'rate prime
Bless with an age exempt from scorn or crime;

---

l.271. his feeble powers attend to neither lute nor lyre.
l.291. Mrs. Thrale said that lines 291-8 were written with J's own mother in mind.

The Vanity of Human Wishes

An age that melts with unperceived decay,
And glides in modest Innocence away;
Whose peaceful day Benevolence endears,
Whose night congratulating Conscience cheers;
The gen'ral fav'rite as the gen'ral friend:
Such age there is, and who shall wish its end?
   Yet ev'n on this her load Misfortune flings,
To press the weary minutes' flagging wings: 300
New sorrow rises as the day returns,
A sister sickens, or a daughter mourns.
Now kindred Merit fills the sable bier,
Now lacerated Friendship claims a tear.
Year chases year, decay pursues decay,
Still drops some joy from with'ring life away;
New forms arise, and diff'rent views engage,
Superfluous lags the vet'ran on the stage,
Till pitying Nature signs the last release,
And bids afflicted worth retire to peace.   310
   But few there are whom hours like these await,
Who set unclouded in the gulfs of fate.
From Lydia's monarch should the search descend,
By Solon cautioned to regard his end,
In life's last scene what prodigies surprise,
Fears of the brave, and follies of the wise?
From Marlb'rough's eyes the streams of dotage flow
And Swift expires a driv'ler and a show.
   The teeming mother, anxious for her race,
Begs for each birth the fortune of a face: 320
Yet Vane could tell what ills from beauty spring;
And Sedley cursed the form that pleased a king.
Ye nymphs of rosy lips and radiant eyes,
Whom Pleasure keeps too busy to be wise,
Whom Joys with soft varieties invite,
By day the frolic, and the dance by night,

---

l.313. Lydia's monarch: Croesus.
l.317f. The Duke of Marlborough suffered two strokes of paralysis before he died in 1722. In his *Life of Swift* J described the Dean's last years in somewhat exaggerated terms.
l.321. Vane: Said to refer to Anne Vane, mistress of Frederick, Prince of Wales; she died in 1736.
l.322. Catherine Sedley (1657-1717) was mistress of the Duke of York, who as James II created her Countess of Dorchester; at the Revolution of 1688 her father turned against James.

Who frown with vanity, who smile with art,
And ask the latest fashion of the heart,
What care, what rules, your heedless charms shall save,
Each nymph your rival, and each youth your slave? 330
Against your fame with fondness hate combines,
The rival batters, and the lover mines.
With distant voice neglected Virtue calls,
Less heard and less, the faint remonstrance falls;
Tired with contempt, she quits the slipp'ry reign,
And Pride and Prudence take her seat in vain.
In crowd at once, where none the pass defend,
The harmless Freedom and the private Friend.
The guardians yield, by force superior plied:
By Int'rest, Prudence; and by Flatt'ry, Pride. 340
Here beauty falls betrayed, despised, distressed,
And hissing Infamy proclaims the rest.
   Where then shall Hope and Fear their objects find?
Must dull Suspense corrupt the stagnant mind?
Must helpless man, in ignorance sedate,
Roll darkling down the torrent of his fate?
Must no dislike alarm, no wishes rise,
No cries attempt the mercies of the skies?
Enquirer, cease, petitions yet remain,
Which heav'n may hear, nor deem religion vain. 350
Still raise for good the supplicating voice,
But leave to heav'n the measure and the choice.
Safe in his pow'r, whose eyes discern afar
The secret ambush of a specious pray'r.
Implore his aid, in his decisions rest,
Secure whate'er he gives, he gives the best.
Yet when the sense of sacred presence fires,
And strong devotion to the skies aspires,
Pour forth thy fervors for a healthful mind,
Obedient passions, and a will resigned; 360
For love, which scarce collective man can fill;
For patience sov'reign o'er transmuted ill;
For faith, that panting for a happier seat,

---

l.361. Though the broad meaning of this line emerges clearly enough, the grammatical structure and the precise meaning are difficult to fix. It may either be taken as "collective man can scarce satisfy love," or as "love can scarce fill c. m.," but in the latter case how are we to interpret "fill"?

Counts death kind Nature's signal of retreat:
These goods for man the laws of heav'n ordain,
These goods he grants, who grants the pow'r to gain;
With these celestial Wisdom calms the mind,
And makes the happiness she does not find.

William Shenstone

1714: born 18 November at The Leasowes, in rural Worcestershire, "the eldest son of a plain uneducated country gentleman . . . who farmed his own estate"; attended a dame school (kept by Sarah Lloyd, the "schoolmistress") and the Solihull Grammar School near Birmingham

1732: to Pembroke College, Oxford; left without taking a degree in 1736

1735: on coming of age inherited The Leasowes and £300 a year

1737: *Poems upon Various Occasions. Written for the Entertainment of the Author, and Printed for the Amusement of a Few Friends, Prejudiced in His Favour* published anonymously at Oxford (contained a short early version of *The Schoolmistress*)

1739-45: at The Leasowes but made excursions to London, Bath, and elsewhere

1741: *The Judgment of Hercules, A Poem* published anonymously

1742: *The Schoolmistress* published anonymously

1745: took up permanent residence at The Leasowes, which he made a model of landscape gardening

1748: began contributing to and later helped to choose poems for the various volumes of Robert Dodsley's *Collection of Poems* (the 2nd ed. of vol. i, 1748, contained an expanded version of *The Schoolmistress*)

1757: began correspondence with Thomas Percy, whom he aided in choosing and editing material for the *Reliques of Ancient English Poetry* (1765)

1763:   died 11 February
1764:   *The Works in Verse and Prose* published and edited by Dodsley

"DIVIDING the world into an hundred parts," Shenstone wrote in his *Essays on Men, Manners, and Things*, "I am apt to believe the calculation might be thus adjusted: Pedants 15, Persons of common sense 40, Wits 15, Fools 15, Persons of a wild uncultivated taste 10, Persons of original taste, improved by art 5." He was among the five, cultivating his "just relish of beauty" as writer, artist, landscape gardener, player on the harpsichord, and collector. In his polished letters ("I look upon my Letters as some of my chef-d'œuvres") he served as arbiter of elegance for others. One of the few to take his century's often repeated advice to cultivate one's garden, he landscaped his small estate as a *ferme ornée* in the picturesque style ("landskip should contain variety enough to form a picture upon canvas: and this is no bad test, as I think the landskip painter is the gardener's best designer") and made it, as a duchess said, "the most perfect model of rural elegance." One of his many admirers wrote to him:

> You give innocent pleasure to yourself and instruction as well as pleasure to others by the amusements you follow. Your pen, your pencil, your taste and your sincere unartful conduct in life (things which make you appear idle) give such an example as it were to be wished might be more generally followed—few have the capacity, fewer have the honesty to spend their time so usefully as well as unblameably.

Shenstone's writings fill but two volumes, one of aphoristic prose, one of poetry. His "Pegasus," he knew, "is one of those dull horses that will not bear to be hurried. Allow him but his time, and he may jog on safely; but urge him to move faster, and he is sure to break one's neck." His poems are a spectrum of polite verse: elegies,* odes, songs, ballads, levities or pieces of humor, and moral pieces. And there is *The Schoolmistress*, that minor masterpiece, which is difficult to classify.

---

* Shenstone wrote twenty-six elegies, all in the elegiac pentameter quatrain (perhaps prompted by James Hammond's *Love Elegies*, 1743), and "A Prefactory Essay on Elegy." Although not published until after his death, the elegies were in manuscript circulation and may have come to Gray's attention. Shenstone extended the scope of the elegy by introducing a new variety of subject matter.

Originally a rather obvious youthful burlesque of Spenser, in imitation of Pope's *The Alley* (Pope "made me consider [Spenser] ludicrously"), *The Schoolmistress* evolved, through successive revisions, into a mature comic work in which burlesque and imitation, the mock-heroic and the realistic, laughter and sentiment were delicately balanced. As he reread *The Faerie Queene*, Shenstone discovered that Spenser, in spite of his "detestable plan," "obviousness of allegory," "bad subject," and "inexpressibly confused action," possessed "some particulars . . . that charm one. Those which afford the greatest scope for a ludicrous imitation are his simplicity and obsolete phrase; and yet these are what give one a very singular pleasure in the perusal." In short, "I am now . . . from trifling and laughing at him, really in love with him." "The true burlesque of Spenser (whose characteristic is simplicity [i.e., naïveté]) seems to consist in a simple representation of such things as one laughs to see or to observe one's self, rather than in any monstrous contrast betwixt the thoughts and the words."

But as he became more sympathetic to Spenser's "peculiar tenderness of sentiment, visible throughout his works," and as he tried to write "more in Spenser's way, yet more independent [of] the antique phrase," he began to fear that "people of wit without taste" would "mistake burlesque for the very foolishness it exposes." To protect himself, he added a "ludicrous index" and a motto "purely to show (fools) that I am in jest." He was quite aware of other burlesques and imitations of Spenser and his relation to them:

> My *Schoolmistress*, I suppose, is much more in Spenser's way than any one would choose to write in, that writes quite gravely, in which case the dialect and stanza of Spenser is hardly preferable to modern heroic. I look upon my poem as somewhat more grave than Pope's *Alley*, and a good deal less than Mr. Thomson's *Castle* [*of Indolence*, 1748]. At least I meant it so, or rather I meant to screen the ridicule which might fall on so low a subject (though perhaps a picturesque one) by pretending to simper all the time I was writing.

In *The Schoolmistress*, Johnson observed, "we are entertained at once with two imitations, of nature in the sentiments, of the original author in the style, and between them the mind is kept in perpetual employment."

THE SCHOOLMISTRESS

IN IMITATION OF SPENSER

Ah me! full sorely is my heart forlorn,
To think how modest worth neglected lies,
While partial Fame doth with her blasts adorn
Such deeds alone, as pride and pomp disguise;
Deeds of ill sort, and mischievous emprize!
Lend me thy clarion, goddess! let me try
To sound the praise of merit, ere it dies;
Such as I oft have chauncèd to espy,
Lost in the dreary shades of dull obscurity.

In every village marked with little spire, 10
Embowered in trees, and hardly known to fame,
There dwells, in lowly shed and mean attire,
A matron old, whom we schoolmistress name;
Who boasts unruly brats with birch to tame;
They grieven sore, in piteous durance pent,
Awed by the power of this relentless dame;
And ofttimes, on vagaries idly bent,
For unkempt hair, or task unconned, are sorely shent.

And all in sight doth rise a birchen tree,
Which Learning near her little dome did stowe; 20
Whilom a twig of small regard to see,
Though now so wide its waving branches flow,
And work the simple vassals mickle woe;
For not a wind might curl the leaves that blew,
But their limbs shuddered, and their pulse beat low;

The Schoolmistress. The text is that of the third and fullest version. The poem bears an epigraph from Virgil (*Aeneid* vi. 426-27): "Voices are heard and loud wailing, the souls of infants weeping on the threshold." l.18. shent: reproached, scolded. l.20. stowe: place.

And, as they looked, they found their horror grew,
And shaped it into rods, and tingled at the view.

So have I seen (who has not, may conceive)
A lifeless phantom near a garden placed;
So doth it wanton birds of peace bereave, 30
Of sport, of song, of pleasure, of repast;
They start, they stare, they wheel, they look aghast:
Sad servitude! such comfortless annoy
May no bold Briton's riper age e'er taste!
Ne superstition clog his dance of joy,
Ne vision empty, vain, his native bliss destroy.

Near to this dome is found a patch so green,
On which the tribe their gambols do display;
And at the door imprisoning board is seen,
Lest weakly wights of smaller size should stray; 40
Eager, perdie, to bask in sunny day!
The noises intermixed, which thence resound,
Do learning's little tenement betray:
Where sits the dame, disguised in look profound,
And eyes her fairy throng, and turns her wheel around.

Her cap, far whiter than the driven snow,
Emblem right meet of decency does yield:
Her apron dyed in grain, as blue, I trowe,
As is the harebell that adorns the field:
And in her hand, for scepter, she does wield 50
Tway birchen sprays: with anxious fear entwined,
With dark distrust, and sad repentance filled;
And steadfast hate, and sharp affliction joined,
And fury uncontrolled, and chastisement unkind.

Few but have kenned, in semblance meet portrayed,
The childish faces of old Eol's train,
Libs, Notus, Auster; these in frowns arrayed,
How then would fare or earth, or sky, or main,
Were the stern god to give his slaves the rein?

---

l.56. Eol: Aeolus, god of the winds.
l.57. Libs . . . Auster: the west- southwest wind, the southwest wind, the south wind.

The Schoolmistress

    And were not she rebellious breasts to quell,   60
    And were not she her statutes to maintain,
    The cot no more, I ween, were deemed the cell
Where comely peace of mind, and decent order dwell.

    A russet stole was o'er her shoulders thrown;
    A russet kirtle fenced the nipping air;
    'Twas simple russet, but it was her own;
    'Twas her own country bred the block so fair;
    'Twas her own labor did the fleece prepare;
    And, sooth to say, her pupils ranged around,
    Through pious awe, did term it passing rare;   70
    For they in gaping wonderment abound,
And think, no doubt, she been the greatest wight on ground.

    Albeit ne flattery did corrupt her truth,
    Ne pompous title did debauch her ear;
    Goody, good-woman, gossip, n'aunt, forsooth,
    Or dame, the sole additions she did hear;
    Yet these she challenged, these she held right dear;
    Ne would esteem him act as mought behove,
    Who should not honored eld with these revere:
    For never title yet so mean could prove,   80
But there was eke a mind which did that title love.

    One ancient hen she took delight to feed,
    The plodding pattern of the busy dame;
    Which, ever and anon, impelled by need,
    Into her school, begirt with chickens, came;
    Such favor did her past deportment claim;
    And, if neglect had lavished on the ground
    Fragment of bread, she would collect the same;
    For well she knew, and quaintly could expound,
What sin it were to waste the smallest crumb she found.   90

    Herbs too she knew, and well of each could speak
    That in her garden sipped the silvery dew;
    Where no vain flower disclosed a gaudy streak,
    But herbs for use and physic, not a few,
    Of gray renown, within those borders grew:

---

l.76. additions: titles.

The tufted basil, pun-provoking thyme,
Fresh baum, and marigold of cheerful hue;
The lowly gill, that never dares to climb
And more I fain would sing, disdaining here to rhyme.
   Yet euphrasy may not be left unsung,   100
That gives dim eyes to wander leagues around;
And pungent radish, biting infant's tongue;
And plantain ribbed, that heals the reaper's wound;
And marjoram sweet, in shepherd's posie found;
And lavender whose spikes of azure bloom
Shall be erewhile in arid bundles bound,
To lurk amidst the labors of her loom,
And crown her kerchiefs clean with mickle rare perfume.

   And here trim rosmarine, that whilom crowned
The daintiest garden of the proudest peer;   110
Ere, driven from its envied site, it found
A sacred shelter for its branches here;
Where edged with gold its glittering skirts appear.
Oh, wassel days! Oh, customs meet and well!
Ere this was banished from its lofty sphere:
Simplicity then sought this humble cell,
Nor ever would she more with thane and lordling dwell.

   Here oft the dame, on Sabbath's decent eve,
Hymnèd such psalms as Sternhold forth did mete;
If winter 'twere, she to her hearth did cleave,   120
But in her garden found a summer seat:
Sweet melody! to hear her then repeat
How Israel's sons, beneath a foreign king,
While taunting foemen did a song entreat,
All, for the nonce untuning every string,
Uphung their useless lyres—small heart had they to sing.

   For she was just, and friend to virtuous lore,
And passed much time in truly virtuous deed;

---

l.97. baum: balsam plant.
l.98. gill: ground ivy.
l.100. euphrasy: eyebright, an herb.
l.109. rosmarine: rosemary, a favorite garden plant in the sixteenth century.

l.119. Thomas Sternhold (d. 1549), with John Hopkins, author of a widely used metrical version of the Psalms.
ll.122-26. Psalm cxxxvii.

The Schoolmistress

And, in those elfins' ears, would oft deplore
The times when truth by popish rage did bleed, 130
And tortious death was true devotion's meed;
And simple faith in iron chains did mourn,
That nould on wooden image place her creed;
And lawny saints in smoldering flames did burn:
Ah! dearest Lord, forefend thilk days should e'er return.

In elbow-chair, like that of Scottish stem
By the sharp tooth of cankering eld defaced,
In which, when he receives his diadem,
Our sovereign prince and liefest liege is placed,
The matron sate; and some with rank she graced, 140
(The source of children's and of courtiers' pride!)
Redressed affronts, for vile affronts there passed,
And warned them not the fretful to deride,
But love each other dear, whatever them betide.

Right well she knew each temper to descry,
To thwart the proud, and the submiss to raise;
Some with vile copper prize exalt on high,
And some entice with pittance small of praise;
And other some with baleful sprig she 'frays:
Even absent, she the reins of power doth hold, 150
While with quaint arts the giddy crowd she sways;
Forewarned, if little bird their pranks behold,
'Twill whisper in her ear, and all the scene unfold.

Lo now with state she utters the command!
Eftsoons the urchins to their tasks repair;
Their books of stature small they take in hand,
Which with pellucid horn securèd are,
To save from finger wet the letters fair;
The work so gay, that on their back is seen,
St. George's high achievements does declare; 160

---

l.131. tortious: unjust.
l.134. lawny: clad in lawn, a cloth used for the sleeves of a bishop's official dress.
l.136. The Coronation Chair in Westminster Abbey; beneath it is the Stone of Scone, brought from Scotland by Edward I.
l.157. hornbooks, stamped with a device of St. George and the Dragon.

On which thilk wight that has y-gazing been
Kens the forthcoming rod, unpleasing sight, I ween!

Ah, luckless he, and born beneath the beam
Of evil star! it irks me whilst I write!
As erst the bard by Mulla's silver stream,
Oft, as he told of deadly dolorous plight,
Sighed as he sung, and did in tears indite.
For brandishing the rod, she doth begin
To loose the brogues, the stripling's late delight!
And down they drop; appears his dainty skin,   170
Fair as the furry coat of whitest ermilin.

Oh, ruthful scene! when from a nook obscure,
His little sister doth his peril see:
All playful as she sate, she grows demure;
She finds full soon her wonted spirits flee;
She meditates a prayer to set him free;
Nor gentle pardon could this dame deny,
(If gentle pardon could with dames agree)
To her sad grief that swells in either eye,
And wrings her so that all for pity she could die.   180

Not longer can she now her shrieks command,
And hardly she forbears, through awful fear,
To rushen forth, and, with presumptuous hand,
To stay harsh justice in its mid-career.
On thee she calls, on thee her parent dear!
(Ah! too remote to ward the shameful blow!)
She sees no kind domestic visage near,
And soon a flood of tears begins to flow,
And gives a loose at last to unavailing woe.

But ah! what pen his piteous plight may trace?   190
Or what device his loud laments explain?
The form uncouth of his disguisèd face?
The pallid hue that dyes his looks amain?
The plenteous shower that does his cheek distain?
When he, in abject wise, implores the dame,

---

l.165. Mulla: Spenser's name for the Awbeg, a river in his native Ireland.
l.169. brogues: trousers.
l.171. ermilin: ermine.

The Schoolmistress

    Ne hopeth aught of sweet reprieve to gain;
    Or when from high she levels well her aim,
And through the thatch his cries each falling stroke proclaim.

    The other tribe, aghast, with sore dismay,
    Attend, and conn their tasks with mickle care;   200
    By turns, astonied, every twig survey,
    And from their fellow's hateful wounds beware,
    Knowing, I wist, how each the same may share;
    Till fear has taught them a performance meet,
    And to the well-known chest the dame repair;
    Whence oft with sugared cates she doth 'em greet,
And gingerbread y-rare; now, certes, doubly sweet!

    See to their seats they hye with merry glee,
    And in beseemly order sitten there;
    All but the wight of bum y-gallèd, he   210
    Abhorreth bench, and stool, and fourm, and chair;
    (This hand in mouth y-fixed, that rends his hair;)
    And eke with snubs profound, and heaving breast,
    Convulsions intermitting! does declare
    His grievous wrong, his dame's unjust behest,
And scorns her offered love, and shuns to be caressed.

    His face besprent with liquid crystal shines,
    His blooming face, that seems a purple flower
    Which low to earth its drooping head declines,
    All smeared and sullied by a vernal shower.   220
    Oh, the hard bosoms of despotic power!
    All, all, but she, the author of his shame,
    All, all, but she, regret this mournful hour:
    Yet hence the youth, and hence the flower shall claim,
If so I deem aright, transcending worth and fame.

    Behind some door, in melancholy thought,
    Mindless of food, he, dreary caitiff! pines;
    Ne for his fellows' joyaunce careth aught,
    But to the wind all merriment resigns;
    And deems it shame, if he to peace inclines;   230

---

l.206. cates: cakes.   l.213. snubs: sobs.
l.211. fourm: bench.   l.217. besprent: sprinkled.

And many a sullen look ascance is sent,
Which for his dame's annoyance he designs;
And still the more to pleasure him she's bent,
The more doth he, perverse, her 'haviour past resent.

Ah me! how much I fear lest pride it be!
But if that pride it be, which thus inspires,
Beware, ye dames, with nice discernment see,
Ye quench not too the sparks of nobler fires:
Ah! better far than all the Muses' lyres,
All coward arts, is valor's generous heat; 240
The firm fixed breast which fit and right requires,
Like Vernon's patriot soul; more justly great
Than craft that pimps for ill, or flowery false deceit.

Yet nursed with skill, what dazzling fruits appear!
Even now sagacious foresight points to show
A little bench of heedless bishops here,
And there a chancellor in embryo,
Or bard sublime, if bard may e'er be so,
As Milton, Shakespeare, names that ne'er shall die!
Though now he crawl along the ground so low, 250
Nor weeting how the Muse should soar on high,
Wisheth, poor starveling elf! his paper kite may fly.

And this perhaps, who, censuring the design,
Low lays the house which that of cards doth build,
Shall Dennis be! if rigid fates incline,
And many an epic to his rage shall yield;
And many a poet quit the Aonian field;
And, soured by age, profound he shall appear,
As he who now with 'sdainful fury thrilled
Surveys mine work; and levels many a sneer, 260
And furls his wrinkly front, and cries, "What stuff is here!"

But now Dan Phoebus gains the middle sky,
And Liberty unbars her prison door;

---

l.242. Admiral Edward Vernon, a naval hero to those opposed to the Admiralty under Walpole's ministry.
l.255. John Dennis (1657-1734), the critic.
l.257. the Aonian field: where Helicon, the mountain home of the Muses, is situated.

And like a rushing torrent out they fly,
And now the grassy cirque han covered o'er
With boisterous revel rout and wild uproar;
A thousand ways in wanton rings they run;
Heaven shield their short-lived pastimes, I implore!
For well may freedom, erst so dearly won,
Appear to British elf more gladsome than the sun. 270
Enjoy, poor imps! enjoy your sportive trade;
And chase gay flies, and cull the fairest flowers,
For when my bones in grass-green sods are laid;
For never may ye taste more careless hours
In knightly castles or in ladies' bowers.
Oh, vain to seek delight in earthly thing!
But most in courts where proud ambition towers;
Deluded wight! who weens fair peace can spring
Beneath the pompous dome of kesar or of king.

See in each sprite some various bent appear! 280
These rudely carol most incondite lay;
Those sauntering on the green, with jocund leer
Salute the stranger passing on his way;
Some builden fragile tenements of clay;
Some to the standing lake their courses bend,
With pebbles smooth at duck and drake to play;
Thilk to the huxter's savory cottage tend,
In pastry kings and queens the allotted mite to spend.

Here, as each season yields a different store,
Each season's stores in order rangèd been; 290
Apples with cabbage-net y-covered o'er,
Galling full sore the unmoneyed wight, are seen;
And gooseb'rie clad in livery red or green;
And here of lovely dye, the Catherine pear,
Fine pear! as lovely for thy juice, I ween:
Oh, may no wight e'er pennyless come there,
Lest smit with ardent love he pine with hopeless care!

See! cherries here, ere cheeries yet abound,
With thread so white in tempting posies tied,

---

l.279. kesar: caesar, emperor.

Scattering like blooming maid their glances round, 300
With pampered look draw little eyes aside;
And must be bought, though penury betide.
The plum all azure and the nut all brown,
And here each season do those cakes abide,
Whose honored names the inventive city own,
Rendering through Britain's isle Salopia's praises known.
Admired Salopia! that with venial pride
Eyes her bright form in Severn's ambient wave,
Famed for her loyal cares in perils tried,
Her daughters lovely, and her striplings brave: 310
Ah! midst the rest, may flowers adorn his grave,
Whose art did first these dulcet cates display!
A motive fair to Learning's imps he gave,
Who cheerless o'er her darkling region stray;
Till Reason's morn arise, and light them on their way.

---

l.306. Salopia: Shropshire; its chief city, Shrewsbury, on the banks of the Severn, was famous for its cakes.

Thomas Gray

1716: born 26 December at father's house in Cornhill, London, the only surviving child of the twelve born to his parents; his father, a scrivener and exchange broker, was a man of violent moods, probably unbalanced; Mrs. Gray and her sister, Mary Antrobus, kept a milliner's shop

c. 1725: to Eton at his mother's expense; became one of a group of four Etonians known in their day as the "Quadruple Alliance" (the others being Horace Walpole, Richard West, Thomas Ashton)

1734: in October to Peterhouse, Cambridge, as a pensioner; joined at Cambridge by Ashton and Walpole

1736: G's *Hymeneal* (Latin verses) on marriage of Frederick, Prince of Wales, printed in the Cambridge *Gratulatio Academiae*

1737: wrote *Luna est habitabilis* (Tripos Verses)

September 1738: left Cambridge for father's house in London, having decided two years previously to take no degree

March 1739: beginning of tour to France and Italy with Horace Walpole

1741: quarrel with Walpole at Reggio in May and G's return to London in September via Milan, Lyons, Paris

6 November:	father's death; his mother and aunt Mary eventually retired from Cornhill, joining their sister, Mrs. Jonathan Rogers, in her house at Stoke Poges, Buckinghamshire
winter 1741-42:	in London, studying law and working at his tragedy *Agrippina*
end of May 1742:	to Stoke; *Ode on the Spring* written (sent 1 June to West)
1 June:	death of his friend West
August:	*Eton Ode, Sonnet: on the Death of Richard West, Hymn to Adversity* written; may also have begun *Elegy Written in a Country Church-yard*
October:	return to Peterhouse as a Fellow-commoner
December 1743:	took degree of Bachelor of Laws
November 1745:	reconciliation with Walpole
March 1747:	*Ode on the Death of a Favorite Cat*
30 May:	*Eton Ode* printed
15 January 1748:	*Eton Ode, Ode on the Spring, Ode on the Cat* printed in Dodsley's *Collection of Poems*
November 1749:	his aunt, Mary Antrobus, died
12 June 1750:	*Elegy* finished and sent to Walpole
15 February 1751:	*Elegy* printed
11 March 1753:	Mrs. Gray died
29 March:	publication of *Designs by Mr. R. Bentley for Six Poems by Mr. T. Gray* (contained *Ode on the Spring, Ode on the Cat, Eton Ode, A Long Story, Hymn to Adversity, Elegy*)
5 March 1756:	migrated from Peterhouse to Pembroke College
8 August 1757:	publication of *Odes by Mr. Gray* (*Progress of Poesy* and *The Bard*, given as *Ode I* and *Ode II*)
December:	declined offer of Poet Laureateship
12 March 1768:	Dodsley published *Poems by Mr. Gray*, the first collected edition (*The Fatal Sisters, Descent of Odin,* and the *Triumphs of Owen* first printed here)
28 July:	appointed Regius Professor of Modern History at Cambridge
April 1769:	composed *Installation Ode*

December: met Charles-Victor de Bonstetten, a young Swiss
March 1770: Bonstetten's departure from England
30 July 1771: died at Cambridge; buried beside his mother in churchyard at Stoke Poges

GRAY'S LIFE has by now been fully documented, thanks to his biographers and to the collectors and editors of his correspondence, and his character and personality stand clearly revealed. The only one out of twelve children to survive, he grew up under his mother's anxious care, sheltered by her and her brothers and sisters from a psychopathic father. The modest inheritance he received from his paternal aunt when he was nineteen sufficed to make him financially independent the rest of his life. Happy at Eton, not unhappy as a pensioner at Peterhouse, and always content to lose himself in literary and philological studies ranging from classical through medieval to Renaissance and modern times, he was one of those who find their natural home within the academic setting.

But we are not to conclude that he withdrew from the everyday world because he lacked the capacity to cope with it, or from an age basically uncongenial to a person of his gifts. Though Gray the man struck some observers as amusingly fussy and again as unpleasantly aloof, he was never ineffectual in practical affairs—the day of the impractical poet and artist had not yet dawned. Nor did the Augustan spirit stifle him. He was an eighteenth-century man of taste, responding with great intellectual energy to the ever-widening artistic interests of this time. He observed the social scene—in Cambridge, in London, in the world at large—with unflagging interest, kept an eye on weather and crops, recording his day-to-day observations in a notebook, played Pergolesi and Bononcini on the piano in his room, and in the summer travelled about England and to Scotland to places of historical interest and picturesque charm. Meanwhile, year in and year out, he pursued his literary studies with unremitting faithfulness. When the inspiration came, he was a poet. If it came only briefly and only at rare intervals, that was because it was a matter of the most perfect, the most delicate balancing of all his perceptions and emotional responses. Only in moments of complete unobstruction could he or would he consent to write as artist.

As poet, Gray embodies that aestheticism which is so much in evidence in the mid-decades of the century. The vigour of the great Augustans was giving way to something less robust and forthright, something more discreet, more consciously literary. To a certain extent Gray shares this aestheticism with Collins, though there are significant differences between the two men. From the Wartons Collins had acquired a theory of poetry deriving from a special interpretation of the term imagination, whereas Gray was never directly influenced by this, or by any other particular dogma concerning the nature of the poetic process, his aestheticism lying chiefly in an intense response to the triumphant moments—largely in terms of inspired phrases and images—in the great line extending back to the Greek lyric poets and dramatists.

But they differed in a more important respect. Pastoralism for Collins included the civic theme, and he used the pastoral poem to voice patriotic sentiments of a kind which he himself embraced with ardour. His *Ode on the Popular Superstitions* reveals an intense interest in manners and psychological behaviour. To Collins, society, though it may not be open and viable, is nevertheless astir with immediate concerns and emotions. Gray, though a Whig in his politics, affords a classic example of that elegiac or cosmic Toryism which flourished so widely at this time. Though he was often repelled by his world, he always ended by accepting the *status quo*. His piety was genuine enough, despite the attraction which certain advanced views on traditional religious tenets seem to have held for him at one stage, but it was less a positive force than a revulsion from what he regarded as the dangerous tendencies fostered by such as Hume and Voltaire.

To see only Gray's cosmic Toryism is to approach him and his art in a mood bordering on contemptuousness: here is eighteenth-century futilitarianism in all its complacent frustration. Sympathetic response to Gray begins by perceiving his aesthetic integrity. He recognized unerringly the nature of his own genius, its powers and its limitations. He worked in the only way possible for him, bringing together into ordered equilibrium the civilized emotions and language lying in that body of literature which he knew as a scholar and which he had made his own through his powers of imaginative fusion. What the unsympathetic critic must see as Gray's most serious limitation—i.e. the absence from all his work of any perception of a large human destiny—the sympathetic viewer regards as imaginative acquiescence in the time-honored sentiments concerning human experience, human virtue, and man's inevitable commitment to suffering. The *Elegy* is not marred for us by any gnawing sense of futility.

Gray's style and language have long since gone out of fashion, but we can still understand the rationale behind them. The greater part of his verse was cast in the form of ode and elegy, an area of poetic composition in which English poets had long used a manner and diction consciously raised above everyday speech by means of Latinisms, stock poetic words, abstractions and personifications, classical allusions, periphrases, compound adjectives, etc. But this style was ordinarily restricted to epic, ode, and pastoral. Elsewhere, as in satiric verse, a plain style was indicated, practically indistinguishable from educated conversation, and when Gray gave himself a poetic holiday by writing in the satiric strain in the *Hymn to Ignorance*, *On Lord Holland's Seat*, and *The Candidate* he laid aside his special "language of poetry." When he used this special language, he never forgot what he was doing nor why. His *Ode on the Cat* is the wittiest of parodies both on himself in his high poetic moments and of the artificial diction, a clear acknowledgment of the peculiarities of his own serious style. And, as Professor Tillotson has so effectively shown, when a poet of Gray's stature employed the higher style and this artificial poetic diction of the eighteenth century, he achieved frequently an originality of effect obscured for us by our mistaken assumption that he is merely availing himself of the clichés at hand.

It is easy to underestimate Gray's energy, to forget that both as scholar and man of taste his interests were genuine, wide-ranging, sustained through a lifetime. And surely it is poetic energy of a remarkable sort that accounts for the diversity of his achievement. We cannot speak of Gray's poetic development, for he did not develop in the usual sense. His earliest English poem, the *Ode on the Spring*, is as finished as anything he ever composed. But he did proceed from the little ode—*On the Spring, Eton College*— to elegy, to Pindaric ode, and finally to imitation of medieval verse, Welsh and Scandinavian. The differences of tone and manner involved here, more considerable than may at first appear, demanded extraordinary readjustments.

ODE ON A DISTANT PROSPECT OF ETON COLLEGE

"Ἄνθρωπος· ἱκανὴ πρόφασις εἰς
τὸ δυστυχεῖν.
MENANDER.

Ye distant spires, ye antique towers,
That crown the watry glade,
Where grateful Science still adores
Her Henry's holy Shade;
And ye, that from the stately brow
Of Windsor's heights th' expanse below
Of grove, of lawn, of mead survey,
Whose turf, whose shade, whose flowers among
Wanders the hoary Thames along
His silver-winding way.   10

Ah happy hills, ah pleasing shade,
Ah fields beloved in vain,

Ode . . .: The first great creative period in Gray's life occurred in 1742. At the end of May he had gone down to Stoke, where he had composed his Ode on the Spring, sending it off to his friend Richard West, only to learn some days later of West's death on 1 June. Gray suffered a profound shock, the imaginative reverberations of which run through the three poems written in August at Stoke: the Hymn to Adversity, the Sonnet on the Death of West, and the Eton Ode. The Eton Ode, published in 1747 at Horace Walpole's urging, was the first of Gray's English poems to appear in print.
Of the six poems by Gray given in the present volume, all save the Sonnet on the Death of West appeared in the collected edition which Dodsley issued in 1768. The 1768 text has been used here as a basis for the five pieces in Dodsley; the text of the Sonnet, never published in Gray's lifetime, is that of the Pembroke MS.
MENANDER: "Because I am a man—a sufficient excuse for being miserable."
1.3. Science: knowledge in general.
1.4. G's note in the 1768 ed.: "King Henry the Sixth, Founder of the College."

Ode on a Distant Prospect of Eton College

    Where once my careless childhood strayed,
A stranger yet to pain!
I feel the gales, that from ye blow,
A momentary bliss bestow,
    As waving fresh their gladsome wing,
    My weary soul they seem to sooth,
    And, redolent of joy and youth,
To breathe a second spring.   20

    Say, Father Thames, for thou hast seen
Full many a sprightly race
Disporting on thy margent green
The paths of pleasure trace,
    Who foremost now delight to cleave
    With pliant arm thy glassy wave?
    The captive linnet which enthrall?
    What idle progeny succeed
To chase the rolling circle's speed,
Or urge the flying ball?   30

    While some on earnest business bent
Their murm'ring labours ply
'Gainst graver hours, that bring constraint
To sweeten liberty:
Some bold adventurers disdain
The limits of their little reign,
And unknown regions dare descry:
Still as they run they look behind,
They hear a voice in every wind,
And snatch a fearful joy.   40

    Gay hope is theirs by fancy fed,
Less pleasing when possest;
The tear forgot as soon as shed,
The sunshine of the breast:
Theirs buxom health of rosy hue,
Wild wit, invention ever-new,
And lively chear of vigour born;
The thoughtless day, the easy night,

---

l.19. G (1768): "And bees their honey redolent of spring. Dryden's *Fable on the Pythag. System.*"

    The spirits pure, the slumbers light,
That fly th' approach of morn.   50

    Alas, regardless of their doom,
The little victims play!
No sense have they of ills to come,
Nor care beyond to-day:
Yet see how all around 'em wait
The Ministers of human fate,
And black Misfortune's baleful train!
Ah, shew them where in ambush stand
To seize their prey the murth'rous band!
Ah, tell them, they are men!   60

    These shall the fury Passions tear,
The vulturs of the mind,
Disdainful Anger, pallid Fear,
And Shame that sculks behind;
Or pineing Love shall waste their youth,
Or Jealousy with rankling tooth,
That inly gnaws the secret heart,
And Envy wan, and faded Care,
Grim-visaged comfortless Despair,
And Sorrow's piercing dart.   70

    Ambition this shall tempt to rise,
Then whirl the wretch from high,
To bitter Scorn a sacrifice,
And grinning Infamy.
The strings of Falshood those shall try,
And hard Unkindness' altered eye,
That mocks the tear it forced to flow;
And keen Remorse with blood defiled,
And moody Madness laughing wild
Amid severest woe.   80

    Lo, in the vale of years beneath
A griesly troop are seen,
The painful family of Death,

---

l.79. G (1768): "—Madness laughing in his ireful mood. *Dryden's Fable of Palamon and Arcite.*"

l.83. family: the attendants or ministers of Death.

More hideous than their Queen:
This racks the joints, this fires the veins,
That every labouring sinew strains,
Those in the deeper vitals rage:
Lo, Poverty, to fill the band,
That numbs the soul with icy hand,
And slow-consuming Age.

To each his suff'rings: all are men,
Condemned alike to groan,
The tender for another's pain;
Th' unfeeling for his own.
Yet ah! why should they know their fate?
Since sorrow never comes too late,
And happiness too swiftly flies.
Thought would destroy their paradise.
No more; where ignorance is bliss,
'Tis folly to be wise.

SONNET

ON THE DEATH OF RICHARD WEST

In vain to me the smileing Mornings shine,
  And redning Phœbus lifts his golden Fire:
The Birds in vain their amorous Descant joyn;
  Or chearful Fields resume their green Attire:
These Ears, alas! for other Notes repine,
  A different Object do these Eyes require.
My lonely Anguish melts no Heart, but mine;
  And in my Breast the imperfect Joys expire.
Yet Morning smiles the busy Race to chear,
  And new-born Pleasure brings to happier Men: 10
The Fields to all their wonted Tribute bear:
  To warm their little Loves the Birds complain:
I fruitless mourn to him, that cannot hear,
  And weep the more because I weep in vain.

Sonnet . . . : Concerning the composition and text of this *Sonnet*, see note on p. 84.

In his 1800 preface, Wordsworth singled out this sonnet of Gray's as an example of lamentably elaborate poetic diction, the only lines of any value being, he declared, 6, 7, 8, 13, and 14. Professor Butt's retort (*The Augustan Age*, p. 114) is effective: the simple language of those five lines is the more effective because of the contrast with the elaborate diction of the rest of the sonnet.

ELEGY

WRITTEN IN A COUNTRY CHURCH-YARD

The Curfew tolls the knell of parting day,
The lowing herd wind slowly o'er the lea,
The plowman homeward plods his weary way,
And leaves the world to darkness and to me.

Now fades the glimmering landscape on the sight,
And all the air a solemn stillness holds,
Save where the beetle wheels his droning flight,
And drowsy tinklings lull the distant folds;

Save that from yonder ivy-mantled tow'r
The mopeing owl does to the moon complain
Of such, as wand'ring near her secret bow'r,
Molest her ancient solitary reign.

Beneath those rugged elms, that yew-tree's shade,
Where heaves the turf in many a mould'ring heap,

Elegy . . . : The precise facts concerning the composition of the *Elegy* remain in doubt. William Mason, Gray's friend and biographer, believed that the greater part of it was written during the summer of 1742, when Gray's grief over West's death was still fresh. Mr. Ketton-Cremer, in his authoritative biography of Gray (see bibliography), believes that only the opening stanzas were composed in 1742. It seems likely that the greater part was worked out at intervals between 1746 and 1750, and we know that it was completed in 1750 (G's letter to Walpole of 12 June 1750).

The MS. now at Eton College, probably the original draft, shows that at one stage the *Elegy* consisted of 22 stanzas, the first 18 being those preserved in the printed version, the last 4 having been ultimately replaced by the last 14 of the printed version. The change thus greatly altered the *Elegy*'s structure and conclusion. The poem was first printed (without the author's name, and with a short preface by Walpole) by Dodsley in February 1751.
l.6. i.e., a solemn stillness holds the air.

Each in his narrow cell for ever laid,
The rude Forefathers of the hamlet sleep.

The breezy call of incense-breathing Morn,
The swallow twitt'ring from the straw-built shed,
The cock's shrill clarion, or the echoing horn,
No more shall rouse them from their lowly bed.   20

For them no more the blazing hearth shall burn,
Or busy housewife ply her evening care:
No children run to lisp their sire's return,
Or climb his knees the envied kiss to share.

Oft did the harvest to their sickle yield,
Their furrow oft the stubborn glebe has broke;
How jocund did they drive their team afield!
How bowed the woods beneath their sturdy stroke!

Let not Ambition mock their useful toil,
Their homely joys, and destiny obscure;   30
Nor Grandeur hear with a disdainful smile,
The short and simple annals of the poor.

The boast of heraldry, the pomp of pow'r,
And all that beauty, all that wealth e'er gave,
Awaits alike th' inevitable hour.
The paths of glory lead but to the grave.

Nor you, ye Proud, impute to These the fault,
If Mem'ry o'er their Tomb no Trophies raise,
Where thro' the long-drawn isle and fretted vault
The pealing anthem swells the note of praise.   40

Can storied urn or animated bust
Back to its mansion call the fleeting breath?
Can Honour's voice provoke the silent dust,
Or Flatt'ry sooth the dull cold ear of Death?

---

l.16. rude: unlettered.
l.26. glebe: the ground, the sod.
l.35. i.e., the inevitable hour awaits alike all that beauty and wealth ever gave.

Elegy Written in a Country Church-yard

Perhaps in this neglected spot is laid
Some heart once pregnant with celestial fire;
Hands, that the rod of empire might have swayed,
Or waked to extasy the living lyre.

But Knowledge to their eyes her ample page
Rich with the spoils of time did ne'er unroll; 50
Chill Penury repressed their noble rage,
And froze the genial current of the soul.

Full many a gem of purest ray serene,
The dark unfathomed caves of ocean bear:
Full many a flower is born to blush unseen,
And waste its sweetness on the desert air.

Some village-Hampden, that with dauntless breast
The little Tyrant of his fields withstood;
Some mute inglorious Milton here may rest,
Some Cromwell guiltless of his country's blood. 60

Th' applause of list'ning senates to command,
The threats of pain and ruin to despise,
To scatter plenty o'er a smiling land,
And read their hist'ry in a nation's eyes,

Their lot forbad: nor circumscribed alone
Their growing virtues, but their crimes confined;
Forbad to wade through slaughter to a throne,
And shut the gates of mercy on mankind,

The struggling pangs of conscious truth to hide,
To quench the blushes of ingenuous shame, 70
Or heap the shrine of Luxury and Pride
With incense kindled at the Muse's flame.

Far from the madding crowd's ignoble strife,
Their sober wishes never learned to stray;

---

l.52. genial: in the double sense of kindly and generative.
l.57. John Hampden (1594-1643), parliamentary leader in both the Short and Long Parliaments.
l.70. ingenuous: artless, natural.
l.73. madding: acting madly, frenzied.

Along the cool sequestered vale of life
They kept the noiseless tenor of their way.

Yet ev'n these bones from insult to protect
Some frail memorial still erected nigh,
With uncouth rhimes and shapeless sculpture decked,
Implores the passing tribute of a sigh.   80

Their name, their years, spelt by th' unlettered muse,
The place of fame and elegy supply:
And many a holy text around she strews,
That teach the rustic moralist to die.

For who to dumb Forgetfulness a prey,
This pleasing anxious being e'er resigned,
Left the warm precincts of the chearful day,
Nor cast one longing ling'ring look behind?

On some fond breast the parting soul relies,
Some pious drops the closing eye requires;   90
Ev'n from the tomb the voice of Nature cries,
Ev'n in our Ashes live their wonted Fires.

For thee, who mindful of th' unhonoured Dead
Dost in these lines their artless tale relate;
If chance, by lonely contemplation led,
Some kindred Spirit shall inquire thy fate,

Haply some hoary-headed Swain may say,
'Oft have we seen him at the peep of dawn
'Brushing with hasty steps the dews away
'To meet the sun upon the upland lawn.   100

'There at the foot of yonder nodding beech
'That wreathes its old fantastic roots so high,
'His listless length at noontide would he stretch,
'And pore upon the brook that babbles by.

---

l.81. composed or cut in the stone by an illiterate person.
l.85. probably means: who ever resigned this life as a prey to forgetfulness?
l.87. cf. Milton, *Paradise Lost* III. 88: "not far off Heaven in the precincts of light."

'Hard by yon wood, now smiling as in scorn,
'Mutt'ring his wayward fancies he would rove,
'Now drooping, woeful wan, like one forlorn,
'Or crazed with care, or crossed in hopeless love.

'One morn I missed him on the customed hill,
'Along the heath and near his fav'rite tree;
'Another came; nor yet beside the rill,
'Nor up the lawn, nor at the wood was he;

'The next with dirges due in sad array
'Slow thro' the church-way ath we saw him born.
'Approach and read (for thou can'st read) the lay,
'Graved on the stone beneath yon aged thorn.'

THE EPITAPH

Here rests his head upon the lap of Earth
A Youth to Fortune and to Fame unknown.
Fair Science frowned not on his humble birth,
And Melancholy marked him for her own.

Large was his bounty, and his soul sincere,
Heav'n did a recompence as largely send:
He gave to Mis'ry all he had, a tear,
He gained from Heav'n ('twas all he wished) a friend.

No farther seek his merits to disclose,
Or draw his frailties from their dread abode,
(There they alike in trembling hope repose,)
The bosom of his Father and his God.

---

l.107. woeful wan: both woeful and wan.

THE PROGRESS OF POESY

NOTE: Gray considered his two Pindaric odes, *The Progress of Poesy* and *The Bard*, as superior to all his other work. They were published as *Odes, by Mr. Gray* by Dodsley in 1757, the first book to be printed at the press recently installed by Walpole at Strawberry Hill. Walpole had urged Gray to supply notes, but he refused. Notes, he wrote, "are signs of weakness and obscurity. If a thing cannot be understood without them, it had better not be understood at all." For the 1768 edition he did, however, consent to furnish a number for both *Odes*, along with this short Advertisement: "When the Author first published this and the following Ode, he was advised, even by his Friends, to subjoin some few explanatory Notes; but had too much respect for the understanding of his Readers to take that liberty."

The two *Odes* reflect everywhere the studies in which Gray had been immersing himself: *The Progress of Poesy*, his studies of Pindar and Lysias; *The Bard*, his researches into Welsh poetry.

The Progress of Poesy was, Gray said, "wrote by fits and starts at very distant intervals." His first reference to it occurs in a letter to Walpole in the summer of 1752, where he mentions "a high Pindaric upon stilts," wanting but 17 lines of having an end. It was finished and sent to Walpole at the close of 1754.

The greater part of *The Bard* was composed in 1755 with unusual rapidity. "I felt myself the Bard," Gray later remarked. But it remained unfinished until May 1757.

THE PROGRESS OF POESY

A PINDARIC ODE

Φωνᾶντα συνετοῖσιν· ἐς
Δὲ τὸ πᾶν ἑρμηνέων χατίζει.
PINDAR, Olymp. II.

I. 1.

AWAKE, Æolian lyre, awake,
And give to rapture all thy trembling strings.
From Helicon's harmonious springs
A thousand rills their mazy progress take:
The laughing flowers, that round them blow,
Drink life and fragrance as they flow.
Now the rich stream of music winds along
Deep, majestic, smooth, and strong,
Thro' verdant vales, and Ceres' golden reign:
Now rowling down the steep amain,   10
Headlong, impetuous, see it pour:
The rocks, and nodding groves rebellow to the roar.

Pindar: The motto was probably intended for both P of P and The Bard. In 1757 it was merely φωνᾶτα συνετοῖσιν (vocal to the intelligent alone); it was expanded in the 1768 ed. (ἐς δὲ τὸ πᾶν etc.: but for the crowd they need interpreters).
l.1. Æolian lyre: Pindar's lyre. The following portions of Gray's note in the 1768 ed., a note in connection with Pindar's poetry, sums up this opening paragraph of the P of P: "The various sources of poetry, which gives life and lustre to all its touches, are here described; its quiet majestic progress enriching every subject (otherwise dry and barren) with a pomp of diction and luxuriant harmony of numbers; and its more rapid and irresistible course, when swoln and hurried away by the conflict of tumultous passions."

I. 2.

 Oh! Sovereign of the willing soul,
Parent of sweet and solemn-breathing airs,
Enchanting shell! the sullen Cares,
And frantic Passions hear thy soft controul.
On Thracia's hills the Lord of War,
Has curbed the fury of his car,
And droptd his thirsty lance at thy command.
Perching on the scept'red hand
Of Jove, thy magic lulls the feathered king
With ruffled plumes, and flagging wing:
Quenched in dark clouds of slumber lie
The terror of his beak, and light'nings of his eye.

I. 3.

 Thee the voice, the dance, obey,
Tempered to thy warbled lay.
O'er Idalia's velvet-green
The rosy-crownèd Loves are seen
On Cytherea's day
With antic Sports, and blue-eyed Pleasures,
Frisking light in frolic measures;
Now pursuing, now retreating,
Now in circling troops they meet:
To brisk notes in cadence beating
Glance their many-twinkling feet.
Slow melting strains their Queen's approach declare:
Where'er she turns the Graces homage pay.
With arms sublime, that float upon the air,
In gliding state she wins her easy way:
O'er her warm cheek, and rising bosom, move
The bloom of young Desire, and purple light of Love.

---

l.2. G's note on this paragraph (1768): "Power of harmony to calm the turbulent sallies of the soul. The thoughts are borrowed from the first Pythian of Pindar."
l.15. cf. Collins's *Ode to Pity*, note to l.42.
l.21. the feathered king: the eagle, Jove's bird.
l.3. G's note on this paragraph (1768): "Power of harmony to produce all the graces of motion in the body."
l.27. Idalia: a town in Cyprus where there was a temple to Venus.
l.29. Cytherea: Venus.

The Progress of Poesy

II. 1.

Man's feeble race what Ills await,
Labour, and Penury, the racks of Pain,
Disease, and Sorrow's weeping train,
And Death, sad refuge from the storms of Fate!
The fond complaint, my Song, disprove,
And justify the laws of Jove.
Say, has he giv'n in vain the heav'nly Muse?
Night, and all her sickly dews,
Her Spectres wan, and Birds of boding cry,   50
He gives to range the dreary sky:
Till down the eastern cliffs afar
Hyperion's march they spy, and glitt'ring shafts of war.

II. 2.

In climes beyond the solar road,
Where shaggy forms o'er ice-built mountains roam,
The Muse has broke the twilight-gloom
To chear the shivering Native's dull abode.
And oft, beneath the od'rous shade
Of Chili's boundless forests laid,
She deigns to hear the savage Youth repeat   60
In loose numbers wildly sweet
Their feather-cinctured Chiefs, and dusky Loves.
Her track, where'er the Goddess roves,
Glory pursue, and generous Shame,
Th' unconquerable Mind, and Freedom's holy flame.

II. 3.

Woods, that wave o'er Delphi's steep,
Isles, that crown th' Egæan deep,

II.1. G's note on this paragraph (1768): "To compensate the real and imaginary ills of life, the Muse was given to Mankind by the same Providence that sends the Day by its chearful presence to dispel the gloom and terrors of the Night."
l.51. gives: permits.
l.53. Hyperion: the sun.

II.2. G's note on this paragraph (1768): "Extensive influence of poetic Genius over the remotest and most uncivilized nations: its connection with liberty, and the virtues that naturally attend on it . . ."
II.3. G's note on this paragraph (1768): "Progress of Poetry from

Fields, that cool Illissus laves,
Or where Mæander's amber waves
In lingering Lab'rinths creep, 70
How do your tuneful Echoes languish,
Mute, but to the voice of Anguish?
Where each old poetic Mountain
Inspiration breathed around:
Ev'ry shade and hallowed Fountain
Murmured deep a solemn sound:
Till the sad Nine in Greece's evil hour
Left their Parnassus for the Latian plains.
Alike they scorn the pomp of tyrant-Power,
And coward Vice, that revels in her chains. 80
When Latium had her lofty spirit lost,
They sought, oh Albion! next thy sea-encirclèd coast.

III. 1.

Far from the sun and summer-gale,
In thy green lap was Nature's Darling laid,
What time, where lucid Avon strayed,
To Him the mighty Mother did unveil
Her aweful face: The dauntless Child
Stretched forth his little arms, and smiled.
This pencil take (she said) whose colours clear
Richly paint the vernal year: 90
Thine too these golden keys, immortal Boy!
This can unlock the gates of Joy;
Of Horrour that, and thrilling Fears,
Or ope the sacred source of sympathetic Tears.

Greece to Italy, and from Italy to England. Chaucer was not unacquainted with the writings of Dante or of Petrarch. The Earl of Surrey and Sir Thomas Wyatt had travelled in Italy, and formed their taste there; Spenser imitated the Italian writers; Milton improved on them: but this School expired soon after the Restoration, and a new one arose on the French model, which has subsisted ever since."
l.68. Illissus: a river running through Athens.
l.69. Mæander: a river flowing through Phrygia.
l.83. in England, far from the sunny South.
l.84. G (1768): "Shakespear."
l.89. pencil: the painter's brush.

III. 2.

Nor second He, that rode sublime
Upon the seraph-wings of Extasy,
The secrets of th' Abyss to spy.
He passed the flaming bounds of Place and Time:
The living Throne, the saphire-blaze,
Where Angels tremble, while they gaze,   100
He saw; but blasted with excess of light,
Closed his eyes in endless night.
Behold, where Dryden's less presumptuous car,
Wide o'er the fields of Glory bear
Two Coursers of ethereal race,
With necks in thunder cloathed, and long-resounding pace.

III. 3.

Hark, his hands the lyre explore!
Bright-eyed Fancy hovering o'er
Scatters from her pictured urn
Thoughts, that breath, and words, that burn.   110
But ah! 'tis heard no more—
Oh! Lyre divine, what daring Spirit
Wakes thee now? Tho' he inherit
Nor the pride, nor ample pinion,
That the Theban Eagle bear
Sailing with supreme dominion
Thro' the azure deep of air:
Yet oft before his infant eyes would run
Such forms, as glitter in the Muse's ray
With orient hues, unborrowed of the Sun: 120

---

l.95. second He: G (1768): "Milton."
l.99. G (1768) refers to *Ezekiel* i. 20, 26, 28.
l.105. G (1768): "Meant to express the stately march and sounding energy of Dryden's rhimes."
l.111. G (1768): "We have had in our language no other odes of the sublime kind, than that of Dryden on St. Cecilia's day: for Cowley (who had his merit) yet wanted judgment, style, and harmony, for such a task. That of Pope is not worthy of so great a man. Mr. Mason indeed of late days has touched the true chords, and with a masterly hand, in some of his Choruses,—above all in the last of Caractacus,

Hark! heard ye not yon footstep dread? &c."
l.115. the Theban Eagle: Pindar.

Yet shall he mount, and keep his distant way
Beyond the limits of a vulgar fate,
Beneath the Good how far—but far above the Great.

l.122. vulgar: ordinary, common.
l.123. This last line is easily confusing: far beneath me are the poets of mere competence; far above me are those of the first order.

THE BARD

NOTE: Gray prefaced *The Bard* with this Advertisement: "The following Ode is founded on a Tradition current in Wales, that EDWARD THE FIRST, when he compleated the conquest of that country, ordered all the Bards, that fell into his hands, to be put to death." And in his Commonplace Book, he had written: "The army of Edward I., as they march through a deep valley, and approach Mount Snowden, are suddenly stopped by the appearance of a venerable figure seated on the summit of an inaccessible rock, who, with a voice more than human, reproaches the king with all the desolation and misery which he had brought on his country. . . . His song ended, he precipitates himself from the mountain, and is swallowed up by the river that rolls at its foot."

THE BARD

A PINDARIC ODE

I. 1.

'Ruin seize thee, ruthless King!
'Confusion on thy banners wait,
'Tho' fanned by Conquest's crimson wing
'They mock the air with idle state.
'Helm, nor Hauberk's twisted mail,
'Nor even thy virtues, Tyrant, shall avail
'To save thy secret soul from nightly fears,
'From Cambria's curse, from Cambria's tears!'
Such were the sounds, that o'er the crested pride
Of the first Edward scattered wild dismay, 10
As down the steep of Snowdon's shaggy side
He wound with toilsome march his long array.
Stout Glo'ster stood aghast in speechless trance:
To arms! cried Mortimer, and couched his quiv'ring lance.

I. 2.

On a rock, whose haughty brow
Frowns o'er old Conway's foaming flood,
Robed in the sable garb of woe,
With haggard eyes the Poet stood;
(Loose his beard, and hoary hair
Streamed, like a meteor, to the troubled air) 20
And with a Master's hand, and Prophet's fire,

---

l.8. Cambria: medieval name of Wales.
l.13. Glo'ster: G (1768): "Gilbert de Clare, surnamed the Red, Earl of Gloucester and Hertford, son-in-law to King Edward."
l.14. Mortimer: G (1768): "Edmond de Mortimer, Lord of Wigmore."

Struck the deep sorrows of his lyre.
'Hark, how each giant-oak, and desert cave,
'Sighs to the torrent's aweful voice beneath!
'O'er thee, oh King! their hundred arms they wave,
'Revenge on thee in hoarser murmurs breath;
'Vocal no more, since Cambria's fatal day,
'To high-born Hoel's harp, or soft Llewellyn's lay.

I. 3.

'Cold is Cadwallo's tongue,
'That hushed the stormy main: 30
'Brave Urien sleeps upon his craggy bed:
'Mountains, ye mourn in vain
'Modred, whose magic song
'Made huge Plinlimmon bow his cloud-topped head.
'On dreary Arvon's shore they lie,
'Smeared with gore, and ghastly pale:
'Far, far aloof th' affrighted ravens fail;
'The famished Eagle screams, and passes by.
'Dear lost companions of my tuneful art,
'Dear, as the light that visits these sad eyes, 40
'Dear, as the ruddy drops that warm my heart,
'Ye died amidst your dying country's cries—
'No more I weep. They do not sleep.
'On yonder cliffs, a griesly band,
'I see them sit, they linger yet,
'Avengers of their native land:
'With me in dreadful harmony they join,
'And weave with bloody hands the tissue of thy line.'

---

l.28. Hoel: a famous bard, son of Owen Gwynedd, prince of North Wales.
l.28. Llewellyn: described as a "tender-hearted prince" in a Welsh poem about him.
ll.29-33. Cadwallo, Urien, Modred: names apparently chosen by Gray as typical for Welsh bards.
l.34. Plinlimmon: a mountain in Cardigan, Wales.
l.35. Arvon's shore: G (1768): "The shores of Caernarvonshire. . . ."
l.35. they: the bards whom Edward had put to death.

II. 1.

"Weave the warp, and weave the woof,
"The winding-sheet of Edward's race.   50
"Give ample room, and verge enough
"The characters of hell to trace.
"Mark the year, and mark the night,
"When Severn shall re-eccho with affright
"The shrieks of death, thro' Berkley's roofs that ring,
"Shrieks of an agonizing King!
"She-Wolf of France, with unrelenting fangs,
"That tear'st the bowels of thy mangled Mate,
"From thee be born, who o'er thy country hangs
"The scourge of Heav'n. What Terrors round him wait!   60
"Amazement in his van, with Flight combined,
"And sorrow's faded form, and solitude behind.

II. 2.

"Mighty Victor, mighty Lord,
"Low on his funeral couch he lies!
"No pitying heart, no eye, afford
"A tear to grace his obsequies.
"Is the sable Warriour fled?
"Thy son is gone. He rests among the Dead.
"The Swarm, that in thy noon-tide beam were born?
"Gone to salute the rising Morn.   70
"Fair laughs the Morn, and soft the Zephyr blows,
"While proudly riding o'er the azure realm
"In gallant trim the gilded Vessel goes;
"Youth on the prow, and Pleasure at the helm;

---

l.49. Double quotation marks enclose the passage of 52 lines which follows, marking the "dreadful harmony" made by the bard and the "griesly band" as they sing together.
l.54. G (1768): "Edward the Second, cruelly butchered in Berkley-Castle."
l.57. G (1768): "Isabel of France, Edward the Second's adulterous Queen."
l.59. G (1768): "Triumphs of Edward the Third in France."
l.64. G (1768): "Death of that King, abandoned by his Children, and even robbed in his last moments by his Courtiers and his Mistress."
l.67. the sable Warrior: G (1768): "Edward, the Black Prince, dead some time before his Father."
l.71. G (1768): "Magnificance of Richard the Second's reign . . ."

The Bard

"Regardless of the sweeping Whirlwind's sway,
"That, hushed in grim repose, expects his evening-prey.

II. 3.

"Fill high the sparkling bowl,
"The rich repast prepare,
"Reft of a crown, he yet may share the feast:
"Close by the regal chair   80
"Fell Thirst and Famine scowl
"A baleful smile upon their baffled Guest.
"Heard ye the din of battle bray,
"Lance to lance, and horse to horse?
"Long Years of havock urge their destined course,
"And thro' the kindred squadrons mow their way.
"Ye Towers of Julius, London's lasting shame,
"With many a foul and midnight murther fed,
"Revere his Consort's faith, his Father's fame,
"And spare the meek Usurper's holy head.   90
"Above, below, the rose of snow,
"Twined with her blushing foe, we spread:
"The bristled Boar in infant-gore
"Wallows beneath the thorny shade.
"Now, Brothers, bending o'er th' accursed loom
"Stamp we our vengeance deep, and ratify his doom.

III. 1.

"Edward, lo! to sudden fate
"(Weave we the woof. The thread is spun)

---

l.81. In one of the four notes he consented to insert in the 1757 ed. of the *Odes*, G gave his reader the following information: "Richard the Second, (as we are told by Archbishop Scroop and the confederate Lords in their manifesto, by Thomas of Walsingham, and all the older Writers,) was starved to death. The story of his assassination by Sir Piers of Exon, is of much later date."
l.83. G (1768): "Ruinous civil wars of York and Lancaster."

l.87. the oldest part of the Tower of London.
l.89. Consort: Margaret of Anjou, Henry VI's queen consort.
l.89. Father: Henry V.
l.90. the meek Usurper: G (1768): "Henry the Sixth very near being canonized. The line of Lancaster had no right of inheritance to the Crown."
l.91. G (1768): "The white and red roses, devices of York and Lancaster."
l.93. Richard III, known as The Boar.

"Half of thy heart we consecrate.
"(The web is wove. The work is done.)" 100
'Stay, oh stay! nor thus forlorn
'Leave me unblessed, unpitied, here to mourn:
'In yon bright track, that fires the western skies,
'They melt, they vanish from my eyes.
'But oh! what solemn scenes on Snowdon's height
'Descending slow their glitt'ring skirts unroll?
'Visions of glory, spare my aching sight,
'Ye unborn Ages, crowd not on my soul!
'No more our long-lost Arthur we bewail.
'All-hail, ye genuine Kings, Britannia's Issue, hail! 110

III. 2.

'Girt with many a Baron bold
'Sublime their starry fronts they rear;
'And gorgeous Dames, and Statesmen old
'In bearded majesty, appear.
'In the midst a Form divine!
'Her eye proclaims her of the Briton-Line;
'Her lyon-port, her awe-commanding face,
'Attempered sweet to virgin-grace.
'What strings symphonious tremble in the air,
'What strains of vocal transport round her play! 120
'Hear from the grave, great Taliessin, hear;
'They breathe a soul to animate thy clay.
'Bright Rapture calls, and soaring, as she sings,
'Waves in the eye of Heav'n her many-coloured wings.

---

l.99. G (1757): "Eleanor of Castile died a few years after the conquest of Wales. The heroic proof she gave of her affection for her Lord is well known. . . ."
l.104. the griesly band, now vanishing from the Bard's sight.
l.109. G (1768): "It was the common belief of the Welch nation, that King Arthur was still alive in Fairy-Land, and should return again to reign over Britain."
l.110. G (1768): "Both Merlin and Taliessin had prophesied, that the Welch should regain their sovereignty over this island; which seemed to be accomplished in the House of Tudor."
l.115. Queen Elizabeth I.
l.121. G (1757): "Taliessin, Chief of the Bards, flourished in the VIth century. . . ."

III. 3.

'The verse adorn again
'Fierce War, and faithful Love,
'And Truth severe, by fairy Fiction drest.
'In buskined measures move
'Pale Grief, and pleasing Pain,
'With Horrour, Tyrant of the throbbing breast.   130
'A Voice, as of the Cherub-Choir,
'Gales from blooming Eden bear;
'And distant warblings lessen on my ear,
'That lost in long futurity expire.
'Fond impious Man, think'st thou, yon sanguine cloud,
'Raised by thy breath, has quenched the Orb of day?
'To-morrow he repairs the golden flood,
'And warms the nations with redoubled ray.
'Enough for me: With joy I see
'The different doom our Fates assign.   140
'Be thine Despair, and scept'red Care,
'To triumph, and to die, are mine.'
He spoke, and headlong from the mountain's height
Deep in the roaring tide he plunged to endless night.

---

l.128. Shakespeare. "The succession of Poets after Mil-
l.131. Milton. ton's time."
l.133. distant warblings: G (1768):

THE FATAL SISTERS

NOTE: In the collected edition of his poems which Gray authorized Dodsley to print in 1768, there appeared for the first time three of the adaptations from Old Norse and Welsh poetry with which Gray had been occupied in the years immediately following the appearance of his two Pindaric *Odes* in 1757. The three pieces were *The Fatal Sisters* (a paraphrase of *Darraðar Lióð*, or *Lay of Darts*, an Icelandic poem of the eleventh century, which was available to Gray in Latin translation in a book by a Danish scholar, Thomas Bartholin, printed Copenhagen 1689), *The Descent of Odin* (based on an Icelandic poem *Vegtams Kviða*, a Latin translation of which was also in Bartholin), and *The Triumphs of Owen* (from the Welsh as translated by the Rev. Evan Evans, a Denbigshire curate).

In 1768 Gray introduced *The Fatal Sisters* with the following Preface:

> In the Eleventh Century *Sigurd*, Earl of the Orkney-Islands, went with a fleet of ships and a considerable body of troops into Ireland, to the assistance of *Sictryg with the silken beard*, who was then making war on his father-in-law *Brian*, King of Dublin: the Earl and all his forces were cut to pieces, and *Sictryg* was in danger of a total defeat; but the enemy had a greater loss by the death of *Brian*, their King, who fell in the action. On Christmas-day, (the day of the battle,) a Native of *Caithness* in Scotland saw at a distance a number of persons on horseback riding full speed towards a hill, and seeming to enter into it. Curiosity led him to follow them, till looking through an opening in the rocks he saw twelve gigantic figures resembling women: they were all employed about a loom; and as they wove, they sung the following dreadful Song; which when they had finished, they tore the web into twelve pieces, and (each taking her portion) galloped Six to the North and as many to the South.

Gray likewise assisted the readers of 1768 with a Note of explanation concerning the Fatal Sisters: "The *Valkyriur* were female Divinities, Servants of *Odin* (or *Woden*) in the Gothic mythology. Their name signifies *Chusers of the slain*. They were mounted on swift horses, with drawn swords in their hands; and in the throng of battle selected such as were destined to slaughter, and conducted them to *Valhalla*, the hall of *Odin*, or paradise of the Brave; where they attended the banquet, and served the departed Heroes with horns of mead and ale."

THE FATAL SISTERS

AN ODE FROM THE NORSE-TONGUE

Now the storm begins to lower,
(Haste, the loom of Hell prepare,)
Iron-sleet of arrowy shower
Hurtles in the darkened air.

Glitt'ring lances are the loom,
Where the dusky warp we strain,
Weaving many a Soldier's doom,
Orkney woe, and *Randver's* bane.

See the griesly texture grow,
('Tis of human entrails made,)
And the weights, that play below,
Each a gasping Warriour's head.

1.8. We know that G took over the phrase "Randver's bane" from the Latin of Bartholin. The original Icelandic speaks of "the friends of Randvérr's slayer," i.e., the Valkyrie, friends of Odin.

Shafts for shuttles, dipt in gore,
Shoot the trembling cords along.
Sword, that once a Monarch bore,
Keep the tissue close and strong.

Mista black, terrific Maid,
Sangrida, and *Hilda* see,
Join the wayward work to aid:
'Tis the woof of victory. 20

Ere the ruddy sun be set,
Pikes must shiver, javelins sing,
Blade with clattering buckler meet,
Hauberk crash, and helmet ring.

(Weave the crimson web of war)
Let us go, and let us fly,
Where our Friends the conflict share,
Where they triumph, where they die.

As the paths of fate we tread,
Wading thro' th' ensanguined field: 30
Gondula, and *Geira*, spread
O'er the youthful King your shield.

We the reins to slaughter give,
Ours to kill, and ours to spare:
Spite of danger he shall live.
(Weave the crimson web of war.)

They, whom once the desart-beach
Pent within its bleak domain,
Soon their ample sway shall stretch
O'er the plenty of the plain. 40

Low the dauntless Earl is laid,
Gored with many a gaping wound:
Fate demands a nobler head;
Soon a King shall bite the ground.

---

l.32. the youthful King: "Sictryg with the silken beard," referred to in G's Preface (see note on page 108).
l.37. the Northmen, destined to take over the interior parts of Ireland.
l.41. apparently Sigurd.
l.44. Brian, King of Dublin.

Long his loss shall Eirin weep,
Ne'er again his likeness see;
Long her strains in sorrow steep,
Strains of Immortality!

Horror covers all the heath,
Clouds of carnage blot the sun. 50
Sisters, weave the web of death;
Sisters, cease, the work is done.

Hail the task, and hail the hands!
Songs of joy and triumph sing!
Joy to the victorious bands;
Triumph to the younger King.

Mortal, thou that hear'st the tale,
Learn the tenour of our song.
Scotland, thro' each winding vale
Far and wide the notes prolong. 60

Sisters, hence with spurs of speed:
Each her thundering faulchion wield;
Each bestride her sable steed.
Hurry, hurry to the field.

l.56. Sictryg.

Mark Akenside

1721: born at Newcastle-upon-Tyne of Nonconformist parents; his father was a butcher
1737: began contributing verses to *The Gentleman's Magazine* under pseudonyms of "Marcus" or "Britannius"
1739: to the University of Edinburgh to study theology, but quickly abandoned theology for medicine
1742: returned to Newcastle; at work on a long didactic-philosophic poem, *The Pleasures of Imagination*
1744: publication by Dodsley of the *Pleasures*, a great and immediate success; in April to Leyden as a medical student; obtained degree there in May; returned to England and practiced as a physician in Northampton
1745: *Odes on Several Subjects*
1745-70: made independent through the generosity of his friend, Jeremiah Dyson, clerk to the House of Commons; set up practice in London, achieving considerable recognition; received a degree from Cambridge University; became a Fellow of the Royal College of Physicians, a Fellow of the Royal Society, physician to Christ's and to St. Thomas's hospitals, and in 1761 one of the Physicians-in-Ordinary to the Queen
1757-70: at work on a revised version of the *Pleasures*
1770: died 23 June
1772: *The Poems of Mark Akenside, M.D.*, edited by Dyson, including the unfinished revision of *The Pleasures of Imagination*, entitled *The Pleasures of the Imagination*

As a youth in Newcastle, Akenside acquired from his Nonconformist environment and from writers like Shaftesbury and Hutcheson the enthusiastic spirit of the English Enlightenment, with its assurance (arising from a confidence in the Divine order and the Divine beneficence), its good-will, and its hope for the enrichment of life. His years at Edinburgh confirmed these views. At fifteen Akenside was already writing poetry—short verse pieces conforming to the traditional kinds, belletristic in nature, exhibiting strong intelligence, marked rhetorical control, and some talent. He continued to write this sort of poetry for a good many years. What distinguishes *The Pleasures of Imagination* from his other compositions is that here the impelling force is his philosophic ideas, which his poetic skill is enlisted to express.

The Pleasures of Imagination achieved, in its time, a very great success, being as well-known as *An Essay on Man, The Seasons*, and *Night Thoughts*. His *Odes*, the first of which appeared in 1745, have merit and preceded the odes of the Wartons, Gray, and Collins. They even influenced Keats. Akenside's verse epistles, satires, and political pieces are vigorous and skillfully controlled. One feels, however, that Akenside's intelligence greatly exceeded his poetic talent, especially so in *The Pleasures of Imagination* which remains his major achievement. *The Pleasures* deserves attention as an example of eighteenth-century didactic poetry, as a statement of a widely-diffused order of ideas, cosmologic, aesthetic, and ethical, and as an expression of that delight in beauty which the Age of Taste was fostering with dedicated enthusiasm.

Analysis of the ideas set forth in the poem reveals the eclectic nature of Akenside's mind.* But however illogically he mixes Platonic idealism and modern empiricism, he does achieve something of a synthesis by virtue of the emotional quality he confers on his subject. He analyzes beauty, but he has experienced it too. Here is the eighteenth-century Man of Taste, a person somewhat different in sensibility and range of experience from the better known Man of Feeling. *The Pleasures of Imagination* is not easy

---

* Akenside did not claim that the philosophic ideas he was presenting were original, and in his footnotes to *T.P. of I.* he cites many of his sources. He relies heavily on Addison's series of essays on the imagination (*Spectator*, nos. 411-421), and draws in various ways and degrees upon Platonic theories, Locke, Leibniz, Shaftesbury and Hutcheson. In form he chiefly follows Lucretius' *De rerum natura*, though he is of course conscious of Pope's *Essay* as the foremost modern example of the didactic-philosophic poem.

reading. The exposition is complex and sometimes confusing, and the style now strikes us as unfortunately artificial and mannered.*

---

* In his foreword A discusses "the manner or turn of composition" in the poem: he has had in mind the style of Virgil's *Georgics*, Horace's "epistolary way," and the example of Pope. Yet, he adds, "the subject . . . tending almost constantly to admiration and enthusiasm, seem'd rather to demand a more open, pathetic and figur'd style." In his effort to attain feeling, sublimity, and stylistic ceremoniousness, as well as in his choice of blank verse, he is clearly influenced by the Miltonic stylistic tradition which persists in so many of the long blank-verse poems of this period.

from THE PLEASURES OF IMAGINATION

from BOOK THE FIRST

With what attractive charms this goodly frame
Of Nature touches the consenting hearts
Of mortal men; and what the pleasing stores
Which beauteous Imitation thence derives
To deck the poet's or the painter's toil,—
My verse unfolds. Attend, ye gentle powers
Of musical delight! and while I sing
Your gifts, your honours, dance around my strain.
Thou, smiling queen of every tuneful breast,
Indulgent Fancy! from the fruitful banks   10
Of Avon, whence thy rosy fingers cull
Fresh flowers and dews to sprinkle on the turf
Where Shakespeare lies, be present; and with thee
Let Fiction come, upon her vagrant wings
Wafting ten thousand colours through the air,
Which, by the glances of her magic eye,
She blends and shifts at will, thro' countless forms,
Her wild creation. Goddess of the lyre,
Which rules the accents of the moving sphere,
Wilt thou, eternal Harmony, descend   20
And join this festive train? for with thee comes
The guide, the guardian of their lovely sports,
Majestic Truth; and where Truth deigns to come,
Her sister Liberty will not be far.
Be present, all ye Genii, who conduct

Book the First . . . : A states his purpose in his foreword: to explain how nature itself (i.e. the outward world) and the imitations of nature given by the various arts afford us pleasure as they work upon us through the faculty of our imagination. In these opening lines, constituting the Invocation, Fancy (i.e. the poetic imagination, here associated with Shakespeare) and Diction (i.e. artistic invention) are seen as working in co-operation with Truth, or that vision of Eternal Harmony.

The wandering footsteps of the youthful bard,
New to your springs and shades; who touch his ear
With finer sounds; who heighten to his eye
The bloom of Nature, and before him turn
The gayest, happiest attitude of things.   30

　　　　　　　　　* * *

　　From Heaven my strains begin; from Heaven descends   56
The flame of genius to the human breast,
And love, and beauty, and poetic joy,
And inspiration. Ere the radiant sun
Sprang from the east, or 'mid the vault of night   60
The moon suspended her serener lamp;
Ere mountains, woods, or streams adorned the globe,
Or Wisdom taught the sons of men her lore;
Then lived the Almighty One: then, deep-retired
In his unfathomed essence, viewed the forms,
The forms eternal of created things;
The radiant sun, the moon's nocturnal lamp,
The mountains, woods, and streams, the rolling globe,
And Wisdom's mien celestial. From the first
Of days, on them his love divine he fixed,   70
His admiration; till in time complete
What he admired and loved, his vital smile
Unfolded into being. Hence the breath
Of life informing each organic frame,
Hence the green earth, and wild resounding waves;
Hence light and shade alternate, warmth and cold;
And clear autumnal skies and vernal showers,
And all the fair variety of things.
　　But not alike to every mortal eye
Is this great scene unveiled. For since the claims   80
Of social life to different labours urge
The active powers of man, with wise intent

1.56. The universe has been designed according to the uncreated images in the mind of the Eternal One. Men are differently constituted, but some have been granted the power to perceive this Eternal Harmony. (These latter, thanks to their imaginative acuity and their awareness of Truth, seem to constitute for A not only the creative artists but more generally the Men of Taste, all of whom experience imaginative delight to a peculiar degree.)

The hand of Nature on peculiar minds
Imprints a different bias, and to each
Decrees its province in the common toil.
To some she taught the fabric of the sphere,
The changeful moon, the circuit of the stars,
The golden zones of heaven: to some she gave
To weigh the moment of eternal things,
Of time, and space, and fate's unbroken chain,   90
And will's quick impulse: others by the hand
She led o'er vales and mountains, to explore
What healing virtue swells the tender veins
Of herbs and flowers; or what the beams of morn
Draw forth, distilling from the clifted rind
In balmy tears. But some, to higher hopes
Were destined; some within a finer mould
She wrought, and tempered with a purer flame.
To these the Sire Omnipotent unfolds
The world's harmonious volume, there to read   100
The transcript of Himself. On every part
They trace the bright impressions of his hand:
In earth or air, the meadow's purple stores,
The moon's mild radiance, or the virgin's form
Blooming with rosy smiles, they see portrayed
That uncreated beauty, which delights
The Mind supreme. They also feel her charms,
Enamoured; they partake the eternal joy.

*   *   *

Thus was Beauty sent from heaven,   372
The lovely ministress of Truth and Good
In this dark world; for Truth and Good are one,

---

l.372. In the preceding lines A, following Addison's discussion in the *Spectator*, has distinguished three varieties of imaginative response: the sublime, the wonderful, and the fair or beautiful. In the present passage he confers a special importance on Beauty: it should be the mistress of Truth and Good; i.e., our creative powers should be reunited with ethical philosophy. They have long been separated, and in a note to l. 30 of Book II, A remarks that philosophy and imagination were never more widely separated than "at the revolution, when *Locke* stood at the head of one party, and *Dryden* of the other." The union of Beauty, Truth, and the Good is set forth in the Platonic vision in the concluding lines of this passage.

And Beauty dwells in them, and they in her,
With like participation. Wherefore, then,
O sons of earth! would ye dissolve the tie?
O wherefore, with a rash, impetuous aim,
Seek ye those flowery joys with which the hand
Of lavish Fancy paints each flattering scene   380
Where Beauty seems to dwell; nor once inquire
Where is the sanction of eternal Truth,
Or where the seal of undeceitful good,
To save your search from folly! Wanting these,
Lo! Beauty withers in your void embrace,
And with the glittering of an idiot's toy
Did Fancy mock your vows. Nor let the gleam
Of youthful hope that shines upon your hearts
Be chilled or clouded at this awful task,
To learn the lore of undeceitful good,   390
And Truth eternal. Though the poisonous charms
Of baleful Superstition guide the feet
Of servile numbers, through a dreary way
To their abode, through deserts, thorns, and mire;
And leave the wretched pilgrim all forlorn
To muse at last amid the ghostly gloom
Of graves, and hoary vaults, and cloistered cells;
To walk with spectres through the midnight shade,
And to the screaming owl's accursed song
Attune the dreadful workings of his heart;   400
Yet be not ye dismayed. A gentler star
Your lovely search illumines. From the grove
Where Wisdom talked with her Athenian sons,
Could my ambitious hand entwine a wreath
Of Plato's olive with the Mantuan bay,
Then should my powerful verse at once dispel
Those monkish horrors; then in light divine
Disclose the Elysian prospect, where the steps
Of those whom Nature charms, through blooming walks,   410
Through fragrant mountains and poetic streams,
Amid the train of sages, heroes, bards,
Led by their wingèd Genius, and the choir
Of laurelled science and harmonious art,
Proceed exulting to the eternal shrine,
Where Truth conspicuous with her sister-twins,

The undivided partners of her sway,
With good and beauty reigns.

* * *

         For what are all
The forms which brute, unconscious matter wears,
Greatness of bulk, or symmetry of parts?
Not reaching to the heart, soon feeble grows
The superficial impulse; dull their charms,
And satiate soon, and pall the languid eye.
Not so the moral species, nor the powers
Of genius and design; the ambitious mind
There sees herself: by these congenial forms
Touched and awakened, with intenser act
She bends each nerve, and meditates well pleased
Her features in the mirror. For of all
The inhabitants of earth, to man alone
Creative Wisdom gave to lift his eye
To Truth's eternal measures; thence to frame
The sacred laws of action and of will,
Discerning justice from unequal deeds,
And temperance from folly. But beyond
This energy of Truth, whose dictates bind
Assenting reason, the benignant Sire,
To deck the honoured paths of just and good,
Had added bright Imagination's rays:
Where Virtue, rising from the awful depth
Of Truth's mysterious bosom, doth forsake
The unadorned condition of her birth;
And, dressed by Fancy in ten thousand hues,
Assumes a various feature, to attract,
With charms responsive to each gazer's eye,
The hearts of men. Amid his rural walk,
The ingenuous youth, whom solitude inspires
With purest wishes, from the pensive shade
Beholds her moving, like a virgin muse
That wakes her lyre to some indulgent theme

---

l.526. Imagination reflects the natural world and delights us in so doing, but it moves us most deeply when it combines with the moral faculty and touches upon the things of moral experience.

>   Of harmony and wonder; while among
>   The herd of servile minds, her strenuous form   560
>   Indignant flashes on the patriot's eye,
>   And through the rolls of memory appeals
>   To ancient honour, or in act serene,
>   Yet watchful, raises the majestic sword
>   Of public Power, from dark Ambition's reach
>   To guard the sacred volume of the laws.

* * *

1.566. *T. P. of I.* consists of three books. Bk. II deals with sources of pleasure other than the three—the sublime, the wonderful, the beautiful—discussed in Bk. I. These other sources include "discovery of truth," the perception of contrivance and design in nature, and the emotions arising from the passions, wherein "nature speaks her genuine language." Bk. III contains a lengthy discussion of still further pleasures, especially those arising from our portrayal of the ridiculous. This passage is important in the history of the eighteenth-century discussion of humor, ridicule, and satire. The latter part of Bk. III discusses the role of association in human experience and "the nature and conduct of taste."

The expanded version of the poem, *The P. of the I.,* was never finished: there are four books, of which only the first two were completed.

William Collins

1721: born at Chichester, where his father, a well-known hatter, was mayor
1733: admitted to Winchester College as a scholar "on the foundation"; here Joseph Warton was his contemporary and close friend; C's poem, entitled "Sonnet" and signed "Delicatulus," printed in *Gentleman's Magazine*, October 1739; said to have composed much of his *Persian Eclogues* while still at Winchester
1740: in March, admitted as a Commoner of Queen's College, Oxford, but according to tradition remained at Winchester, being elected in the summer as a scholar at New College, Oxford, where however there was no vacancy
1741: in July, elected to a Demyship at Magdalen College, Oxford
1742: *Persian Eclogues* published
1743: graduated B.A.; in December his *Verses Humbly Ad-*

The documented facts concerning C's life have only gradually come to light. The *Memoirs of Collins* given by W. May Thomas in his edition of the *Poetical Works of William Collins* was as accurate as possible when it appeared in 1858. The brief biographical account given by W. C. Bronson in his edition of the *Poems* (1898) was, in turn, up-to-date. H. O. White supplied new information in 1927 ("The Letters of William Collins," *R E S*, III) and again in 1930 ("William Collins and Miss Bundy," *R E S*, VI), and all this was embodied by E. G. Ainsworth in his *Poor Collins* (1937; see bibliography). P. L. Carver furnished the most recent information in a remarkable series of notes in *N & Q*, 19 Aug. 1939 through 14 Oct., though his *Drafts and Fragments of Verse* (see bibliography), edited in 1956 by J. S. Cunningham (from the Warton papers in the Trinity College, Oxford, library), must henceforth be taken into account in considering C's artistic career.

dress'd to Sir Thomas Hanmer appeared; quitted the University for London

1744: entered into the gay life of London, lodging with the Bundys in King's Square Court, Soho; described at this time by John Mulso as "entirely an Author, & hardly speaks out of Rule . . . ;" a second edition of the verses *To Sir Thomas Hanmer* appeared, with the addition of the *Song from Cymbeline* ("To fair Fidele's grassy tomb"); on his own initiative, sometime before September, determined to take Holy Orders, and asked the Duke of Richmond for assistance in obtaining a curacy; offered one by Mr. Green, rector of Birdham; back in London, dissuaded from entering the Church by a Mr. Hardham, a tobacconist and enthusiastic lover of the drama; under Hardham's influence, may now have tried to write a tragedy, eventually giving this up; turned to a translation with commentary of Aristotle's *Poetics*; published proposals for a work advertised in Dublin at close of year as *A Review of the Advancement of Learning from 1300 to 1521*; engaged to furnish lives for the newly established *Biographica Britannica*

1745: early this year an uncle, Charles Collins, died, leaving C an inheritance; in the spring or early summer, before the possibility of coming into possession, there very likely occurred the episode, reported by Samuel Johnson, of C's pursuit by the bailiffs and his escape, through Johnson's help in securing an advance from a publisher "on the credit of a translation of Aristotle's Poetics"; in the summer, visited another uncle, Lt. Col. Edmund Martin, in Flanders, presumably to offer his services as a soldier at the moment of crisis brought on by the presence of the Young Pretender in the north, but his uncle apparently considered him unfit for service with the army; back in England by September

1746: in May met Joseph Warton at the Gilford races, where he and Warton determined to publish their odes in a joint volume; in May, still waiting for his inheritance to become available, C was arrested for debt at the suit of Miss Bundy at his lodgings in King's Square Court; 7 June his *Ode to a Lady* (to be included in *Odes on Several Subjects*) printed in Dodsley's *Museum*; in August once more in Flanders, presumably travelling for pleasure; late December (dated 1747) C's *Odes on Several Descriptive and Allegoric Subjects* appeared (Warton's *Odes on Various Subjects* printed separately—it is said at the insistence of the publisher—at about the same time)

1747: saw much of James Thomson at Richmond; by November was concerned with arrangements for a literary journal, originally conceived of as the "Clarendon Review" to be printed at Oxford, now referred to as the *Friendly Examiner, or Letters of Polémon and Philèthus or, the Plain Dealer* . . .

1749: *Ode Occasion'd by the Death of Mr. Thomson* printed in July; in autumn met John Home, and probably began the *Ode on the Popular Superstitions of the Highlands of Scotland*

1750: Thomas Warton saw C in London, "before his illness," C talking of the still-intended history of the *Revival of Learning* (i.e., *Review of the Advancement of Learning*), and of the still-projected *Clarendon Review*; *The Passions* set to music by Dr. William Hayes, Professor of Music at Oxford

1751: in London, seriously ill

1754: according to one report, went to France and later to Bath trying to regain health; said to have been confined in McDonald's madhouse at Chelsea, and removed from there by his sister to Chichester; J. and T. Warton visited him in September at Chichester; in November went to Oxford for a change of air, but his disabilities overcame him, and probably on this occasion Gilbert White saw him "under Merton wall, in a very affecting situation, struggling, and conveyed by force, in the arms of two or three men, towards the parish of St. Clement, in which was a house that took in such unhappy objects . . ."; from this time on C was apparently confined at Chichester

1757: *Persian Eclogues* reprinted (as *Oriental Eclogues*)

1759: died at Chichester, 12 June

1788: *An Ode on the Popular Superstitions of the Highlands of Scotland* first printed in *Transactions of the Royal Society of Edinburgh*, the short gaps in the ms. being supplied by Dr. Alexander Carlyle, the missing stanza V and first part of VI by Henry MacKenzie

1956: *William Collins: Drafts and Fragments of Verse*

OUR MOST RECENT information substantially discredits the older, traditional picture of Collins as an impecunious poet living from hand to mouth, pursued by bailiffs, and threatened with imprisonment for debt. He was, as a matter of fact, fairly well-to-do by the standards of his time, inheriting property from both his mother, whose death occurred in 1744 not long after his arrival in London, and from an uncle, Charles Collins, who died shortly afterwards. Collins's financial difficulties (Samuel Johnson once rescued him from the bailiffs; on another occasion he was arrested for debt at the suit of Miss Bundy, at whose house he lodged) could scarcely have been grimly serious ones and seem to have been occasioned by delays in settling the estates. He was not, as long believed, dependent upon his uncle in the army, Col. Martin.

From all accounts Collins was a delightful person. Dr. Johnson called him "poor dear Collins." Joseph and Thomas Warton held him in deep affection. He "was an acceptable companion everywhere," wrote John Ragsdale, another friend. His letter to John Gilbert Cooper (10 November 1747) has charming touches and it is a pity that only two of Collins's letters have thus far turned up. Unquestionably he was a dedicated artist. His constant revisions reveal his extraordinary sense of design and style. But the fragmentary nature of his achievement and the manner in which, to use the disparaging words of Gilbert White, his contemporary at Oxford, he "was always planning schemes" which "were carried no farther than the drawing up proposals" should not be attributed to flightiness or ineffectuality. Obviously Collins suffered from some physical maladjustment which no one understood, and what was taken for "madness" was very likely the direct result of this physical condition. Johnson seems to have guessed at this, for in the *Life* he observed that Collins's disorder "was not alienation of mind, but general laxity and feebleness, a deficiency rather of his vital than intellectual powers." A few days in a modern medical clinic would probably have given him ultimate freedom from his neuropsychological disturbances and restored his normal energy.

Collins enjoyed almost no reputation during his lifetime, but interest in him increased rapidly during the last four decades of the century, and by 1818, when Hazlitt was expressing his glowing appreciation, his place among the true poets had become assured. Our own century has been concerned with the more precise analysis of his art. It seemed important fifty years ago to determine the "pre-romantic" elements in his poetry. There undoubtedly are some, but Mr. Tillyard probably reflects the current prevailing opinion when he insists that Collins was entirely a man of his age, addressing his poetry to an eighteenth-century audience. The most significant recent studies of Collins give us a clearer understanding of his intentions by way of his poetic theory and his concept of the ode. His poetry was a "poetry of the imagination," in the sense which Joseph Warton and Addison used that term.

The volume issued in December 1746, precisely entitled *Odes on Several Descriptive and Allegoric Subjects*, contains twelve poems. These are not independent odes, but make up a planned whole. The central subject of the volume is the different kinds of literary art (tragedy, pastoral, Miltonic verse of sublimity, patriotic poetry, comedy, with the art of music being added at the end) and the affective qualities inherent in each. These different kinds and the emotional effects peculiar to each are presented in a variety of ode forms.

Traditionally there were two types of English odes, the impressively elaborate and sublime (the Pindaric, Cowleyan, or Great Ode), and the quieter, Horatian type with love its appropriate subject. The descriptive-allegorical ode was a new and important variant, permitting Collins to use a variety of odic forms and thus to achieve an exquisite modulation of mood as he passes from one poem and subject to another.

It is difficult today to come to terms with Collins's intentions. The delicacy of his effects, particularly in "How sleep the Brave" and the *Ode to Evening*, has always been felt, but more or less in spite of his language, the form of his verse, his pictorialism, and his allegorization. If we can convince ourselves that his artistic strategy springs from a reasoned and sometimes subtle theory, if we will in short learn to construe the idiom of this mid-eighteenth century poetic art, we shall discover in Collins a controlled and hence civilized and humanized emotion of surprising depth.

ODE TO PITY

O THOU, the friend of man, assigned
With balmy hands his wounds to bind,
And charm his frantic woe:
When first Distress, with dagger keen,
Broke forth to waste his destined scene,
His wild unsated foe!

By Pella's bard, a magic name,
By all the griefs his thought could frame,
Receive my humble rite:
Long, Pity, let the nations view
Thy sky-worn robes of tend'rest blue,
And eyes of dewy light!

But wherefore need I wander wide
To old Ilissus' distant side,
Deserted stream, and mute?
Wild Arun too has heard thy strains,
And Echo, midst my native plains,
Been soothed by Pity's lute.

Ode to Pity: This and the following *Ode to Fear* are concerned with the emotional effects of tragedy. Collins, said to have been engaged on a translation of Aristotle's *Poetics*, of course had Aristotle's pity and fear in mind, and doubtless also the hints dropped by Addison in his papers on the imagination. The verse form of this ode, the traditional six-line romance stanza, is in no sense Pindaric.
l.7. Pella's bard: the 1746 edition noted the following: "*Euripides*, of whom *Aristotle* pronounces, on a Comparison of him with *Sophocles,* That he was the greater Master of the tender Passions, ἦν τραγικώτερος." Euripides died in Pella. Aristotle says merely that Euripides seems the most tragic of the poets.
l.14. Ilissus: flowed through Athens.
l.16. Arun: 1746 note: "The River *Arun* runs by the Village in *Sussex,* where *Otway* had his *Birth.*"
l.17. Chichester, C's birthplace, was near the valley of the Arun.

Ode to Pity

    There first the wren thy myrtles shed
    On gentlest Otway's infant head,   20
        To him thy cell was shown;
    And while he sung the female heart,
    With youth's soft notes unspoiled by art,
        Thy turtles mixed their own.

    Come, Pity, come! By Fancy's aid,
    E'en now my thoughts, relenting maid,
        Thy temple's pride design:
    Its southern site, its truth complete,
    Shall raise a wild enthusiast heat
        In all who view the shrine.   30

    There Picture's toils shall well relate
    How Chance, or hard involving Fate,
        O'er mortal Bliss prevail:
    The buskined Muse shall near her stand,
    And sighing prompt her tender hand,
        With each disastrous tale.

    There let me oft, retired by day,
    In dreams of passion melt away,
        Allowed with thee to dwell:
    There waste the mournful lamp of night,   40
    Till, Virgin, thou again delight
        To hear a British shell!

---

l.19. the wren: gentlest of the birds.
l.20. Otway: the dramatist Thomas Otway (1651-1685).
l.24. turtles: the turtle dove.

l.40. waste: use up.
l.42. shell: Hermes was said to have invented the lyre by using the shell of a tortoise.

ODE TO FEAR

STROPHE

THOU, to whom the world unknown
With all its shadowy shapes is shown;
Who see'st appalled the unreal scene,
While Fancy lifts the veil between:
   Ah Fear! ah frantic Fear!
   I see, I see thee near!
I know thy hurried step, thy haggard eye!
Like thee I start, like thee disordered fly,
For lo what monsters in thy train appear!
Danger, whose limbs of giant mould   10
What mortal eye can fixed behold?
Who stalks his round, an hideous form,
Howling amidst the midnight storm,
Or throws him on the ridgy steep
Of some loose hanging rock to sleep:
And with him thousand Phantoms joined,
Who prompt to deeds accursed the mind:
And those, the Fiends who, near allied,
O'er Nature's wounds and wrecks preside;
Whilst Vengeance, in the lurid air,   20
Lifts her red arm, exposed and bare:
On whom that rav'ning Brood of Fate,
Who lap the blood of Sorrow, wait:
Who, Fear, this ghastly train can see,
And look not madly wild, like thee?

Ode to Fear: The form of this ode, suggestive of the Greek, places it in the tradition of the Great Ode of the Pindaric-Cowleyan-Drydenic tradition.
l.22. rav'ning Brood: 1746 note: "Alluding to the Κύνας ἀφύκτους of *Sophocles.* See the ELECTRA."

EPODE

In earliest Greece, to thee, with partial choice,
    The grief-full Muse addrest her infant tongue;
The maids and matrons, on her awful voice,
    Silent and pale in wild amazement hung.

Yet he, the bard who first invoked thy name,   30
    Disdained in Marathon its power to feel:
For not alone he nursed the poet's flame,
    But reached from Virtue's hand the patriot's steel.

But who is he whom later garlands grace,
    Who left awhile o'er Hybla's dews to rove,
With trembling eyes thy dreary steps to trace,
    Where thou and Furies shared the baleful grove?

Wrapt in thy cloudy veil the incestuous queen
    Sighed the sad call her son and husband heard,
When once alone it broke the silent scene,   40
    And he, the wretch of Thebes, no more appeared.

O Fear, I know thee by my throbbing heart:
    Thy withering power inspired each mournful line:
Though gentle Pity claim her mingled part,
    Yet all the thunders of the scene are thine!

ANTISTROPHE

Thou who such weary lengths hast past,
Where wilt thou rest, mad nymph, at last?

---

l.30. 1746 note: "Æschylus."
l.31. Æschylus fought at Marathon.
l.34. later garlands: Sophocles was some thirty years younger than Æschylus.
l.35. left awhile: ceased for a space.
l.35. Sophocles was called "the Attic bee"; Hybla, in Sicily, was noted for honey; the meaning of the entire line is that in the *Oedipus Colloneus* Sophocles departed from his usual tone.

l.37. the baleful grove: *Oedipus Colloneus* takes place by the grove of the Furies.
l.38. thy cloudy veil: a voice spoke from a cloud.
l.38. the incestuous queen: 1746 edition: "Jocasta." Actually, it was not Jocasta's voice that "sighed the sad call" but the god's.
l.39. her son and husband: Oedipus, both Jocasta's son and her husband.

Say, wilt thou shroud in haunted cell,
Where gloomy Rape and Murder dwell?
  Or in some hollowed seat,
    'Gainst which the big waves beat, 50
Hear drowning seamen's cries, in tempests brought?
Dark power, with shuddering, meek, submitted thought,
Be mine to read the visions old
Which thy awakening bards have told:
And, lest thou meet my blasted view,
Hold each strange tale devoutly true;
Ne'er be I found, by thee o'erawed,
In that thrice-hallowed eve abroad
When ghosts, as cottage maids believe, 60
Their pebbled beds permitted leave,
And goblins haunt, from fire, or fen,
Or mine, or flood, the walks of men!
  O thou whose spirit most possest
The sacred seat of Shakespeare's breast!
By all that from thy prophet broke,
In thy divine emotions spoke,
Hither again thy fury deal,
Teach me but once like him to feel;
His cypress wreath my meed decree, 70
And I, O Fear, will dwell with thee!

ODE ON THE POETICAL CHARACTER

1

As once, if, not with light regard,
I read aright that gifted bard
(Him whose school above the rest
His loveliest elfin queen has blest),
One, only one, unrivaled Fair
Might hope the magic girdle wear,
At solemn turney hung on high,
The wish of each love-darting eye;

Lo! to each other nymph in turn applied,
As if, in air unseen, some hovering hand,   10

Ode on the Poetical Character: This is similar in form to the *Ode to Fear.* There has been much discussion regarding its general meaning and the reading of various passages and phrases. It has often been taken as C's central statement concerning the poetic imagination. The girdle or cestus, likened to the magic girdle in the *Faerie Queene,* Bk. IV, is being woven by God in the presence of "the loved enthusiast," who is Young Fancy (i.e. the imagination). Sec. 2 does not make this process entirely clear. Some have found the description audacious in the extreme; others insist that the Creator and the Loved Enthusiast are merely conversing earnestly while the cestus, given ultimately to Milton, is being woven, the Loved Enthusiast then breaking into song "from out the veiling cloud." Who is the "richhaired Youth of Morn"? Clearly he is the poet, says Garrod; to others he is just as clearly the sun. What meanings we find in the second half of Sec. 2 will depend on how we take the *Ode* as a whole. Is it about the poetic imagination in the broadest sense? If the twelve odes of the 1746 volume constitute a designed whole which distinguishes various kinds of poetry and the appropriate affects of each kind, then it would seem reasonable to take this *Ode on the Poetical Character,* the entire closing section of which is devoted to Milton, as a statement of Miltonic sublime poetry; and from this it would follow that "ecstatic Wonder," truth with its tarsel eyes, and the "bright uncounted Powers" are attributes of this particular kind of poetry.

l.5. The 1746 ed. specifies Florimel in the *Faerie Queene,* Bk. IV. In Spenser, however, it was Amoret, not Florimel, who was the "unrivaled fair."

l.6. the cest of sec. 2, the "hollowed work" given to Milton.

Some chaste and angel friend to virgin fame,
　With whispered spell had burst the starting band,
It left unblest her loathed, dishonoured side;
　Happier, hopeless Fair, if never
　Her baffled hand with vain endeavour
Had touched that fatal zone to her denied!

Young Fancy thus, to me divinest name,
　To whom, prepared and bathed in heaven,
　The cest of amplest power is given:
　To few the godlike gift assigns,
　To gird their blest prophetic loins, 20
And gaze her visions wild, and feel unmixed her flame!

2

The band, as fairy legends say,
Was wove on that creating day,
When He, who called with thought to birth
Yon tented sky, this laughing earth,
And drest with springs and forests tall,
And poured the main engirting all,
Long by the loved Enthusiast wooed,
Himself in some diviner mood, 30
Retiring, sat with her alone,
And placed her on his sapphire throne;
The whiles, the vaulted shrine around,
Seraphic wires were heard to sound,
Now sublimest triumph swelling,
Now on love and mercy dwelling;
And she, from out the veiling cloud,
Breathed her magic notes aloud:
And thou, thou rich-haired Youth of Morn,
And all thy subject life was born! 40
The dangerous Passions kept aloof,
Far from the sainted growing woof:
But near it sat ecstatic Wonder,
Listening the deep applauding thunder;
And Truth, in sunny vest arrayed,

By whose the tarsel's eyes were made;
All the shadowy Tribes of Mind,
In braided dance, the murmurs joined,
And all the bright uncounted Powers
Who feed on Heaven's ambrosial flowers.   50
Where is the bard whose soul can now
Its high presuming hopes avow?
Where he who thinks, with rapture blind,
This hallowed work for him designed?

3

High on some cliff, to heaven up-piled,
Of rude access, of prospect wild,
Where, tangled round the jealous steep,
Strange shades o'erbrow the valleys deep,
And holy Genii guard the rock,
Its glooms embrown, its springs unlock,   60
While on its rich ambitious head,
An Eden, like his own, lies spread:

I view that oak, the fancied glades among,
By which as Milton lay, his evening ear,
From many a cloud that dropped ethereal dew,
Nigh sphered in heaven, its native strains could hear,
On which that ancient trump he reached was hung:
    Thither oft, his glory greeting,
    From Waller's myrtle shades retreating,
With many a vow from Hope's aspiring tongue,   70

My trembling feet his guiding steps pursue;
    In vain—Such bliss to one alone
    Of all the sons of soul was known;
    And Heaven and Fancy, kindred powers,
    Have now o'erturned the inspiring bowers;
    Or curtained close such scene from every future view.

---

l.46. tarsel: male falcon.
ll.55-62. Atop the cliff lies Milton's symbolic domain, "an Eden, like his own." C's description is based on Milton's Paradise as described in *P. L.* IV.

l.63. see *Il Penseroso*, ll. 59, 60.
l.69. The "I" who speaks is rejecting the love poetry of Edmund Waller (1605-1687) for poetry of the Miltonic sublime order.
l.72. Milton.

ODE

WRITTEN IN THE BEGINNING OF THE YEAR 1746

How sleep the brave, who sink to rest,
By all their country's wishes blest!
When Spring, with dewy fingers cold,
Returns to deck their hallowed mold,
She there shall dress a sweeter sod
Than Fancy's feet have ever trod.

By fairy hands their knell is rung;
By forms unseen their dirge is sung;
There Honour comes, a pilgrim gray,
To bless the turf that wraps their clay; 10
And Freedom shall a while repair,
To dwell a weeping hermit there!

Ode . . . : In early 1746 England was looking back at three bloody military engagements— those at Fontenoy (May 1745), Preston Pans (September 1745), and Falkirk (January 1746). This ode introduces the patriotic theme, variously treated in the odes To Mercy, To Liberty, To a Lady, and To Peace. "How sleep the brave," in octosyllabic couplets broken into two stanzas, suggests the traditional Latin form which, in distinction from the Pindaric, the English ode had often assumed. In C's mind these verses would seem to constitute a variant of pastoral poetry, which induces a mood of peace and tranquillity and extends to themes pertaining to civil order. This ode is allegorical by virtue of the figures appearing in the second section, but unlike most of the other odes of the 1746 volume it gives no analysis of how a certain affect is bestowed—it is this affect.
l.6. In the sense "than Fancy's feet have ever before trod."

ODE TO EVENING

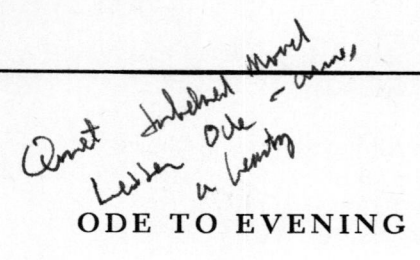

If ought of oaten stop, or pastoral song,
May hope, chaste Eve, to soothe thy modest ear,
   Like thy own solemn springs,
   Thy springs, and dying gales;

O nymph reserved, while now the bright-haired sun
Sits in yon western tent, whose cloudy skirts,
   With brede ethereal wove,
   O'erhang his wavy bed:

Now air is hushed, save where the weak-eyed bat
With short shrill shriek flits by on leathern wing;   10
   Or where the beetle winds
   His small but sullen horn,

As oft he rises 'midst the twilight path,
Against the pilgrim born in heedless hum:
   Now teach me, maid composed,
   To breathe some softened strain,

Whose numbers, stealing through thy darkening vale,
May not unseemly with its stillness suit;

The *Ode to Evening* is a statement about pastoral poetry, and as in "How sleep the brave" C uses a form that associates the piece with the quieter, Latin ode. The stanza here employed is that of Milton's translation of the *Fifth Ode* of Horace. The text given here embodies the variations occurring in the Dodsley *Collection* of 1748 save that in the final stanza the original version of 1746 has been preserved as the better.

l.7. brede: braid or embroidery; Blunden adds that *brede* carries an allusion to the colors of the rainbow.

l.14. The pilgrim, as Garrod remarks, "is only, in plain English, a man out for a walk," and he asks who is borne, pilgrim or beetle?

> As, musing slow, I hail
> Thy genial loved return!

For when thy folding-star arising shows
His paly circlet, at his warning lamp
> The fragrant Hours, and Elves
> Who slept in flowers the day,

And many a nymph who wreathes her brows with sedge,
And sheds the freshening dew, and, lovelier still,
> The pensive Pleasures sweet,
> Prepare thy shadowy car.

Then lead, calm votress, where some sheety lake
Cheers the lone heath, or some time-hallowed pile,
> Or upland fallows grey,
> Reflect its last cool gleam.

But when chill blustering winds, or driving rain,
Forbid my willing feet, be mine the hut,
> That from the mountain's side,
> Views wilds, and swelling floods,

And hamlets brown, and dim-discovered spires;
And hears their simple bell, and marks o'er all
> Thy dewy fingers draw
> The gradual dusky veil.

While Spring shall pour his showers, as oft he wont,
And bathe thy breathing tresses, meekest Eve!
> While Summer loves to sport
> Beneath thy lingering light;

While sallow Autumn fills thy lap with leaves;
Or Winter, yelling through the troublous air,
> Affrights thy shrinking train,
> And rudely rends thy robes;

---

l.32. It is difficult to know what is reflecting what.

Ode to Evening

    So long, regardful of thy quiet rule,
    Shall Fancy, Friendship, Science, smiling Peace,   50

    Thy gentlest influence own,
    And love thy favourite name!

---

l.52. C's ending has often been pronounced markedly ineffective. But if pastoralism embraces, by way of its tranquillity, a social and humanistic concern, then it is possible to follow the logic of these concluding lines; and it becomes clear that Evening's "favorite name" would be Peace, Tranquillity, or some synonym.

AN ODE ON THE POPULAR SUPERSTITIONS OF THE HIGHLANDS OF SCOTLAND

CONSIDERED AS THE SUBJECT OF POETRY

I

Home, thou return'st from Thames, whose Naiads long
    Have seen thee ling'ring, with a fond delay,
Mid those soft friends, whose hearts, some future day,
    Shall melt, perhaps, to hear thy tragic song.
Go, not unmindful of that cordial youth,
    Whom, long endeared, thou leavs't by Lavant's side;
Together let us wish him lasting truth,
    And joy untained with his destined bride.
Go! nor regardless, while these numbers boast
    My short-lived bliss, forget my social name;   10

An Ode on the Popular Superstitions . . . .: The present text is based on that in the 1788 *Trans. Royal Soc. of Edinburgh*, Dr. Alex. Carlyle's suggested reading for the short gaps in the ms. being omitted, and the two missing lines (in stanzas XI and XIII), noted in the *Trans.*, being indicated. The *Ode* was apparently composed in the latter part of 1749, shortly after C's introduction at Winchester to John Home (1722-1808), a Scot and minister of the Kirk, who had come to England in a vain effort to persuade Garrick to produce his tragedy *Agis*. C's prophecy at the beginning of st. I was to be partially fulfilled, for in 1755 H returned to London with *Douglas*, another tragedy again refused by Garrick but produced with great effect at Covent Garden in 1757. The closing lines of st. II show that C regarded the kind of poetry he is here describing as essentially pastoral: it sustains "the rural faith"; reflecting unsophisticated emotions it touches our hearts directly. C was indebted for much of his material to his conversations with Home and to two books by Martin Martin, *A Late Voyage to St. Kilda* (1698) and *A Description of the Western Islands of Scotland* (1703; rev. 1716).
l.5. John Barrow, through whom C had met H.
l.6. Lavant: river in Sussex.

Ode on the Popular Superstitions of Scotland

But think far off how, on the southern coast,
 I met thy friendship with an equal flame!
Fresh to that soil thou turn'st, whose ev'ry vale
 Shall prompt the poet, and his song demand:
To thee thy copious subjects ne'er shall fail;
 Thou need'st but take the pencil to thy hand,
And paint what all believe who own thy genial land.

II

There must thou wake perforce thy Doric quill,
 'Tis Fancy's land to which thou sett'st thy feet;
Where still, 'tis said, the fairy people meet   20
 Beneath each birken shade on mead or hill.
There each trim lass that skims the milky store
 To the swart tribes their creamy bowl allots;
By night thy sip it round the cottage-door,
 While airy minstrels warble jocund notes.
There every herd, by sad experience, knows
 How, winged with fate, their elf-shot arrows fly;
When the sick ewe her summer food foregoes,
 Or, stretched on earth, the heart-smit heifers lie.
Such airy beings awe th' untutored swain: 30
 Nor thou, though learn'd, his homelier thoughts neglect;
Let thy sweet muse the rural faith sustain:
 These are the themes of simple, sure effect,
That add new conquests to her boundless reign,
And fill, with double force, her heart-commanding strain.

III

Ev'n yet preserved, how often may'st thou hear,
 Where to the pole the Boreal mountains run,
Taught by the father to his list'ning son
 Strange lays, whose power had charmed a Spencer's ear.
At ev'ry pause, before thy mind possest,   40
 Old Runic bards shall seem to rise around,
With uncouth lyres, in many-coloured vest,

---

l.17. all . . . who own: natives of Scotland.
l.18. Doric: simple, natural, in the manner of Greek pastoral poetry.
l.23. the swart tribes: the Brownies, referred to by Martin in his *Description*; and by Milton in *L'Allegro*.
l.26. a popular belief, also cited by Martin.

　　　　Their matted hair with boughs fantastic crowned:
　　Whether thou bid'st the well-taught hind repeat
　　　　The choral dirge that mourns some chieftain brave,
　　When ev'ry shrieking maid her bosom beat,
　　　　And strewed with choicest herbs his scented grave;
　　Or whether, sitting in the shepherd's shiel,
　　　　Thou hear'st some sounding tale of war's alarms;
　　When, at the bugle's call, with fire and steel,　　　　　　　50
　　　　The sturdy clans poured forth their bony swarms,
　　And hostile brothers met to prove each other's arms.

　　　　　　　　　　IV

　　'Tis thine to sing, how framing hideous spells
　　　　In Sky's lone isle the gifted wizzard seer,
　　Lodged in the wintry cave with [　　]
　　　　Or in the depth of Uist's dark forests dwells:
　　How they, whose sight such dreary dreams engross,
　　　　With their own visions oft astonished droop,
　　When o'er the wat'ry strath or quaggy moss
　　　　They see the gliding ghosts unbodied troop.　　　　　　60
　　Or if in sports, or on the festive green,
　　　　Their [　　] glance some fated youth descry,
　　Who, now perhaps in lusty vigour seen
　　　　And rosy health, shall soon lamented die.
　　For them the viewless forms of air obey,
　　　　Their bidding heed, and at their beck repair.
　　They know what spirit brews the stormful day,
　　　　And heartless, oft like moody madness stare
　　To see the phantom train their secret work prepare.

　　　　　　　[Stanza V missing.]

　　　　　　　　　　VI

　　　　[The first eight lines missing.]
　　What though far off, from some dark dell espied　　　　　95
　　　　His glimm'ring mazes cheer th' excursive sight,
　　Yet turn, ye wand'rers, turn your steps aside,
　　　　Nor trust the guidance of that faithless light;

---

l.48. shiel: hut.　　　　　　　　l.57. Martin discussed this "second
ll.54-56. Sky and Uist: islands of the　　sight."
Hebrides.

Ode on the Popular Superstitions of Scotland

For watchful, lurking 'mid th' unrustling reed,
    At those mirk hours the wily monster lies,
And listens oft to hear the passing steed,
    And frequent round him rolls his sullen eyes,
If chance his savage wrath may some weak wretch surprise.

VII

Ah, luckless swain, o'er all unblest indeed!
    Whom late bewildered in the dank, dark fen,
Far from his flocks and smoking hamlet then!
    To that sad spot [   ]:
On him enraged, the fiend, in angry mood,
    Shall never look with pity's kind concern,
But instant, furious, raise the whelming flood
    O'er its drowned bank, forbidding all return.
Or, if he meditate his wished escape
    To some dim hill that seems uprising near,
To his faint eye the grim and grisly shape,
    In all its terrors clad, shall wild appear.
Meantime, the wat'ry surge shall around him rise,
    Poured sudden forth from ev'ry swelling source.
What now remains but tears and hopeless sighs?
    His fear-shook limbs have lost their youthly force,
And down the waves he floats, a pale and breathless corse.

VIII

For him, in vain, his anxious wife shall wait,
    Or wander forth to meet him on his way;
For him, in vain, at to-fall of the day,
    His babes shall linger at th' unclosing gate!
Ah, ne'er shall he return! Alone, if night
    Her travelled limbs in broken slumbers steep,
With dropping willows drest, his mournful sprite
    Shall visit sad, perchance, her silent sleep:
Then he, perhaps, with moist and wat'ry hand,
    Shall fondly seem to press her shudd'ring cheek,
And with his blue swoln face before her stand,
    And, shiv'ring cold, these piteous accents speak:
Pursue, dear wife, thy daily toils pursue
    At dawn or dusk, industrious as before;
Nor e'er of me one hapless thought renew,

While I lie welt'ring on the oziered shore,
Drown'd by the Kaelpie's wrath, nor e'er shall aid thee
 more!

IX

Unbounded is thy range; with varied stile
 Thy muse may, like those feath'ry tribes which spring
From their rude rocks, extend her skirting wing 140
 Round the moist marge of each cold Hebrid isle,
To that hoar pile which still its ruin shows:
 In whose small vaults a pigmy-folk is found,
Whose bones the delver with his spade upthrows,
 And culls them, wond'ring, from the hallowed ground!
Or thither where beneath the show'ry west
 The mighty kings of three fair realms are laid:
Once foes, perhaps, together now they rest.
 No slaves revere them, and no wars invade:
Yet frequent now, at midnight's solemn hour, 150
 The rifted mounds their yawning cells unfold,
And forth the monarchs stalk with sov'reign pow'r
 In pageant robes, and wreathed with sheeny gold,
And on their twilight tombs aerial council hold.

X

But O! o'er all, forget not Kilda's race,
 On whose bleak rocks, which brave the wasting tides,
Fair Nature's daughter, Virtue, yet abides.
 Go, just, as they, their blameless manners trace!
Then to my ear transmit some gentle song
 Of those whose lives are yet sincere and plain, 160
Their bounded walks the rugged cliffs along,
 And all their prospect but the wintry main.
With sparing temp'rance, at the needful time,
 They drain the sainted spring, or, hunger-prest,
Along th' Atlantic rock undreading climb,

---

l.137. Kaelpie: a water spirit.
l.143. Martin (*Des.*) has a passage on this "abundance of small bones" in the Island of Benbecula, said by some to be the bones of birds, by others of pigmies.
l.147. Martin (*Des.*): Kings of Scotland, Ireland, and Norway were said to be buried on the island of Iona.
l.155. Kilda's race: St. Kilda, remotest of the islands; Martin (*Late V.*) described the inhabitants as free of all vices.

Ode on the Popular Superstitions of Scotland

And of its eggs despoil the Solan's nest.
Thus blest in primal innocence they live,
Sufficed and happy with that frugal fare
Which tasteful toil and hourly danger give.
Hard is their shallow soil, and bleak and bare;   170
Nor ever vernal bee was heard to murmur there!

XI

Nor need'st thou blush, that such false themes engage
Thy gentle mind, of fairer stores possest;
For not alone they touch the village breast,
But filled in elder time th' historic page.
There Shakespeare's self, with ev'ry garland crowned,
[   ]
In musing hour, his wayward sisters found,
And with their terrors drest the magic scene.
From them he sung, when mid his bold design,   180
Before the Scot afflicted and aghast,
The shadowy kings of Banquo's fated line,
Through the dark cave in gleamy pageant past.
Proceed, nor quit the tales which, simply told,
Could once so well my answ'ring bosom pierce;
Proceed, in forceful sounds and colours bold
The native legends of thy land rehearse;
To such adapt thy lyre and suit thy powerful verse.

XII

In scenes like these, which, daring to depart
From sober truth, are still to nature true,   190
And call forth fresh delight to fancy's view,
Th' heroic muse employed her Tasso's art!
How have I trembled, when at Tancred's stroke,
Its gushing blood the gaping cypress poured;
When each live plant with mortal accents spoke,
And the wild blast up-heaved the vanished sword!
How have I sat, when piped the pensive wind,
To hear his harp, by British Fairfax strung.

---

l.169. tasteful toil: toil that makes food tasteful.
l.192. Tasso (1544-1595): ref. to his poem, *Jerusalem Delivered*. The English tr. by Edward Fairfax (1600) had been rptd. 1749, and C wrote an unptd. *Epistle* to the editor.

Prevailing poet, whose undoubting mind
   Believed the magic wonders which he sung! 200
Hence at each sound imagination glows;
Hence his warm lay with softest sweetness flows;
   Melting it flows, pure, num'rous, strong and clear,
And fills th' impassioned heart, and wins th' harmonious ear.

XIII

ALL hail, ye scenes that o'er my soul prevail,
   Ye [   ] friths and lakes which, far away,
Are by smooth Annan filled, or past'ral Tay,
   Or Don's romantic springs, at distance, hail!
The time shall come when I, perhaps, may tread
   Your lowly glens, o'erhung with spreading broom, 210
Or o'er your stretching heaths by fancy led:
   [   ]
Then will I dress once more the faded bow'r,
   Where Johnson sat in Drummond's [   ] shade;
Or crop from Tiviot's dale each [   ]
   And mourn on Yarrow's banks [.]
Meantime, ye Pow'rs, that on the plains which bore
   The cordial youth, on Lothian's plains attend
Where'er he dwell, on hill, or lowly muir,
   To him I lose, your kind protection lend, 220
And, touched with love like mine, preserve my absent friend.

---

ll.207-208. Annan, Tay, Don: rivers in Scotland.
l.214. In 1619 Ben Jonson visited the poet Wm. Drummond at Hawthornden, near Edinburgh.
l.215f. Tiviot, Yarrow: rivers of the Border Country.
l.218. Edinburgh is situated in the county of Lothian.

Christopher Smart

1722: born Shipbourne, Kent; his father being the steward of Fairlawn, estate of William, Viscount Vane
1733: on death of father sent to Durham by his mother; often at Raby Castle, seat of Henry Vane, Lord Barnard, who showed him great kindness
October 1739: to Pembroke Hall, Cambridge; won reputation for his Latin verses, publishing a Latin version of Pope's *Ode on St. Cecilia's Day* (1743); took B.A. 1744; elected Fellow of Pembroke July 1745; certain of his English verses appeared 1746
1747: M.A.; in financial trouble and arrested in October for debt; freed by help of friends; left Cambridge for a time, but in October 1748 was reappointed to his academic post
summer 1749: to London to make his way as literary man; associated with publisher John Newbery, writing for the latter's magazines, *The Student* and *The Midwife*
June 1752: *Poems on Several Occasions* (containing the georgic, *The Hop-Garden*)
c. 1752: married Anna Carnan, Newbery's step-daughter
1753: *The Hilliad*, directed against Dr. John Hill
1756: prose translation of complete works of Horace; *Hymn to the Supreme Being on Recovery from a Dangerous Fit of Illness*; began contributing to *The Universal Visiter and Monthly Memorialist*, a magazine undertaken by Smart and Richard Rolt, but fell ill shortly after

1756-63: mental illness, taking the form of religious mania; confined for a while at St. Luke's Hospital; in illness compiled the ms. (containing *Jubilate Agno*) printed 1939 as *Rejoice in the Lamb. A Song from Bedlam*
6 April 1763: *A Song to David*
1765: *A Translation of the Psalms of David* (containing *Hymns and Spiritual Songs* and *Song to David*)
1767: *The Works of Horace* (a verse translation)
1768: *Parables of Our Lord and Saviour Jesus Christ, done into familiar verse*
26 April 1770: in King's Bench Prison for debt, where he completed *Hymns for the Amusement of Children* (1770)
20 May 1771: died in prison

JUDGED BY outward circumstances, Smart's life was anything but happy. Achieving success and youthful renown at Cambridge, a fellow of his College by twenty-three, at twenty-five he had begun to lose place through his inability to cope with everyday life. He proceeded to London and to a career as professional writer. There he made many friends, wrote and published a considerable amount of verse, and enjoyed some success; but his career was broken off by the onset of mental illness, exhibiting itself as religious mania, and during the next five years he was at intervals under necessary and forcible restraint. It was during this period that he wrote that strangest of poems, *Jubilate Agno*, of which nothing was known till the present century.

His greatest work, *A Song to David*, which was probably composed in 1759 and 1760, made no great impression when published in 1763, and his concluding eight years were marked by disregard in spite of the high quality of his later verse. He ended life as a broken little man, indigent, seeking charity from his friends, yet to him the world was overwhelmingly beautiful, and in his joyfulness, in sanity as previously in madness, he continued to write poems expressing his thankfulness.

Up to the time of his breakdown, Smart exhibited the sort of poetic talent by no means unusual among the verse writers of the age. Possessed of diversity and metrical versatility, he practiced the recognized "kinds" with adroitness, while in his artificial diction, imagery, and syntax he acknowledged Milton's preponderant influence upon his style. Occasionally—notably in his georgic *The Hop-Garden*—he caught suddenly and in a few direct and flashing words some recollected impression of things once seen. Undoubtedly his genius was maturing steadily, but it would seem that only after emerging from his long period of mental illness did he become fully aware of a new energy and of a poetic manner and technique adequate to carry it.

A *Song to David* is, in lyricism, unmatched in the entire period. Here is true grandiloquence, unmarked by the clichés associated with the conventional Miltonic sublimity. Instead of the traditional, patterned language we have magnificently direct imagery reflecting the beauty of the world in its entire range, and instead of sonorities intended to echo *Paradise Lost*, a sweeping power which is Hebraic in both style and spirit. As Mr. Brittain has pointed out, the directness and frequent peculiarity of the phrasing result from a conscious following of Horatian practice and precept. "For my talent," Smart wrote in *Jubilate Agno*, "is to give an impression upon words by punching, that when the reader casts his eye upon 'em, he takes up the image from the mould which I have made." And again (in *The Works of Horace*): "*Impression* . . . is a talent or gift of almighty God, by which a genius is empowered to throw an emphasis on a word or a sentence in such wise, that it cannot escape any reader of good sense, and true critical sagacity."

A SONG TO DAVID

NOTE: The *Song* is a sustained chant, of praise to David, of gratitude to God the Creator of the universe. Its reference to David are chiefly Biblical, drawing constantly upon I and II Samuel. It is a work of great complexity and of an intricate formal design. The chief structural principle seems to be the ordering of the stanzas in groups of three, seven, or multiples thereof. Smart himself described briefly the main sections in a headnote in the original edition. Detailed studies of the structure have been made by both Havens and Brittain (see bibliography). The comments here reflect the latter's analysis. Stanzas 1-3 comprise the Invocation; 4-17, David's twelve virtues, with a stanza devoted to each; 18-26, the subjects sung by David; 27-29, what he achieved by his singing; 30-38, David's intellectual achievement, his "science" being a comprehensive knowledge of the work of God during the seven days of creation; 39, regarded by Brittain as a transitional stanza; 40-48, described by Smart as "an exercise upon the decalogue"; 49-51, according to Brittain a transition from the first part of the *Song*, devoted to David, to the immediately succeeding sections, which are a lyric of praise and gratitude to God; 52-63, in Smart's words, "an exercise upon the seasons, and the right use of them," three stanzas being given to each of the four seasons (the word ADORATION occurs in each stanza, but each time changes its line position so that it goes, as it were, through two cycles); 64, transitional; 65-71, the five senses, one stanza for each sense (ADORATION here keeps its place in the first line of each stanza); 72-86, "an amplification in five degrees" wrought up to a conclusion (Smart), David being again the central subject, with each of the five degrees—gratitude, faith, prayer, purity of heart, salvation through Christ—set forth in a sub-unit of three stanzas.

A SONG TO DAVID

I

O THOU, that sit'st upon a throne,
With harp of high majestic tone,
   To praise the King of kings;
And voice of heav'n-ascending swell,
Which, while its deeper notes excell,
   Clear, as a clarion, rings:

II

To bless each valley, grove and coast,
And charm the cherubs to the post
   Of gratitude in throngs;
To keep the days on Zion's mount,
And send the year to his account,
   With dances and with songs:

III

O Servant of God's holiest charge,
The minister of praise at large,
   Which thou may'st now receive;
From thy blest mansion hail and hear,
From topmost eminence appear
   To this the wreath I weave.

IV

Great, valiant, pious, good, and clean,
Sublime, contemplative, serene,
   Strong, constant, pleasant, wise!
Bright effluence of exceeding grace;
Best man!—the swiftest and the race,
   The peril, and the prize!

V

Great—from the lustre of his crown,
From Samuel's horn, and God's renown,
   Which is the people's voice;
For all the host, from rear to van,
Applauded and embraced the man—
   The man of God's own choice.　　　　　30

VI

Valiant—the word, and up he rose;
The fight—he triumphed o'er the foes,
   Whom God's just laws abhor;
And, armed in gallant faith, he took
Against the boaster, from the brook,
   The weapons of the war.

VII

Pious—magnificent and grand;
'Twas he the famous temple planned;
   (The seraph in his soul:)
Foremost to give his Lord his dues,　　　　　40
Foremost to bless the welcome news,
   And foremost to condole.

VIII

Good—from Jehudah's genuine vein,
From God's best nature good in grain,
   His aspect and his heart;
To pity, to forgive, to save,
Witness En-gedi's conscious cave,
   And Shimei's blunted dart.

IX

Clean—if perpetual prayer be pure,
And love, which could itself inure　　　　　50
   To fasting and to fear—
Clean in his gestures, hands, and feet,

---

l.26.　I Samuel xvi.　　　　　l.47.　I Samuel xxiv.
l.35.　the boaster: Goliath.　l.48.　II Samuel xvi and xix.
l.38.　I Chronicles xxviii.

To smite the lyre, the dance compleat,
To play the sword and spear.

X

Sublime—invention ever young,
Of vast conception, tow'ring tongue,
   To God the eternal theme;
Notes from yon exaltations caught,
Unrivaled royalty of thought,
   O'er meaner strains supreme. 60

XI

Contemplative—on God to fix
His musings, and above the six
   The sabbath-day he blest;
'Twas then his thoughts self-conquest pruned,
And heavenly melancholy tuned,
   To bless and bear the rest.

XII

Serene—to sow the seeds of peace,
Rememb'ring, when he watched the fleece,
   How sweetly Kidron purled—
To further knowledge, silence vice,
And plant perpetual paradise,
   When God had calmed the world. 70

XIII

Strong—in the Lord, who could defy
Satan, and all his powers that lie
   In sempiternal night;
And hell, and horror, and despair
Were as the lion and the bear
   To his undaunted might.

XIV

Constant—in love to God, THE TRUTH,
Age, manhood, infancy, and youth— 80
   To Jonathan his friend

---

l.69. Kidron: stream near Bethlehem.   l.77. I Samuel xvii.

    Constant, beyond the verge of death;
    And Ziba, and Mephibosheth,
       His endless fame attend.

XV

Pleasant—various as the year;
Man, soul, and angel, without peer,
    Priest, champion, sage and boy;
In armour, or in ephod clad,
His pomp, his piety was glad;
    Majestic was his joy.   90

XVI

Wise—in recovery from his fall,
Whence rose his eminence o'er all,
    Of all the most reviled;
The light of Israel in his ways,
Wise are his precepts, prayer and praise,
    And counsel to his child.

XVII

His muse, bright angel of his verse,
Gives balm for all the thorns that pierce,
    For all the pangs that rage;
Blest light, still gaining on the gloom,   100
The more than Michal of his bloom,
    Th' Abishag of his age.

XVIII

He sung of God—the mighty source
Of all things—the stupendous force
    On which all strength depends;
From whose right arm, beneath whose eyes,
All period, pow'r, and enterprise
    Commences, reigns, and ends.

---

l.83. II Samuel xvi and xix.
l.88. ephod: garment worn by the high priest.
l.101. Michal: David's wife.
l.102. Abishag: a Shunammite woman who cared for David in his final illness.

A Song to David

XIX

Angels—their ministry and meed,
Which to and fro with blessings speed,
   Or with their citterns wait;
Where Michael with his millions bows,
Where dwells the seraph and his spouse
   The cherub and her mate.

XX

O David, scholar of the Lord!
Of God and Love—the Saint elect
   For infinite applause—
To rule the land, and briny broad,
To be laborious in his laud,
   And heroes in his cause.

XXI

The world—the clustering spheres he made,
The glorious light, the soothing shade,
   Dale, champaign, grove, and hill;
The multitudinous abyss,
Where secrecy remains in bliss,
   And wisdom hides her skill.

XXII

Trees, plants, and flow'rs—of virtuous root;
Gem yielding blossom, yielding fruit,
   Choice gums and precious balm;
Bless ye the nosegay in the vale,
And with the sweetness of the gale
   Enrich the thankful psalm.

XXIII

Of fowl—e'en ev'ry beak and wing
Which chear the winter, hail the spring,
   That live in peace or prey;
They that make music, or that mock,

---

l.111. citterns: harps.
l.112. Revelation xii.
    l.123. champaign: flat open country.

The quail, the brave domestic cock,
The raven, swan, and jay.

XXIV

Of fishes—ev'ry size and shape,
Which nature frames of light escape,   140
   Devouring man to shun:
The shells are in the wealthy deep,
The shoals upon the surface leap,
   And love the glancing sun.

XXV

Of beasts—the beaver plods his task;
While the sleek tigers roll and bask,
   Nor yet the shades arouse:
Her cave the mining coney scoops;
Where o'er the mead the mountain stoops,
   The kids exult and brouse.   150

XXVI

Of gems—their virtue and their price,
Which hid in earth from man's device,
   Their darts of lustre sheathe;
The jasper of the master's stamp,
The topaz blazing like a lamp,
   Among the mines beneath.

XXVII

Blest was the tenderness he felt
When to his graceful harp he knelt,
   And did for audience call;
When Satan with his hand he quelled   160
And in serene suspense he held
   The frantic throes of Saul.

XXVIII

His furious foes no more maligned
As he such melody divined,
   And sense and soul detained;

---
l.162. I Samuel xvi.

Now striking strong, now soothing soft,
He sent the godly sounds aloft,
  Or in delight refrained.

XXIX

When up to heaven his thoughts he piled
From fervent lips fair Michal smiled,
  As blush to blush she stood;
And chose herself the queen, and gave
Her utmost from her heart, 'so brave,
  And plays his hymns so good.'

XXX

The pillars of the Lord are seven,
Which stand from earth to topmost heav'n;
  His wisdom drew the plan;
His WORD accomplished the design,
From brightest gem to deepest mine,
  From CHRIST enthroned to man.

XXXI

Alpha, the cause of causes, first
In station, fountain, whence the burst
  Of light, and blaze of day;
Whence bold attempt, and brave advance,
Have motion, life, and ordinance,
  And heaven itself its stay.

XXXII

Gamma supports the glorious arch
On which angelic legions march,
  And is with sapphires paved;
Thence the fleet clouds are sent adrift,
And thence the painted folds, that lift
  The crimson veil, are waved.

XXXIII

Eta with living sculpture breathes,
With verdant carvings, flow'ry wreathes

---

l.175. "the monuments of God's works in the first week" (Smart), or the seven pillars of wisdom (cf. Proverbs ix.1).

Of never-wasting bloom;
In strong relief his goodly base
All instruments of labour grace,
　The trowel, spade, and loom.

XXXIV

Next Theta stands to the Supreme—
Who formed, in number, sign, and scheme,
　Th' illustrious lights that are;
And one addressed his saffron robe,
And one, clad in a silver globe,
　Held rule with ev'ry star.

XXXV

Iota's tuned to choral hymns
Of those that fly, while he that swims
　In thankful safety lurks;
And foot, and chapitre, and niche,
The various histories enrich
　Of God's recorded works.

XXXVI

Sigma presents the social droves,
With him that solitary roves,
　And man of all the chief;
Fair on whose face, and stately frame,
Did God impress his hallowed name,
　For ocular belief.

XXXVII

OMEGA! GREATEST and the BEST,
Stands sacred to the day of rest,
　For gratitude and thought;
Which blessed the world upon his pole,
And gave the universe his goal,
　And closed th' infernal draught.

XXXVIII

O DAVID, scholar of the Lord!
Such is thy science, whence reward
　And infinite degree;

A Song to David

O strength, O sweetness, lasting ripe!
God's harp thy symbol, and thy type
   The lion and the bee!

XXXIX

There is but one who ne'er rebelled,
But One by passion unimpelled,
   By pleasures uninticed;
He from himself his semblance sent,
Grand object of his own content,
   And saw the God in CHRIST.

XL

Tell them, I am, JEHOVA said
To MOSES; while earth heard in dread,
   And, smitten to the heart,
At once above, beneath, around,
All Nature, without voice or sound,
   Replied, 'O Lord, THOU ART.'

XLI

Thou art—to give and to confirm,
For each his talent and his term;
   All flesh thy bounties share:
Thou shalt not call thy brother fool;
The porches of the Christian school
   Are meekness, peace, and pray'r.

XLII

Open, and naked of offence,
Man's made of mercy, soul, and sense;
   God armed the snail and wilk;
Be good to him that pulls thy plough;
Due food and care, due rest, allow
   For her that yields thee milk.

XLIII

Rise up before the hoary head,
And God's benign commandment dread,

---
l.227. type: symbolic representation.   l.235. Exodus iii.
l.228. Judges xiv.   l.249. wilk: whelk.

Which says thou shalt not die:
'Not as I will, but as thou wilt,'
Prayed He whose conscience knew no guilt;
  With whose blessed pattern vie.

XLIV

Use all thy passions!—love is thine,
And joy, and jealousy divine;   260
  Thine hope's eternal fort,
And care thy leisure to disturb,
With fear concupiscence to curb,
  And rapture to transport.

XLV

Act simply, as occasion asks;
Put mellow wine in seasoned casks;
  Till not with ass and bull:
Remember thy baptismal bond;
Keep from commixtures foul and fond,
  Nor work thy flax with wool.   270

XLVI

Distribute: pay the Lord his tithe,
And make the widow's heart-strings blithe;
  Resort with those that weep:
As you from all and each expect,
For all and each thy love direct,
  And render as you reap.

XLVII

The slander and its bearer spurn,
And propagating praise sojourn
  To make thy welcome last;
Turn from Old Adam to the New;   280
By hope futurity pursue;
  Look upwards to the past.

XLVIII

Controul thine eye, salute success,
Honour the wiser, happier bless,
  And for thy neighbour feel;

Grutch not of mammon and his leaven,
Work emulation up to heaven
  By knowledge and by zeal.

XLIX

O DAVID, highest in the list
Of worthies, on God's ways insist,
  The genuine word repeat:
Vain are the documents of men,
And vain the flourish of the pen
  That keeps the fool's conceit.

L

PRAISE above all—for praise prevails;
Heap up the measure, load the scales,
  And good to goodness add:
The generous soul her saviour aids,
But peevish obloquy degrades;
  The Lord is great and glad.

LI

For ADORATION all the ranks
Of angels yield eternal thanks,
  And DAVID in the midst;
With God's good poor, which last and least
In man's esteem, thou to thy feast,
  O blessèd bridegroom, bidst.

LII

For ADORATION seasons change,
And order, truth, and beauty range,
  Adjust, attract, and fill:
The grass the polyanthus cheques;
And polished porphyry reflects,
  By the descending rill.

LIII

Rich almonds colour to the prime
For ADORATION; tendrils climb,

---

l.286. Grutch: begrudge.

And fruit-trees pledge their gems;
And Ivis with her gorgeous vest,
Builds for her eggs her cunning nest,
   And bell-flowers bow their stems.

LIV

With vinous syrup cedars spout;
From rocks pure honey gushing out,
   For ADORATION springs:
All scenes of painting crowd the map
Of nature; to the mermaid's pap
   The scalèd infant clings.

LV

The spotted ounce and playsome cubs
Run rustling 'mongst the flow'ring shrubs,
   And lizards feed the moss;
For ADORATION beasts embark,
While waves upholding halcycon's ark
   No longer roar and toss.

LVI

While Israel sits beneath his fig,
With coral root and amber sprig
   The weaned advent'rer sports;
Where to the palm the jasmine cleaves,
For ADORATION 'mongst the leaves
   The gale his peace reports.

LVII

Increasing days their reign exalt,
Nor in the pink and mottled vault
   The opposing spirits tilt;
And, by the coasting reader spied,
The silverlings and crusions glide
   For ADORATION gilt.

---

l.316. Ivis: the humming bird.
l.325. ounce: leopard.

l.341. silverlings: tarpons; crusions: carp.

LVIII

For ADORATION rip'ning canes
And cocoa's purest milk detains
  The western pilgrim's staff;
Where rain in clasping boughs inclosed,
And vines with oranges disposed,
  Embow'r the social laugh.

LIX

Now labour his reward receives,
For ADORATION counts his sheaves
  To peace, her bounteous prince;
The nectarine his strong tint imbibes,
And apples of ten thousand tribes,
  And quick peculiar quince.

LX

The wealthy crops of whit'ning rice,
'Mongst thyine woods and groves of spice,
  For ADORATION grow;
And, marshalled in the fencèd land,
The peaches and pomegranates stand,
  Where wild carnations blow.

LXI

The laurels with the winter strive;
The crocus burnishes alive
  Upon the snow-clad earth:
For ADORATION myrtles stay
To keep the garden from dismay,
  And bless the sight from dearth.

LXII

The pheasant shows his pompous neck;
And ermine, jealous of a speck,
  With fear eludes offence:
The sable, with his glossy pride,
For ADORATION is described,
  Where frosts the waves condense.

---

l.356. Revelation xviii.12: thyme wood yields a resin (gum sandarac).

LXIII

The cheerful holly, pensive yew,
And holy thorn, their trim renew;
  The squirrel hoards his nuts;
All creatures batten o'er their stores,
And careful nature all her doors
  For ADORATION shuts.

LXIV

For ADORATION, DAVID'S psalms
Lift up the heart to deeds of alms; 380
  And he, who kneels and chants,
Prevails his passions to controul,
Finds meat and med'cine to the soul,
  Which for translation pants.

LXV

For ADORATION, beyond match,
The scholar bullfinch aims to catch
  The soft flute's iv'ry touch;
And, careless on the hazel spray,
The daring redbreast keeps at bay
  The damsel's greedy clutch. 390

LXVI

For ADORATION, in the skies,
The Lord's philosopher espies
  The Dog, the Ram, and Rose;
The planets ring, Orion's sword;
Nor is his greatness less adored
  In the vile worm that glows.

LXVII

For ADORATION, on the strings
The western breezes work their wings,
  The captive ear to sooth.—
Hark! 'Tis a voice—how still, and small— 400

---

l.393. The Dog, Ram, and Rose are constellations.
l.394. The planet's ring: Saturn's ring.
l.397. the strings: i.e., of the Æolian harp.

That makes the cataracts to fall,
Or bids the sea be smooth!

LXVIII

For ADORATION, incense comes
From bezoar, and Arabian gums;
And from the civet's furr:
But as for prayer, or e'er it faints,
Far better is the breath of saints
Than galbanum and myrrh.

LXIX

For ADORATION from the down
Of dam'sins to th' anana's crown, 410
God sends to tempt the taste;
And while the luscious zest invites,
The sense, that in the scene delights,
Commands desire be chaste.

LXX

For ADORATION, all the paths
Of grace are open, all the baths
Of purity refresh;
And all the rays of glory beam
To deck the man of God's esteem,
Who triumphs o'er the flesh. 420

LXXI

For ADORATION, in the dome
Of Christ, the sparrows find an home;
And on his olives perch:
The swallow also dwells with thee,
O man of GOD'S humility,
Within his Saviour CHURCH.

LXXII

Sweet is the dew that falls betimes,
And drops upon the leafy limes;
Sweet, Hermon's fragrant air:

---

l.404. bezoar: a substance found in the stomachs of some animals.
l.408. galbanum: gum-resin.
l.410. anana: the pineapple.

Sweet is the lily's silver bell, 430
And sweet the wakeful tapers smell
  That watch for early pray'r.

LXXIII

Sweet the young nurse with love intense,
Which smiles o'er sleeping innocence;
  Sweet when the lost arrive:
Sweet the musician's ardour beats,
While his vague mind's in quest of sweets,
  The choicest flow'rs to hive.

LXXIV

Sweeter in all the strains of love,
The language of thy turtle dove, 440
  Paired to thy swelling chord;
Sweeter, with ev'ry grace endued,
The glory of thy gratitude,
  Respired unto the Lord.

LXXV

Strong is the horse upon his speed;
Strong in pursuit the rapid glede,
  Which makes at once his game:
Strong the tall ostrich on the ground;
Strong through the turbulent profound
  Shoots xiphias to his aim. 450

LXXVI

Strong is the lion—like a coal
His eyeball—like a bastion's mole
  His chest against the foes:
Strong, the gier-eagle on his sail,
Strong against tide, th' enormous whale
  Emerges as he goes.

LXXVII

But stronger still in earth and air,
And in the sea, the man of pray'r;

---

l.446. glede: the hawk.
l.450. xiphias: the sword-fish.
l.454. the gier-eagle: the eagle or vulture.

And far beneath the tide;
And in the seat to faith assigned,
Where ask is have, where seek is find,
Where knock is open wide.

LXXVIII

Beauteous the fleet before the gale;
Beauteous the multitudes in mail,
Ranked arms and crested heads:
Beauteous the garden's umbrage mild,
Walk, water, meditated wild,
And all the bloomy beds.

LXXIX

Beauteous the moon full on the lawn;
And beauteous, when the veil's withdrawn,
The virgin to her spouse:
Beauteous the temple, decked and filled,
When to the heav'n of heav'ns they build
Their heart-directed vows.

LXXX

Beauteous, yea beauteous more than these,
The shepherd king upon his knees,
For his momentous trust;
With wish of infinite conceit,
For man, beast, mute, the small and great,
And prostrate dust to dust.

LXXXI

Precious the bounteous widow's mite;
And precious, for extreme delight,
The largess from the churl:
Precious the ruby's blushing blaze,
And alba's blest imperial rays,
And pure cerulean pearl.

---

l.466. umbrage: shade.
l.485. alba: this would seem to be the diamond; cf. the white stone or *calculus candidus* (*gemma alba*) of Revelation ii.17.
l.486. cerulean: blue.

LXXXII

Precious the penitential tear;
And precious is the sigh sincere;
  Acceptable to God:
And precious are the winning flow'rs,   490
In gladsome Israel's feast of bow'rs,
  Bound on the hallowed sod.

LXXXIII

More precious that diviner part
Of David, ev'n the Lord's own heart,
  Great, beautiful, and new:
In all things where it was intent,
In all extremes, in each event,
  Proof—answ'ring true to true.

LXXXIV

Glorious the sun in mid career;
Glorious th' assembled fires appear;   500
  Glorious the comet's train:
Glorious the trumpet and alarm;
Glorious th' almighty stretch'd-out arm;
  Glorious th' enraptured main:

LXXXV

Glorious the northern lights a-stream;
Glorious the song, when God's the theme;
  Glorious the thunder's roar:
Glorious hosanna from the den;
Glorious the catholic amen;
  Glorious the martyr's gore: 510

LXXXVI

Glorious—more glorious, is the crown
Of Him that brought salvation down,
  By meekness, called thy Son:
Thou at stupendous truth believed;—
And now the matchless deed's atchieved,
  DETERMINED, DARED, AND DONE.

Joseph Warton

1722: born at Dunsfold, Surrey, son of Thomas Warton senior* and elder brother of Thomas Warton the younger†; received early education at grammar school at Basingstoke, of which his father was headmaster

1735-40: at Winchester College, where he and William Collins were close friends

1740-44: in residence at Oriel College, Oxford, taking his B.A. in March 1744

---

* The three Wartons were closely associated with one another in life and have become so in literary history. The father, Thomas the elder (1688?-1745), was a fellow of Magdalen College, Oxford, and Professor of Poetry (1718-1728), but ceased to reside regularly at Oxford in 1723 on becoming vicar of Basingstoke, Hampshire, and master of the grammar school there. His poetry—dating mostly from Oxford it would seem—was unknown until 1748 when the posthumous *Poems on Several Occasions* appeared, edited by his son Joseph.

† Thomas the younger (1728-1790) was born in Basingstoke. At sixteen he entered Trinity College, Oxford, succeeding after graduation to a fellowship there and remaining a tutor and fellow to the end of his life. His youthful poem, *Ode to a Fountain*, appeared in 1746 in his brother Joseph's *Odes on Various Subjects*; his interesting *Pleasures of Melancholy*, said to have been written in 1745, was printed anonymously in 1747; his *Poems* (1777) contained a number of sonnets and odes, among the latter *The Grave of King Arthur* and *The Crusade*, both reflecting his life-long interest in the medieval scene; in his *Verses on Sir J. Reynolds's Painted Window at New College* (1782), he expressed his appreciation of Reynolds's classical art. In 1785 he became poet-laureate. Though of some significance as a minor poet, he is chiefly remembered as a critic and literary historian: *Observations on the Faerie Queene of Spenser* (1754); *The History of English Poetry, from the close of the eleventh to the commencement of the eighteenth century* (I, 1774; II, 1778; III, 1781); an edition with notes of *Milton's Poems upon Several Occasions* (1785).

1744: took holy orders and went to Basingstoke as his father's curate; *The Enthusiast* published

December 1746: *Odes on Various Subjects*, prefaced by an Advertisement setting forth his poetic intentions;‡ (J. W. and Collins had planned to publish their odes in a joint volume, but this plan fell through and their odes appeared separately but at about the same time, Collins's as *Odes on Several Descriptive and Allegorical Subjects* [1747, but actually published December 1746])

1747: *Ranelagh House: a Satire in Prose in the Manner of Monsieur Le Sage*

1749: *An Ode to Evening; An Ode, occasioned by Mr. West's translation of Pindar*

1753: *The Works of Virgil in Latin and English* (containing J. W.'s translation of the *Eclogues* and *Georgics*, his essays on pastoral poetry, on didactic poetry, on the *Aeneid*, and a life of Virgil); began contributions to *The Adventurer* (twenty-four papers 1753-54); essay on *Simplicity of Taste* in *The World* (no. 26)

1755: appointed second master at Winchester College

1756: *Essay on the Writings and Genius of Pope*
1766: headmaster of Winchester
1773: elected to the Club
1782: *Essay on . . . Pope* (Part II)
1797: *The Works of Pope* (9 vols.)
23 February 1800: died at Wickham, Hampshire

JOSEPH WARTON has often been cited as one of the first to question the prevailing Augustan literary tastes and practices, and in this challenge to the canons of neoclassicism he has been associ-

‡ The Advertisement in full reads: "The Public has been so much accustom'd of late to didactic Poetry alone, and Essays on Moral Subjects, that any work where the imagination is much indulged, will perhaps not be relished or regarded. The author therefore of these poems is in some pain lest certain austere critics should think them too fanciful and descriptive. But as he is convinced that the fashion of moralizing in verse has been carried too far, and as he looks upon Invention and Imagination to be the chief faculties of a Poet, so he will be happy if the following Odes may be look'd upon as an attempt to bring back Poetry into its right channel."

ated with his father and brother. Gosse (in 1915) described Joseph as "the earliest person in the modern world . . . to observe what vain sacrifices had been made by the classicists, and in particular by the English classicists . . ."; and he found in *The Enthusiast* the essence of romantic hysteria.

Today any such view seems to be largely unjustified. It is true that the poetry of all three Wartons and the criticism of the two sons show clearly enough that they registered with unusual sensibility that enlargement of literary and aesthetic taste which was taking place throughout the eighteenth century in consequence of a steadily expanding historical awareness. In the poetry of Thomas the elder we find repeated and explicit emphasis on simplicity of life and taste, as in *Retirement: An Ode*, but this reflects both a classical and a neoclassical attitude. His translations and his imitations of Scandinavian poetry and of Spenser are evidence of the widening responsiveness of the period. His frequent use of the ode form and personification is not a break with tradition but a continuation of a line running from Milton through Dryden and (occasionally) Pope, and his anticipation of Gray in the *Elegy on an Infant* looks back directly to *Lycidas*.

Joseph took up where his father left off, and occasionally both as poet and critic went to extremes. No one, however, can read the body of his verse and critical prose without being firmly persuaded of his essential Augustanism. The often-quoted Advertisement to his *Odes* of 1746 is scarcely the revolutionary pronouncement it has sometimes been taken for. Sixteen years afterwards Hurd, in his *Letters of Chivalry and Romance*, was to distinguish three kinds of poetry: that which has men and manners for its theme; that which addresses itself to the heart and would obtain its end through the passions; and that which addresses itself solely or principally to the imagination, "a young and credulous faculty, which loves to admire and be deceived. . . ." Joseph Warton was one of the most articulate of those who, in the mid-decades, developed under the term "poetry of the imagination" a poetic which was not to invalidate Augustan moral poetry but to justify another kind alongside it. This latter had its roots in classical poetry, in Spenser, in Shakespeare, in Milton; it was essentially description, as in Theocritus, as in *L'Allegro* and *Il Penseroso*. Addison had already made the central statement in his series of *Spectator* papers on the Pleasures of Imagination (nos. 411-421): these pleasures arise from the sense of sight; the primary pleasures, induced by objects actually in view, fall under the three heads of Greatness (the Sublime), the New or Uncommon (the Wonderful), and the Beautiful; the secondary pleasures arise from the action of the mind as it deals with primary impressions and are those the poet gives us as he receives "ideas" from actual objects and ranges these ideas together "in such Figures and Representations as are most likely to hit the Fancy of the Reader"; description can be made to represent "such Objects as are apt to raise a secret Ferment in the Mind of the Reader, and to work, with Violence, upon his Passions" (terror and pity being the passions which serious poetry is chiefly concerned to stir up); there is a kind of writing which, breaking direct contact with Nature, entertains the reader's imagination with characters and actions of persons having no existence (i.e., "the Fairy Way of Writing," presenting fairies, witches, demons, etc.); and poetry can also give us imaginary beings representing, under a visible shape, some passion, appetite, virtue, or vice.

We should view Warton's statement in his Advertisement of 1746, much of his later criticism,* and his own poetic compositions in the light of such observations. If Warton is, after all, only a mediocre poet, he is still important. He helped lay the foundations for what may be regarded as the Aesthetic Movement of the mid-century, and the artistic possibilities of this "poetry of the imagination" were brilliantly realized in the work of Collins, his friend from boyhood and fellow poet.

In its blank verse *The Enthusiast* reflects Thomson's influence, in its descriptive passages the minor verse of Milton. It engages some six different themes in the following order. In the opening passage, Warton carries his father's concept of simplicity to an extreme, by rejecting the landscape gardening of the period in favor of "forests brown," pathless wilds, and the thrush-haunted copse. The second paragraph introduces an associated theme: the emotional effect upon the spectator of natural scenes unspoiled by human artifice, of humble cottages, of Gothic ruins. Here is the picturesque, in Warton's case deriving largely from *L'Allegro* and *Il Penseroso*, but again carried to an extreme. The four succeeding paragraphs develop the theme of primitiveness. Not only is nature

---

* Mr. Trowbridge—cf. his article cited in the bibliography—has analyzed the full range of Warton's theory, which in regard to descriptive, visual imagery was unusual chiefly in emphasizing particularity rather than the sort of abstraction or generality which Johnson, for instance, insisted upon.

superior to art, but early man in his uncomplicated existence was happier than his modern descendant, the latter suffering from feverish luxury. Towards the close of the sixth paragraph he introduces the idea of harmony, the Divine harmony of the universe which, seen in the beauty of nature, harmonizes the mind. Here Warton approaches Akenside. The disparaging reference to Addison leads into the lines on Shakespeare with their implications concerning both the nature of imagination—or "Fair Fancy" —and the course of latter-day English poetry. In the three closing paragraphs the poet follows Milton through experiences similar to those of *L'Allegro* and *Il Penseroso*. The sights and sounds peculiar to daytime are followed by those of the night. Warton again makes the most of the opportunities for emotionalizing the scenes, and in his personifications gives us figures that stand mid-way between those of Milton and Collins.

The Enthusiast does not compel interest as poetry proper, but it claims our attention by reason both of its ideas and of the rhetoric —it is mostly rhetoric rather than genuine poetry—in which these ideas are set forth. The *Ode to Fancy* is largely Miltonic in form and manner. Here too the artificial is being dismissed in favor of wild nature, and the descriptive details are markedly picturesque. To Fancy—i.e., the Imagination—is attributed, more clearly than in *The Enthusiast*, the power of originality in the sense of imaginative inventiveness.*

---

* A few items concerning the two Thomases follow: E. Partridge gives select bibliographies for both in *The Three Wartons* (see bibliography). The 1748 edition of Thomas the elder's poems has been reproduced by the Facsimile Text Society (New York: The Facsimile Text Society; 1930). Collections of T. W. the younger's poems are in the edition of the British poets by Chalmers (1810), Sanford (1819), etc. Selections from both are given by E. Partridge. Clarence Rinaker has a full-length study of T. W. the younger, *T. W. A Biographical and Critical Study* (Urbana: University of Illinois, 1916); shorter essays on T. W. the younger are by W. P. Ker, "T. Warton," *Proceedings of the British Academy*, (1909-10); Edmund Gosse, "Two Pioneers of Romanticism: J. and T. Warton," *Proceedings . . . Br. Academy*, (1915-16); D. N. Smith, "Warton's History of English Poetry," *Proceedings . . . Br. Academy*, (1929); L. C. Martin, "T. W. and the Early Poems of Milton," *Proceedings . . . Br. Academy*, (1934); J. S. Cunningham, "Thomas Warton and William Collins: a Footnote," *Durham Univ. Journal*, XLVI (1953-54).

THE ENTHUSIAST OR
THE LOVER OF NATURE

Rure vero barbaroque laetatur. MARTIAL.
Ut mihi devio
Rupes et vacuum nemus
Mirari libet! HORACE.

Ye green-robed Dryads, oft at dusky eve
By wondering shepherds seen, to forests brown,
To unfrequented meads, and pathless wilds,
Lead me from gardens decked with art's vain pomps.
Can gilt alcoves, can marble-mimic gods,
Parterres embroidered, obelisks, and urns,
Of high relief; can the long, spreading lake
Or vista lessening to the sight; can Stowe
With all her Attic fanes, such raptures raise,
As the thrush-haunted copse, where lightly leaps   10
The fearful fawn the rustling leaves along,
And the brisk squirrel sports from bough to bough,
While from an hollow oak, whose naked roots
O'erhang a pensive rill, the busy bees
Hum drowsy lullabies? The bards of old,
Fair Nature's friends, sought such retreats, to charm
Sweet Echo with their songs; oft too they met
In summer evenings, near sequestered bowers,

Martial: *Epigrams* III lviii.5: "[our friend Faustinus' villa] rejoices in a farm, honest and without artificiality."
Horace: *Odes* III 25.13: Christopher Smart translates into prose as "I love to stray and to gaze with awe upon the unfrequented banks and groves."

l.8. Stowe: the Buckinghamshire residence of Richard Temple, Lord Cobham, was famous for its gardens, the design of which was successively in the hands of three distinguished landscape gardeners, Bridgeman, William Kent, and Brown. Guide-books to the estate began to appear in 1747.

Or mountain-nymph, or Muse, and eager learnt
The moral strains she taught to mend mankind.   20
As to a secret grot Aegeria stole
With patriot Numa, and in silent night
Whispered him sacred laws, he list'ning sat,
Rapt with her virtuous voice, old Tyber leaned
Attentive on his urn, and hushed his waves.
  Rich in her weeping country's spoils, Versailles
May boast a thousand fountains, that can cast
The tortured waters to the distant Heav'ns;
Yet let me choose some pine-topt precipice
Abrupt and shaggy, whence a foamy stream,   30
Like Anio, tumbling roars; or some bleak heath,
Where straggling stands the mournful juniper,
Or yew-tree scathed; while in clear prospect round,
From the grove's bosom spires emerge, and smoke
In bluish wreaths ascends, ripe harvests wave,
Low, lonely cottages, and ruined tops
Of Gothic battlements appear, and streams
Beneath the sun-beams twinkle.—The shrill lark,
That wakes the wood-man to his early task,
Or love-sick Philomel, whose luscious lays   40
Soothe lone night-wanderers, the moaning dove
Pitied by list'ning milk-maid, far excel
The deep-mouthed viol, the soul-lulling lute,
And battle-breathing trumpet. Artful sounds!
That please not like the choristers of air,
When first they hail th' approach of laughing May.
  Can Kent design like Nature? Mark where Thames
Plenty and pleasure pours through Lincoln's meads;
Can the great artist, though with taste supreme
Endued, one beauty to this Eden add?   50
Though he, by rules unfettered, boldly scorns
Formality and Method, round and square
Disdaining, plans irregularly great.
  Creative Titian, can thy vivid strokes,

---

l.21. Aegeria: Livy, I 19.
l.31. Anio: the Aniene River, furnishing Rome with water.
l.47. Kent: William Kent (1684-1748), landscape gardener and architect.
l.48. Lincoln's meads: the Earl of Lincoln's estate at Weybridge, Surrey.
l.54. Titian: the Venetian painter (1477-1576).

Or thine, O graceful Raphael, dare to vie
With the rich tints that paint the breathing mead?
The thousand-coloured tulip, violet's bell
Snow-clad and meek, the vermil-tinctured rose,
And golden crocus?—Yet with these the maid,
Phillis or Phoebe, at a feast or wake, 60
Her jetty locks enamels; fairer she,
In innocence and home-spun vestments dressed,
Than if cerulean sapphires at her ears
Shone pendent, or a precious diamond-cross
Heaved gently on her panting bosom white.
    Yon shepherd idly stretched on the rude rock,
List'ning to dashing waves, and sea-mew's clang
High-hovering o'er his head, who views beneath
The dolphin dancing o'er the level brine,
Feels more true bliss than the proud admiral, 70
Amid his vessels bright with burnished gold
And silken streamers, though his lordly nod
Ten thousand war-worn mariners revere.
And great Aeneas gazed with more delight
On the rough mountain shagged with horrid shades,
(Where cloud-compelling Jove, as fancy dreamed,
Descending, shook his direful Aegis black)
Than if he entered the high Capitol
On golden columns reared, a conquered world
Exhausted, to enrich its stately head. 80
More pleased he slept in poor Evander's cot
On shaggy skins, lulled by sweet nightingales,
Than if a Nero, in an age refined,
Beneath a gorgeous canopy had placed
His royal guest, and bade his minstrels sound
Soft slumb'rous Lydian airs, to soothe his rest.
    Happy the first of men, ere yet confined
To smoky cities; who in sheltering groves,
Warm caves, and deep-sunk vallies lived and loved,
By cares unwounded; what the sun and showers, 90
And genial earth untillaged, could produce,
They gathered grateful, or the acorn brown,
Or blushing berry; by the liquid lapse

---

l.55. Raphael: the Italian painter (1403-1520).
l.74. Aeneas: *Aeneid* VIII.
l.87. Happy . . . men: Lucretius.

Of murm'ring waters called to slake their thirst,
Or with fair nymphs their sun-brown limbs to bathe;
With nymphs who fondly clasped their fav'rite youths,
Unawed by shame, beneath the beechen shade,
Nor wiles, nor artificial coyness knew.
Then doors and walls were not; the melting maid
Nor frown of parents feared, nor husband's threats;   100
Nor had cursed gold their tender hearts allured:
Then beauty was not venal. Injured love,
O! whither, god of raptures, art thou fled?
While Avarice waves his golden wand around,
Abhorred magician, and his costly cup
Prepares with baneful drugs, t'enchant the souls
Of each low-thoughted fair to wed for gain.
   In Earth's first infancy (as sung the bard,
Who strongly painted what he boldly thought),
Though the fierce north oft smote with iron whip   110
Their shiv'ring limbs, though oft the bristly boar
Or hungry lion 'woke them with their howls,
And scared them from their moss-grown caves, to rove
Houseless and cold in dark tempestuous nights;
Yet were not myriads in embattled fields
Swept off at once, nor had the raging seas
O'erwhelmed the found'ring bark and shrieking crew;
In vain the glassy ocean smiled to tempt
The jolly sailor, unsuspecting harm,
For Commerce ne'er had spread her swelling sails,   120
Nor had the wond'ring Nereids ever heard
The dashing oar: then famine, want, and pain,
Sunk to the grave their fainting limbs; but us,
Diseaseful dainties, riot, and excess,
And feverish luxury destroy. In brakes
Or marches wild unknowingly they cropped
Herbs of malignant juice; to realms remote
While we for powerful poisons madly roam,
From every noxious herb collecting death.
What though unknown to those primeval sires   130
The well-arched dome, peopled with breathing forms
By fair Italia's skilful hand, unknown

---

l.108. bard: Lucretius.   l.122: *Paradise Lost* IX.

The shapely column, and the crumbling busts
Of awful ancestors in long descent?
Yet why should man mistaken, deem it nobler
To dwell in palaces, and high-roofed halls,
Than in God's forests, architect supreme!
Say, is the Persian carpet, than the field's
Or meadow's mantle gay, more richly wov'n;
Or softer to the votaries of ease   140
Than bladed grass, perfumed with dew-dropt flow'rs?
O taste corrupt! that luxury and pomp,
In specious names of polished manners veiled
Should proudly banish Nature's simple charms!
All-beauteous Nature! by thy boundless charms
Oppressed, O where shall I begin thy praise,
Where turn th' ecstatic eye, how ease my breast
That pants with wild astonishment and love!
Dark forests, and the op'ning lawn, refreshed
With ever-gushing brooks, hill, meadow, dale,   150
The balmy bean-field, the gay-clovered close,
So sweetly interchanged, the lowing ox,
The playful lamb, the distant water-fall
Now faintly heard, now swelling with the breeze,
The sound of pastoral reed from hazel-bower,
The choral birds, the neighing steed, that snuffs
His dappled mate, stung with intense desire,
The ripened orchard when the ruddy orbs
Betwixt the green leaves blush, the azure skies,
The cheerful Sun that through Earth's vitals pours   160
Delight and health and heat; all, all conspire,
To raise, to soothe, to harmonize the mind,
To lift on wings of praise, to the great Sire
Of being and of beauty, at whose nod
Creation started from the gloomy vault
Of dreary Chaos, while the griesly king
Murmured to feel his boisterous power confined.
   What are the lays of artful Addison,
Coldly correct, to Shakespear's warblings wild?
Whom on the winding Avon's willowed banks   170
Fair Fancy found, and bore the smiling babe
To a close cavern: (still the shepherds show
The sacred place, whence with religious awe

They hear, returning from the field at eve,
Strange whisp'rings of sweet music through the air)
Here, as with honey gathered from the rock,
She fed the little prattler, and with songs
Oft soothed his wond'ring ears, with deep delight
On her soft lap he sat, and caught the sounds.
   Oft near some crowded city would I walk,   180
Listening the far-off noises, rattling cars,
Loud shouts of joy, sad shrieks of sorrow, knells
Full slowly tolling, instruments of trade,
Striking mine ears with one deep-swelling hum.
Or wand'ring near the sea, attend the sounds
Of hollow winds, and ever-beating waves,
Ev'n when wild tempests swallow up the plains,
And Boreas' blasts, big hail, and rains combine
To shake the groves and mountains, would I sit,
Pensively musing on the outrageous crimes   190
That wake heav'n's vengeance: at such solemn hours,
Demons and goblins through the dark air shriek,
While Hecat, with her black-browed sisters nine,
Rides o'er the Earth, and scatters woes and death.
Then too, they say, in drear Aegyptian wilds
The lion and the tiger prowl for prey
With roarings loud! the list'ning traveller
Starts fear-struck, while the hollow-echoing vaults
Of pyramids increase the deathful sounds.
   But let me never fail in cloudless nights,   200
When silent Cynthia in her silver car
Through the blue concave slides, when shine the hills,
Twinkle the streams, and woods look tipped with gold,
To seek some level mead, and there invoke
Old Midnight's sister, Contemplation sage
(Queen of the rugged brow, and stern-fixt eye),
To lift my soul above this little Earth,
This folly-fettered world: to purge my ears,
That I may hear the rolling planets' song,
And tuneful turning spheres: if this be barred,   210
The little Fays that dance in neighbouring dales,
Sipping the night-dew, while they laugh and love,

---

l.211: Fays: as in *Midsummer Night's Dream*.

Shall charm me with aerial notes.—As thus
I wander musing, lo, what awful forms
Yonder appear! sharp-eyed Philosophy
Clad in dun robes, an eagle on his wrist,
First meets my eye; next, virgin Solitude
Serene, who blushes at each gazer's sight;
Then Wisdom's hoary head, with crutch in hand,
Trembling, and bent with age; last, Virtue's self,   220
Smiling, in white arrayed, who with her leads
Sweet Innocence, that prattles by her side,
A naked boy!—Harassed with fear I stop,
I gaze, when Virtue thus—"Whoe'er thou art,
"Mortal, by whom I deign to be beheld
"In these my midnight-walks; depart, and say
"That henceforth I and my immortal train
"Forsake Britannia's isle; who fondly stoops
"To Vice, her favourite paramour."—She spoke,
And as she turned, her round and rosy neck,   230
Her flowing train, and long ambrosial hair,
Breathing rich odours, I enamoured view.
    O who will bear me then to western climes,
(Since Virtue leaves our wretched land) to fields
Yet unpolluted with Iberian swords:
The isles of Innocence, from mortal view
Deeply retired, beneath a plantane's shade,
Where Happiness and Quiet sit enthroned,
With simple Indian swains, that I may hunt
The boar and tiger through savannahs wild,   240
Through fragrant deserts, and through citron-groves?
There, fed on dates and herbs, would I despise
The far-fetched cates of luxury, and hoards
Of narrow-hearted avarice; nor heed
The distant din of the tumultuous world.
So when rude whirlwinds rouse the roaring main,
Beneath fair Thetis sits, in coral caves,
Serenely gay, nor sinking sailors' cries

---

l.229. She spoke: *Aeneid* I 402-405: "Dixit; et averteus rosea cervice refulsit . . ." Dryden translated the passage as follows: "Thus having said, [Venus] turned, and made appear / Her neck refulgent, and disheveled hair, / which, flowing from her shoulders, reached the ground / And widely spread ambrosial scents around. . . ."

Disturb her sportive nymphs, who round her form
The light fantastic dance, or for her hair   250
Weave rosy crowns, or with according lutes
Grace the soft warbles of her honied voice.

ODE TO FANCY

O Parent of each lovely Muse,
Thy spirit o'er my soul diffuse,
O'er all my artless songs preside,
My footsteps to thy temple guide,
To offer at thy turf-built shrine,
In golden cups no costly wine,
No murdered fatling of the flock,
But flowers and honey from the rock.
O Nymph, with loosely-flowing hair,
With buskined leg, and bosom bare,   10
Thy waist with myrtle-girdle bound,
Thy brows with Indian feathers crowned,
Waving in thy snowy hand
An all-commanding magic wand,
Of pow'r to bid fresh gardens blow
'Mid cheerless Lapland's barren snow,
Whose rapid wings thy flight convey
Through air, and over earth and sea,
While the vast, various landscape lies
Conspicuous to thy piercing eyes;   20
O lover of the desert, hail!
Say, in what deep and pathless vale,
Or on what hoary mountain's side,
'Mid fall of waters, you reside,
'Mid broken rocks, a rugged scene,
With green and grassy dales between,
'Mid forests dark of aged oak,
Ne'er echoing with the woodman's stroke,
Where never human art appeared,
Nor ev'n one straw-rooft cot was reared,   30
Where Nature seems to sit alone,
Majestic on a craggy throne;

Ode to Fancy

Tell me the path, sweet wand'rer, tell,
To thy unknown sequestered cell,
Where woodbines cluster round the door,
Where shells and moss o'erlay the floor,
And on whose top an hawthorn blows,
Amid whose thickly-woven boughs
Some nightingale still builds her nest,
Each evening warbling thee to rest; 40
There lay me by the haunted stream,
Rapt in some wild, poetic dream,
In converse while methinks I rove
With Spenser through a fairy grove;
'Till suddenly awoke, I hear
Strange whispered music in my ear,
And my glad soul in bliss is drowned
By the sweetly-soothing sound!
Me, Goddess, by the right-hand lead,
Sometimes through the yellow mead, 50
Where Joy and white-robed Peace resort,
And Venus keeps her festive court,
Where Mirth and Youth each evening meet,
And lightly trip with nimble feet,
Nodding their lily-crownèd heads,
Where Laughter rose-lipped Hebe leads;
Where Echo walks steep hills among,
List'ning to the shepherd's song:
Yet not those flowery fields of joy
Can long my pensive mind employ, 60
Haste, Fancy, from these scenes of folly,
To meet the matron Melancholy,
Goddess of the tearful eye,
That loves to fold her arms, and sigh;
Let us with silent footsteps go
To charnels and the house of woe,
To Gothic churches, vaults, and tombs,
Where each sad night some virgin comes,
With throbbing breast, and faded cheek,
Her promised bridegroom's urn to seek; 70
Or to some abbey's mould'ring tow'rs,
Where, to avoid cold wintry show'rs,
The naked beggar shivering lies,

While whistling tempests round her rise,
And trembles lest the tottering wall
Should on her sleeping infants fall.
  Now let us louder strike the lyre,
For my heart glows with martial fire,
I feel, I feel, with sudden heat,
My big tumultuous bosom beat; 80
The trumpet's clangours pierce my ear,
A thousand widows' shrieks I hear,
Give me another horse, I cry,
Lo! the base Gallic squadrons fly;
Whence is this rage?—what spirit, say,
To battle hurries me away?
'Tis Fancy, in her fiery car,
Transports me to the thickest war,
There whirls me o'er the hills of slain,
Where Tumult and Destruction reign; 90
Where mad with pain, the wounded steed
Tramples the dying and the dead;
Where giant Terror stalks around,
With sullen joy surveys the ground,
And, pointing to th' ensanguined field,
Shakes his dreadful Gorgon-shield!
  O guide me from this horrid scene
To high-archt walks and alleys green,
Which lovely Laura seeks, to shun
The fervours of the mid-day sun; 100
The pangs of absence, O remove!
For thou canst place me near my love,
Canst fold in visionary bliss,
And let me think I steal a kiss,
While her ruby lips dispense
Luscious nectar's quintessence!
When young-eyed Spring profusely throws
From her green lap the pink and rose,
When the soft turtle of the dale
To Summer tells her tender tale, 110
When Autumn cooling caverns seeks,
And stains with wine his jolly cheeks;
When Winter, like poor pilgrim old,
Shakes his silver beard with cold;

At every season let my ear
Thy solemn whispers, Fancy, hear.
O warm, enthusiastic maid,
Without thy powerful, vital aid,
That breathes an energy divine,
That gives a soul to every line,
Ne'er may I strive with lips profane
To utter an unhallowed strain,
Nor dare to touch the sacred string,
Save when with smiles thou bid'st me sing.
O hear our prayer, O hither come
From thy lamented Shakespear's tomb,
On which thou lov'st to sit at eve,
Musing o'er thy darling's grave;
O queen of numbers, once again
Animate some chosen swain,
Who, filled with unexhausted fire,
May boldly smite the sounding lyre,
Who with some new, unequalled song,
May rise above the rhyming throng,
O'er all our list'ning passions reign,
O'erwhelm our souls with joy and pain,
With terror shake, with pity move,
Rouse with revenge, or melt with love,
O deign t' attend his evening walk,
With him in groves and grottos talk;
Teach him to scorn with frigid art
Feebly to touch th' unraptured heart;
Like lightning, let his mighty verse
The bosom's inmost foldings pierce;
With native beauties win applause,
Beyond cold critics' studied laws;
O let each Muse's fame increase,
O bid Britannia rival Greece!

Oliver Goldsmith

❦

1730?: born of Anglo-Irish stock 10 November,* the son of the Rev. Chas. G., curate-in-charge of the parish of Kilkenny West in West Meath, Ireland; the second son of seven surviving children; passed his childhood at the family house near the village of Lissoy (known today as Auburn), situated within his father's parish

c. 1737-45: at various schools at Elphin, Athlone, and Egeworthstown

11 June 1745: admitted as sizar at Trinity College, Dublin

1747: death of father

February 1750: graduated B. A.

1750-52: turned down for ordination in the Church; a tutor in a County Roscommon family; disastrous trip to Cork (perhaps hoping to get to America) and to Dublin (with intention of proceeding to London to study law at the Temple)

September 1752: off finally to Edinburgh to take up study of medicine at the university

c. February 1754: in Edinburgh, pursuing medical studies

c. February 1754: in Leydon, studying medicine

---

* The G family Bible, now lost, gave 10 November, but the year was torn away. Apparently G himself had no exact knowledge of the year of his birth. 1729, '30, and '31 are all possible dates.

early 1755-1756: travelling in Europe, across Flanders to Paris, probably into Germany and Switzerland, certainly to Padua and other Italian cities

c. 1 February 1756: landed penniless at Dover; to London

1756-57: early struggles in London as assistant in an apothecary's shop, physician in Southwork, perhaps a proofreader in Samuel Richardson's printing shop, and an usher in the Rev. John Milner's school for boys at Peckham, Surrey; taken on by Ralph Griffith, proprietor and editor of the *Monthly Review*, for which (April-September '57) he wrote book reviews

1758-59: odd jobs as writer and translator; reviewing— mostly in 1759—for Smollett's *Critical Review*; at work on a survey of literary culture in Europe and England; planned to go out to India, having been promised post of physician with East India Company; to save passage money sought appointment as hospital mate on a warship bound for India, but on presenting himself for examination at Surgeons' Hall on 21 December 1758 was found "not qualified," and his appointment became valueless when news of French victories in India reached England in March 1759

2 April 1759: publication of *An Enquiry into the Present State of Polite Learning in Europe*

1759: now known as "Dr. Goldsmith," though there is no record of his having taken this degree; an increasing number of friends and literary acquaintances, including the Rev. Thomas Percy, and possibly by this date Smollett, Arthur Murphy, Burke, and Johnson; contributor to several magazines and author of the short-lived *Bee* (6 October-24 November)

1760: contributed to Newbery's *Public Ledger*, starting 24 January, a series of "Chinese Letters" which ran through 14 August 1761; many other essays in a variety of periodicals; moved to new quarters in No. 6 Wine Office Court, off Fleet Street and near the Cheshire Cheese

1761: a recorded meeting with Percy and Samuel Johnson on 31 May; probably at this time met Joshua Reynolds

1762: 1 May, publication of the "Chinese Letters" in book form as *The Citizen of the World*; now giving over essay writing and turning to probably better-paying hack work; conversation with Boswell on Christmas day

1764: founding of the club, G being an original member; moved to No. 2 Garden Court, the Temple; publication in June of *An History of England in a Series of Letters from a Nobleman to his Son*; at work on final draft of his poem *The Traveller, or A Prospect of Society*, printed 19 December

1765: 4 June, *Essays by Mr. Goldsmith*, a collection of twenty-five of his previously published essays and two poems; new lodgings at No. 3 King's Bench Walk in the Temple

1766: 12 March, published *The Vicar of Wakefield*

1767: April, *The Beauties of English Poesy, selected by Oliver Goldsmith*

1768: 29 January, first performance of *The Good Natur'd Man*, produced by Colman at Covent Garden; moved to No. 2 Brick Court in the Temple to the rooms he occupied until his death

1768-74: now well-paid for his hack work and compiling, he contracted for many jobs with the publishers (some of the eventual publications resulting from this work being *The Roman History* ['69], a *Life of Dr. Parnell* ['70], a *Life of Henry St. John* ['70], *History of England . . . to the Death of George II* ['71], an abridgment of the *Roman History* ['72], and *History of the Earth, and Animated Nature*, an abridgment of the *History of England*, and *The Grecian History* [all posthumously in '74])

1770: 26 May, publication of *The Deserted Village*; achieved general recognition as one of the foremost living men of letters

1772: in August dangerously ill from an infection of the bladder
1773: January, his *Essays on the Theatre* in *Westminster Magazine*; 15 March, Colman produced *She Stoops to Conquer* at Covent Garden
1774: Garrick's satiric epitaph on G, the spur for G's *Retaliation*, unfinished at his death; 29 March, G fell seriously ill, expiring in the Temple on 4 April; 9 April, buried privately in the Temple Burying Ground; 19 April, *Retaliation* printed
1776: monument to G by Nollekens with Johnson's epitaph erected in Westminster Abbey

"LORD BLESS US, what an anomalous character was his." Thus Mrs. Thrale of Oliver Goldsmith, thereby expressing in her fashion the constant astonishment and bewilderment which seem to have been felt by most of those who knew Goldsmith in his years of triumph. His contemporaries had many things to say about him, and these and other records have been handed down by a long line of conscientious biographers. Yet Goldsmith still eludes us. Partly because he *was* anomalous, an Anglo-Irish curiosity among Englishmen, an *étourdi* as Boswell put it; partly, it would seem, because we have such a mass of miscellaneous and sometimes contradictory information about him. Today our interest lies chiefly in the period from 1756 to 1774, which begins with his forlorn arrival in London, where he gradually achieves literary eminence first as an essayist and then as poet, novelist, and dramatist, and ends with his premature and unexpected death in 1774.

Unquestionably Goldsmith has suffered from the impression handed down by his contemporaries that his literary life was a formless affair, without much inner purpose or artistic logic. But when Johnson wrote in the famous Latin epitaph that Goldsmith left scarcely any kind of writing untouched, and touched nothing that he did not adorn, there are deeper implications than the great Cham was perhaps aware of. It is not just by chance and good luck that an artist is thus successful on diverse occasions and in diverse ways. We can reasonably assume that he has been moved by some steadily-maintained force, some characteristic intuition.

The biographical facts, which we have in superabundance, do not help us much understand his imaginative history. For this we must turn to the writings themselves. Here we see reflected much of the ordered world which the age of reason and reasonableness had created. Goldsmith's prose, for all its delicate modulations, is a balanced one. The conversation in his plays falls into clausal and phrasal patterns of balance and antithesis. In the poems the couplets, the longer verse periods, and the ideas being presented show a similar kind of syntactic and logical ordering. At the same time, however, this order is somehow placed in question. What was it that Goldsmith sensed behind this façade which reason and an established society present? Certainly not horror. The face, rather, of what he thought of as "nature": man shorn of pretense and over-refinement; man accepting life gladly, yet haunted by a vision of a lost home.

Here, if we must give names, is the rococo imagination. More precisely we can point out how, in actual composition, Goldsmith succeeds in introducing various elements that play against the conventional order and balance. In *She Stoops to Conquer*, there are obvious contrasts between characters—e.g., between Mr. and Mrs. Hardcastle, between Marlow and Tony Lumpkin—but Kate Hardcastle, symbol of what is natural and admirable, is not established dialectically. In his earlier play, *The Good Natur'd Man*, and at the end of *The Vicar of Wakefield*, Goldsmith repudiates through comic parody such traditional dramaturgic patterns as the discovery scene and the sudden turn from misfortune to happiness. In *The Traveller*, as elsewhere, is the figure and the idea of the traveller, the homeless one, to whom all places are strange and all conditions artificial. In form *The Deserted Village* has a tight framework, but much of its formal rigorousness dissolves before the bitter nostalgia arising from the memory of a lost Paradise. The constant references by Goldsmith's critics to the thematic poverty of his work overlook these ever-present themes of his imagination and their expression in the diverse media of essay, novel, poem, and drama.

Goldsmith's collected verse is more extensive than we sometimes realize and shows his easy mastery of a number of different genres ranging from the poetical epistle to the ballad. But as a poet he is remembered today chiefly for the two great compositions, *The Traveller* and *The Deserted Village*.

We do not usually think of Goldsmith as a critic. He did as a matter of fact write a good deal of criticism at one time or another; and his scattered observations about poetry, marked by a greater consistency than we might expect, have immediate relevance to his own verse. He disliked blank verse; the new experiments in the ode form; the aesthetic imagery associated with Hurd, Gray, and Mason (though he admired Collins). He gave his critical allegiance wholeheartedly to Dryden, Pope, the minor Augustan poets (Swift, Prior, Addison), and Samuel Johnson; and he was an unquestioning traditionalist in his concept of the double function of poetry to please and instruct.

Indeed, those of his aesthetic convictions which have sometimes been taken as essentially pre-romantic can be better understood as logical—and by no means novel—deductions from this very traditionalism. Poetry, he believed, should be addressed to the many, never to the select few. Poetry should avoid all affectations and passing aesthetic fashions. Poetry should convey strong and vigorous emotions, imprinting on others the sentiments which the poet is possessed of. "Almost all things written from the heart," he observed in a brief comment on a poem by Savage, "have some merit." This insistence that poetry have a general appeal, that its form and language be directly and clearly functional, and that it be rhetorically moving, is perfectly good English classical doctrine.

His poetry squares with his critical principles. In the face of the aesthetic movement of the mid-decades, Goldsmith, along with Johnson, reasserted the traditional line running from Dryden through Pope: verse in couplets, concerned with the broad moral themes of the age, and addressed to educated men everywhere. Goldsmith admits into his verse many of the conventions which mark this line, because he has no reason to challenge them: poetic diction, circumlocution, abstraction and personification. Yet it is Goldsmith's distinction that in taking up this traditional mode he infused into it a new quality of lyrical emotion, simple and direct, and expressed in a language which transforms a generally conventional diction into something close to colloquialism.

The Traveller, which Johnson preferred to *The Deserted Village*, is one of the great panoramic poems in the language, associated with those by Denham, Dyer, Scott, and Byron. It has a curious kind of unity, attained through a blending of an intellectual element—as in the splendidly rhetorical series of descriptive analyses—and the emotional one conferred by the Traveller in meditation. If *The Deserted Village* does not have this balance, if here the emotional element seems more unrestrained, that is because Goldsmith was appealing through pathos against an injustice and materialism that seemed to be undermining the nation. He uses emotion for a rhetorical purpose. But it is genuine emotion, deeply felt. We should not confuse it with the sort of sentimentalism we find in much of the drama of the period, which Goldsmith protested against both as dramatic critic and as playwright. The heart can be betrayed into easy and shallow sentiment. But deep emotion that comes directly from the experiences of life is valid and Goldsmith knew that without it there can be no genuine poetry.

THE TRAVELLER

DEDICATION TO THE REV. HENRY GOLDSMITH

Dear Sir,

I am sensible that the friendship between us can acquire no new force from the ceremonies of a Dedication; and perhaps it demands an excuse thus to prefix your name to my attempts, which you decline giving with your own. But as a part of this Poem was formerly written to you from Switzerland, the whole can now, with propriety, be only inscribed to you. It will also throw a light upon many parts of it, when the reader understands, that it is addressed to a man, who, despising Fame and Fortune, has retired early to Happiness and Obscurity, with an income of forty pounds a year.

I now perceive, my dear brother, the wisdom of your humble choice. You have entered upon a sacred office, where the harvest is great, and the labourers are but few; while you have left the field of Ambition, where the labourers are many, and the harvest not worth carrying away. But of all kinds of ambition, what from the refinement of the times, from different systems of criticism, and from the divisions of party, that which pursues poetical fame is the wildest.

Poetry makes a principal amusement among unpolished nations; but in a country verging to the extremes of refinement, Painting and Music come in for a share. As these offer the feeble mind a less laborious entertainment, they at first rival Poetry, and at length supplant her; they engross all that favour once shown to her, and though but younger sisters, seize upon the elder's birthright.

Yet, however this art may be neglected by the powerful, it is still in greater danger from the mistaken efforts of the learned to improve it. What criticisms have we not heard of late in favour of blank verse, and Pindaric odes, choruses, anapaests and iambics, alliterative care and happy negligence! Every absurdity has now a champion to defend it; and as he is generally much in the wrong, so he has always much to say; for error is ever talkative.

But there is an enemy to this art still more dangerous, I mean Party. Party entirely distorts the judgment, and destroys the taste. When the mind is once infected with this disease, it can only find pleasure in what contributes to increase the distemper. Like the tiger, that seldom desists from pursuing man after having once preyed upon human flesh, the reader, who has once gratified his appetite with calumny, makes, ever after, the most agreeable feast upon murdered reputation. Such readers generally admire some half-witted thing, who wants to be thought a bold man, having lost the character of a wise one. Him they dignify with the name of poet; his tawdry lampoons are called satires, his turbulence is said to be force, and his frenzy fire.

What reception a Poem may find, which has neither abuse, party, nor blank verse to support it, I cannot tell, nor am I solicitous to know. My aims are right. Without espousing the cause of any party, I have attempted to moderate the rage of all. I have endeavoured to show, that there may be equal happiness in states, that are differently governed from our own; that every state has a particular principle of happiness, and that this principle in each may be carried to a mischievous excess. There are few can judge, better than yourself, how far these positions are illustrated in this Poem.

I am, dear Sir,
Your most affectionate Brother,
OLIVER GOLDSMITH.

This letter is in itself an introduction to Goldsmith. The first paragraph adumbrates one of his fundamental themes: the idyllic peace of our first home in contrast with the harsh experience awaiting those who—like the wandering poet—venture into the hostile world. Paragraph 3 expresses Goldsmith's deep concern for national culture, and at the same time his amusing refusal to acknowledge that anything but the art of letters can contribute thereto. Paragraph 4 is a provocative statement of his deep-seated prejudice against the blank-verse poetry now coming into fashion, and against Gray's Pindaric manner. Paragraph 5, referring in a narrow sense to Charles Churchill's politically loaded satires, reflects Goldsmith's settled—and in 18th-century England by no means uncommon—attitude towards the British constitution, which, seen as a balancing of power between the Crown and Parliament, seemed to demand statesmanship in behalf of the general welfare rather than a running battle between opposing political factions. The final paragraph, with its bald statement of the theme to be accorded imaginative treatment in the ensuing poem, would have excited a good deal of interest in 1764, for Goldsmith promises to touch upon a number of questions concerning luxury, the psychology of human desires, and the nature of happiness and civilized taste which were then being extensively debated.

Goldsmith made numerous alterations in the original text of 1764. The present text is based upon the 1774 ed. In 1902 Bertram Dobell thought he had turned up an early version of the poem, departing widely from the hitherto recognized first edition of 1764, and he published his discovery as *A Prospect of Society By Oliver Goldsmith*; but as W. B. Todd showed (in his 1956 study, *A Prospect of Society . . . Reconstructed* [see bibliography]), what Dobell had unearthed was final proof sheets of the poem, "badly bungled, and finally suppressed."

The Traveller is to some extent based on Goldsmith's own continental wanderings, and as he states in his dedicatory letter, some of it was written while he was abroad He may well have had in mind Addison's *Letter from Italy to Lord Halifax* (1705), of which he was to remark in the *Beauties of English Poesy* (1767) that it had "a strain of political thinking that was, at that time, new in our poetry." Goldsmith, however, takes a very different line from Addison, for the latter, finding the Italians languishing under a "proud oppression," is stirred at the thought that Liberty adores and crowns Britannia's isle, and that Britain's fate is to watch over Europe and "hold in balance each contending state."

THE TRAVELLER

OR A PROSPECT OF SOCIETY

REMOTE, unfriended, melancholy, slow,
Or by the lazy Scheldt, or wandering Po;
Or onward, where the rude Carinthian boor,
Against the houseless stranger shuts the door;
Or where Campania's plain forsaken lies,
A weary waste expanding to the skies:
Where'er I roam, whatever realms to see,
My heart untravelled fondly turns to thee;
Still to my brother turns with ceaseless pain,
And drags at each remove a lengthening chain.   10

    Eternal blessings crown my earliest friend,
And round his dwelling guardian saints attend:
Blessed be that spot, where cheerful guests retire
To pause from toil, and trim their ev'ning fire;
Blessed that abode, where want and pain repair,
And every stranger finds a ready chair:
Blessed be those feasts with simple plenty crowned,
Where all the ruddy family around
Laugh at the jests or pranks that never fail,
Or sigh with pity at some mournful tale,
Or press the bashful stranger to his food,   20
And learn the luxury of doing good.

    But me, not destined such delights to share,
My prime of life in wand'ring spent and care,
Impelled, with steps unceasing, to pursue
Some fleeting good, that mocks me with the view;
That, like the circle bounding earth and skies,

1.3. Carinthian: region in southern Austria bordered on the south by the Carnic Alps.

Allures from far, yet, as I follow, flies;
My fortune leads to traverse realms alone,
And find no spot of all the world my own.

E'en now, where Alpine solitudes ascend,
I sit me down a pensive hour to spend;
And, placed on high above the storm's career,
Look downward where a hundred realms appear;
Lakes, forests, cities, plains, extending wide,
The pomp of kings, the shepherd's humbler pride.

When thus Creation's charms around combine,
Amidst the store, should thankless pride repine?
Say, should the philosophic mind disdain
That good, which makes each humbler bosom vain?
Let school-taught pride dissemble all it can,
These little things are great to little man;
And wiser he, whose sympathetic mind
Exults in all the good of all mankind.
Ye glitt'ring towns, with wealth and splendour crowned,
Ye fields, where summer spreads profusion round,
Ye lakes, whose vessels catch the busy gale,
Ye bending swains, that dress the flow'ry vale,
For me your tributary stores combine;
Creation's heir, the world, the world is mine!

As some lone miser visiting his store,
Bends at his treasure, counts, re-counts it o'er;
Hoards after hoards his rising raptures fill,
Yet still he sighs, for hoards are wanting still:
Thus to my breast alternate passions rise,
Pleased with each good that heaven to man supplies:
Yet oft a sigh prevails, and sorrows fall,
To see the hoard of human bliss so small;
And oft I wish, amidst the scene, to find
Some spot to real happiness consigned,
Where my worn soul, each wand'ring hope at rest,
May gather bliss to see my fellows blessed.

But where to find that happiest spot below,
Who can direct, when all pretend to know?

The shudd'ring tenant of the frigid zone
Boldly proclaims that happiest spot his own,
Extols the treasures of his stormy seas,
And his long nights of revelry and ease;
The naked negro, panting at the line,
Boasts of his golden sands and palmy wine, 70
Basks in the glare, or stems the tepid wave,
And thanks his gods for all the good they gave.
Such is the patriot's boast, where'er we roam,
His first, best country ever is, at home.
And yet, perhaps, if countries we compare,
And estimate the blessings which they share,
Though patriots flatter, still shall wisdom find
An equal portion dealt to all mankind,
As different good, by Art or Nature given,
To different nations makes their blessings even. 80

   Nature, a mother kind alike to all,
Still grants her bliss at Labour's earnest call;
With food as well the peasant is supplied
On Idra's cliffs as Arno's shelvy side;
And though the rocky-crested summits frown,
These rocks, by custom, turn to beds of down.
From Art more various are the blessings sent;
Wealth, commerce, honour, liberty, content.
Yet these each other's power so strong contest,
That either seems destructive of the rest. 90
Where wealth and freedom reign contentment fails,
And honour sinks where commerce long prevails.
Hence every state to one loved blessing prone,
Conforms and models life to that alone.
Each to the favourite happiness attends,
And spurns the plan that aims at other ends;
Till, carried to excess in each domain,
This favourite good begets peculiar pain.

   But let us try these truths with closer eyes,
And trace them through the prospect as it lies: 100
Here for a while my proper cares resigned,

---

l.84. Idra: Idria, a town now in n. w. Yugoslavia, noted for its mines.

Here let me sit in sorrow for mankind,
Like yon neglected shrub at random cast,
That shades the steep, and sighs at every blast.

Far to the right where Apennine ascends,
Bright as the summer, Italy extends;
Its uplands sloping deck the mountain's side,
Woods over woods in gay theatric pride;
While oft some temple's mould'ring tops between
With venerable grandeur mark the scene.　　　110

Could Nature's bounty satisfy the breast,
The sons of Italy were surely blest.
Whatever fruits in different climes were found,
That proudly rise, or humbly court the ground;
Whatever blooms in torrid tracts appear,
Whose bright succession decks the varied year;
Whatever sweets salute the northern sky
With vernal lives that blossom but to die;
These here disporting own the kindred soil,
Nor ask luxuriance from the planter's toil;　　　120
While sea-born gales their gelid wings expand
To winnow fragrance round the smiling land.

But small the bliss that sense alone bestows,
And sensual bliss is all the nation knows.
In florid beauty groves and fields appear,
Man seems the only growth that dwindles here.
Contrasted faults through all his manners reign,
Though poor, luxurious, though submissive, vain,
Though grave, yet trifling, zealous, yet untrue;
And e'en in penance planning sins anew.　　　130
All evils here contaminate the mind,
That opulence departed leaves behind;
For wealth was theirs, not far removed the date,
When commerce proudly flourished through the state;
At her command the palace learned to rise,
Again the long-fall'n column sought the skies;
The canvas glowed beyond e'en Nature warm,
The pregnant quarry teemed with human form;
Till, more unsteady than the southern gale,

Commerce on other shores displayed her sail; 140
While nought remained of all that riches gave,
But towns unmanned, and lords without a slave;
And late the nation found with fruitless skill
Its former strength was but plethoric ill.

Yet still the loss of wealth is here supplied
By arts, the splendid wrecks of former pride;
From these the feeble heart and long-fall'n mind
An easy compensation seem to find.
Here may be seen, in bloodless pomp arrayed,
The paste-board triumph and the cavalcade; 150
Processions formed for piety and love,
A mistress or a saint in every grove.
By sports like these are all their cares beguiled,
The sports of children satisfy the child;
Each nobler aim, repressed by long control,
Now sinks at last, or feebly mans the soul;
While low delights, succeeding fast behind,
In happier meanness occupy the mind:
As in those domes, where Caesars once bore sway,
Defaced by time and tottering in decay, 160
There in the ruin, heedless of the dead,
The shelter-seeking peasant builds his shed,
And, wond'ring man could want the larger pile,
Exults, and owns his cottage with a smile.

My soul, turn from them; turn we to survey
Where rougher climes a nobler race display,
Where the bleak Swiss their stormy mansions tread,
And force a churlish soil for scanty bread;
No product here the barren hills afford,
But man and steel, the soldier and his sword; 170
No vernal blooms their torpid rocks array,
But winter ling'ring chills the lap of May;

---

l.150. triumph: In the *Present State of Polite Learning* G had remarked that "the wits . . . of Rome are united into a rural groupe of nymphs and swains, under the appellation of modern Arcadians. Where in the midst of porticos, processions, and cavalcades, abbés turn'd into shepherds, and shepherdesses without sheep, indulge their innocent *divertimenti.*"

l.170. soldier: referring to the Swiss mercenaries, well-known throughout Europe.

The Traveller

>   No Zephyr fondly sues the mountain's breast,
> But meteors glare, and stormy glooms invest.
>
>   Yet still, e'en here, content can spread a charm,
> Redress the clime, and all its rage disarm.
> Though poor the peasant's hut, his feasts though small,
> He sees his little lot the lot of all;
> Sees no contiguous palace rear its head
> To shame the meanness of his humble shed;
> No costly lord the sumptuous banquet deal,
> To make him loathe his vegetable meal;
> But calm, and bred in ignorance and toil,
> Each wish contracting, fits him to the soil.
> Cheerful at morn he wakes from short repose,
> Breasts the keen air, and carols as he goes;
> With patient angle trolls the finny deep,
> Or drives his venturous plough-share to the steep;
> Or seeks the den where snow-tracks mark the way,
> And drags the struggling savage into day.
> At night returning, every labour sped,
> He sits him down the monarch of a shed;
> Smiles by his cheerful fire, and round surveys
> His children's looks, that brighten at the blaze;
> While his loved partner, boastful of her hoard,
> Displays her cleanly platter on the board:
> And haply too some pilgrim, thither led,
> With many a tale repays the nightly bed.
>
>   Thus every good his native wilds impart,
> Imprints the patriot passion on his heart,
> And e'en those ills, that round his mansion rise,
> Enhance the bliss his scanty fund supplies.
> Dear is that shed to which his soul conforms,
> And dear that hill which lifts him to the storms;
> And as a child, when scaring sounds molest,
> Clings close and closer to the mother's breast,
> So the loud torrent, and the whirlwind's roar,
> But bind him to his native mountains more.

---

l.187. angle: fishhook, or fishing line, hook, and bait.   l.190. savage: a wolf or bear.

Such are the charms to barren states assigned;
Their wants but few, their wishes all confined.   210
Yet let them only share the praises due,
If few their wants, their pleasures are but few;
For every want that stimulates the breast,
Becomes a source of pleasure when redrest.
Whence from such lands each pleasing science flies,
That first excites desire, and then supplies;
Unknown to them, when sensual pleasures cloy,
To fill the languid pause with finer joy;
Unknown those powers that raise the soul to flame,
Catch every nerve, and vibrate through the frame.
Their level life is but a smould'ring fire,   220
Unquenched by want, unfanned by strong desire;
Unfit for raptures, or, if raptures cheer
On some high festival of once a year,
In wild excess the vulgar breast takes fire,
Till, buried in debauch, the bliss expire.

But not their joys alone thus coarsely flow:
Their morals, like their pleasures, are but low,
For, as refinement stops, from sire to son
Unaltered, unimproved, the manners run;   230
And love's and friendship's finely-pointed dart
Fall blunted from each indurated heart.
Some sterner virtues o'er the mountain's breast
May sit, like falcons cow'ring on the nest;
But all the gentler morals, such as play
Through life's more cultured walks and charm the way,
These far dispersed, on timorous pinions fly,
To sport and flutter in a kinder sky.

To kinder skies, where gentler manners reign,
I turn; and France displays her bright domain.   240
Gay sprightly land of mirth and social ease,
Pleased with thyself, whom all the world can please,
How often have I led thy sportive choir,
With tuneless pipe, beside the murmuring Loire?
Where shading elms along the margin grew,

---

l.228. low: not refined.

And freshened from the wave the Zephyr flew;
And haply, though my harsh touch falt'ring still,
But mocked all tune, and marred the dancer's skill;
Yet would the village praise my wondrous power,
And dance, forgetful of the noon-tide hour.   250
Alike all ages. Dames of ancient days
Have led their children through the mirthful maze,
And the gay grandsire, skilled in gestic lore,
Has frisked beneath the burthen of threescore.

   So blessed a life these thoughtless realms display,
Thus idly busy rolls their world away:
Theirs are those arts that mind to mind endear,
For honour forms the social temper here:
Honour, that praise which real merit gains,
Or e'en imaginary worth obtains,   260
Here passes current; paid from hand to hand,
It shifts in splendid traffic round the land:
From courts, to camps, to cottages it strays,
And all are taught an avarice of praise;
They please, are pleased, they give to get esteem,
Till, seeming blessed, they grow to what they seem.

   But while this softer art their bliss supplies,
It gives their follies also room to rise;
For praise too dearly loved, or warmly sought,
Enfeebles all internal strength of thought;   270
And the weak soul, within itself unblest,
Leans for all pleasure on another's breast.
Hence ostentation here, with tawdry art,
Pants for the vulgar praise which fools impart;
Here vanity assumes her pert grimace,
And trims her robes of frieze with copper lace;
Here beggar pride defrauds her daily cheer,
To boast one splendid banquet once a year;
The mind still turns where shifting fashion draws,
Nor weighs the solid worth of self-applause.   280

---

l.253. gestic lore: traditional gestures and movements.
l.264. avarice: an insatiable desire.
l.276. copper lace: good-for-nothing ornamental braid.

To men of other minds my fancy flies,
Embosomed in the deep where Holland lies.
Methinks her patient sons before me stand,
Where the broad ocean leans against the land,
And, sedulous to stop the coming tide,
Lift the tall rampire's artificial pride.
Onward, methinks, and diligently slow,
The firm-connected bulwark seems to grow;
Spreads it long arms amidst the wat'ry roar,
Scoops out an empire, and usurps the shore; 290
While the pent ocean rising o'er the pile,
Sees an amphibious world beneath him smile;
The slow canal, the yellow-blossomed vale,
The willow-tufted bank, the gliding sail,
The crowded mart, the cultivated plain,
A new creation rescued from his reign.

Thus, while around the wave-subjected soil
Impels the native to repeated toil,
Industrious habits in each bosom reign,
And industry begets a love of gain. 300
Hence all the good from opulence that springs,
With all those ills superfluous treasure brings,
Are here displayed. Their much-loved wealth imparts
Convenience, plenty, elegance, and arts;
But view them closer, craft and fraud appear,
E'en liberty itself is bartered here.
At gold's superior charms all freedom flies,
The needy sell it, and the rich man buys;
A land of tyrants, and a den of slaves,
Here wretches seek dishonourable graves, 310
And calmly bent, to servitude conform,
Dull as their lakes that slumber in the storm.

Heavens! how unlike their Belgic sires of old!
Rough, poor, content, ungovernably bold;
War in each breast, and freedom on each brow;
How much unlike the sons of Britain now!

---

l.286. rampire: rampart.
l.306. liberty: Mitford's note in his 1831 ed. of the *Poetical Works:* "Slavery was permitted in Holland; children were sold by their parents for a certain number of years."

The Traveller

   Fired at the sound, my genius spreads her wing,
And flies where Britain courts the western spring;
Where lawns extend that scorn Arcadian pride,
And brighter streams than famed Hydaspes glide.
There all around the gentlest breezes stray,
There gentle music melts on ev'ry spray;
Creation's mildest charms are there combined,
Extremes are only in the master's mind!
Stern o'er each bosom reason holds her state,
With daring aims irregularly great,
Pride in their port, defiance in their eye,
I see the lords of human kind pass by,
Intent on high designs, a thoughtful band,
By forms unfashioned, fresh from Nature's hand;
Fierce in their native hardiness of soul,
True to imagined right, above control,
While e'en the peasant boasts these rights to scan,
And learns to venerate himself as man.

   Thine, Freedom, thine the blessings pictured here,
Thine are those charms that dazzle and endear;
Too blessed, indeed, were such without alloy,
But fostered e'en by Freedom ills annoy:
That independence Britons prize too high,
Keeps man from man, and breaks the social tie;
The self-dependent lordlings stand alone,
All claims that bind and sweeten life unknown;
Here by the bonds of nature feebly held,
Minds combat minds, repelling and repelled.
Ferments arise, imprisoned factions roar,
Repressed ambition struggles round her shore,
Till over-wrought, the general system feels
Its motions stop, or frenzy fire the wheels.

   Nor this the worst. As nature's ties decay,
As duty, love, and honour fail to sway,
Fictitious bonds, the bonds of wealth and law,
Still gather strength, and force unwilling awe.
Hence all obedience bows to these alone,

---

l.320. Hydaspes: Horace (*Odes*. I. xxii) refers to "fabulous Hydaspes"; a river in Punjab, India, it is now known as the Jhilum.

And talent sinks, and merit weeps unknown;
Till time may come, when stripped of all her charms,
The land of scholars, and the nurse of arms,
Where noble stems transmit the patriot flame,
Where kings have toiled, and poets wrote for fame,
One sink of level avarice shall lie,
And scholars, soldiers, kings, unhonoured die. 360

  Yet think not, thus when Freedom's ills I state,
I mean to flatter kings, or court the great;
Ye powers of truth, that bid my soul aspire,
Far from my bosom drive the low desire;
And thou, fair Freedom, taught alike to feel
The rabble's rage, and tyrant's angry steel;
Thou transitory flower, alike undone
By proud contempt, or favour's fostering sun,
Still may thy blooms the changeful clime endure,
I only would repress them to secure: 370
For just experience tells, in every soil,
That those who think must govern those that toil;
And all that freedom's highest aims can reach,
Is but to lay proportioned loads on each.
Hence, should one order disproportioned grow,
Its double weight must ruin all below.

  O then how blind to all that truth requires,
Who think it freedom when a part aspires!
Calm is my soul, nor apt to rise in arms,
Except when fast-approaching danger warms: 380
But when contending chiefs blockade the throne,
Contracting regal power to stretch their own;
When I behold a factious band agree
To call it freedom when themselves are free;
Each wanton judge new penal statutes draw,
Laws grind the poor, and rich men rule the law;
The wealth of climes, where savage nations roam,
Pillaged from slaves to purchase slaves at home;
Fear, pity, justice, indignation start,
Tear off reserve, and bare my swelling heart; 390

The Traveller

> Till half a patriot, half a coward grown,
> I fly from petty tyrants to the throne.
>
> Yes, brother, curse with me that baleful hour,
> When first ambition struck at regal power;
> And thus polluting honour in its source,
> Gave wealth to sway the mind with double force.
> Have we not seen, round Britain's peopled shore,
> Her useful sons exchanged for useless ore?
> Seen all her triumphs but destruction haste,
> Like flaring tapers brightening as they waste;   400
> Seen opulence, her grandeur to maintain,
> Lead stern depopulation in her train,
> And over fields where scattered hamlets rose,
> In barren solitary pomp repose?

---

l.394: G makes the same point in the *Vicar of W.* (ch. xix). His views concerning the balanced nature of the British Constitution, the legitimate powers of the crown, and the obstructive nature of political maneuvering, were shared by many of his contemporaries. What distinguishes G in the present passage and elsewhere in his verse and prose is the forthright manner in which he presents a conflict between the men of wealth and the middle and lower classes, a conflict between an excessive and crass materialism and a social tradition which seemed to him to nurture all the lifegiving qualities.

l.404: This passage clearly anticipates the main theme of *The Deserted Village*. But what precisely does G refer to? The enclosure movement persisted throughout the eighteenth century; i.e., the old communal strips, cultivated in common, were being combined into larger holdings by various Acts of Parliament, thus making possible the use of far more efficient methods of farming. Historians agree that the movement was necessary for food production to keep pace with the rising population. But they differ as to how much hardship displaced farmers and villagers suffered. Undoubtedly G had the general enclosure movement in mind in both *The Traveller* and *Deserted Village*, but in both poems he refers not to enclosure for improved farming but to enclosure by rich men who did not hesitate to wipe out entire villages in order to create ostentatious estates. And it may be, as R. S. Crane has suggested in his *New Essays by O. G.* (see bibliography), that G's essay, "The Revolution in Low Life" (*Lloyd's Evening Post*, June 1762), points directly to passages in *The Traveller* and *Deserted Village*. "I spent part of last summer in a little village," wrote G, "distant about fifty miles from town, consisting of near a hundred houses." The villagers are then described in their happiness. But they must shortly leave. "I was informed that a Merchant of immense fortune in London, who had lately purchased the estate on which they lived, intended to lay the whole out in a seat of pleasure for himself." Throughout the Kingdom, G adds, laborious husbandmen have thus been reduced, "and the lands are now either occupied by some general undertaker, or turned into enclosures destined for the purposes of amuse-

Have we not seen, at pleasure's lordly call,
The smiling long-frequented village fall?
Beheld the duteous son, the sire decayed,
The modest matron, and the blushing maid,
Forced from their homes, a melancholy train,
To traverse climes beyond the western main;   410
Where wild Oswego spreads her swamps around,
And Niagara stuns with thund'ring sound?

E'en now, perhaps, as there some pilgrim strays
Through tangled forests, and through dangerous ways;
Where beasts with man divided empire claim,
And the brown Indian marks with murd'rous aim;
There, while above the giddy tempest flies,
And all around distressful yells arise,
The pensive exile, bending with his woe,
To stop too fearful, and too faint to go,   420
Casts a long look where England's glories shine,
And bids his bosom sympathise with mine.

Vain, very vain, my weary search to find
That bliss which only centres in the mind:
Why have I strayed from pleasure and repose,
To seek a good each government bestows?
In every government, though terrors reign,
Though tyrant kings, or tyrant laws restrain,
How small, of all that human hearts endure,
That part which laws or kings can cause or cure.   430
Still to ourselves in every place consigned,
Our own felicity we make or find:
With secret course, which no loud storms annoy,
Glides the smooth current of domestic joy.
The lifted axe, the agonising wheel,

---

ment or luxury." (See H. J. Bell, Jr., "The Deserted Village and G's Social Doctrines," *PMLA*, LIX [1944]; and E. Miner, "The Making of *The Deserted Village*," *HLQ*, XXII [1959].) l.420: This is one of the nine lines of the poem written, according to Boswell, by Johnson (cf. note to

l.429 below).
l.429: In his *Life of J.*, under February 1766, Boswell states that in 1783 Johnson marked line 420 of the poem and the concluding ten lines save the next to the last couplet as his contribution ("These are all of which I can be sure.").

Luke's iron crown, and Damiens bed of steel,
To men remote from power but rarely known,
Leave reason, faith, and conscience, all our own.

l.436. George and Luke Dosa had headed a rebellion in Hungary in 1513; George was condemned to be crowned with a red-hot iron. In 1757 one Robert-François Damien attempted to assassinate Louis XV and was put to death after being tortured on an iron bed or chair.

THE DESERTED VILLAGE

NOTE: Goldsmith dedicated *The Deserted Village* to his friend, Sir Joshua Reynolds. The prefixed letter of dedication reads in part as follows:

How far you may be pleased with the versification and mere mechanical parts of this attempt, I don't pretend to enquire; but I know you will object (and indeed several of our best and wisest friends concur in the opinion) that the depopulation it deplores is no where to be seen, and the disorders it laments are only to be found in the poet's own imagination. To this I can scarce make any other answer than that I sincerely believe what I have written; that I have taken all possible pains, in my country excursions, for these four or five years past, to be certain of what I allege; and that all my views and enquiries have led me to believe those miseries real, which I here attempt to display. But this is not the place to enter into an enquiry, whether the country be depopulating, or not; the discussion would take up much room, and I should prove myself, at best, an indifferent politician, to tire the reader with a long preface, when I want his unfatigued attention to a long poem.

In regretting the depopulation of the country, I inveigh against the increase of our luxuries; and here also I expect the shout of modern politicians against me. For twenty or thirty years past, it has been the fashion to consider luxury as one of the greatest national advantages; and all the wisdom of antiquity in that particular, as erroneous. Still however, I must remain a professed ancient on that head, and continue to think those luxuries prejudicial to states, by which so many vices are introduced, and so many kingdoms have been undone. Indeed so much has been poured out of late on the other side of the question, that, merely for the sake of novelty and variety, one would sometimes wish to be in the right.*

* Concerning the question of "depopulation," raised in the first of these paragraphs, cf. the preceding note to l.404 on the depopulation passage in *The Traveller*. The concluding statement in this paragraph is pure Goldsmith: not confused as we first assume, but genuinely provocative. How are we to take it? Does it mean to say that a poem's value depends wholly upon its execution, and not at all upon its thematic material? G emphatically did not embrace any such belief. He regarded serious theme and effective execution as functionally interdependent. Here he really retracts nothing of his theory of depopulation, but by emphasizing the imaginative element—i.e., poetic statement—he places his theory in the context of human experience portrayed through art. The concluding statement of the second paragraph is again arresting. Was it perhaps at this kind of polyphonic logic that G was sometimes aiming in his disastrous attempts at conversational wit?

THE DESERTED VILLAGE

SWEET AUBURN! loveliest village of the plain,
Where health and plenty cheered the labouring swain,
Where smiling spring its earliest visit paid,
And parting summer's lingering blooms delayed:
Dear lovely bowers of innocence and ease,
Seats of my youth, when every sport could please,
How often have I loitered o'er thy green,
Where humble happiness endeared each scene;
How often have I paused on every charm,
The sheltered cot, the cultivated farm,　　　　　　　　　　　10
The never-failing brook, the busy mill,
The decent church that topped the neighbouring hill,
The hawthorn bush, with seats beneath the shade,
For talking age and whispering lovers made;
How often have I blessed the coming day,
When toil remitting lent its turn to play,
And all the village train, from labour free,
Led up their sports beneath the spreading tree;
While many a pastime circled in the shade,
The young contending as the old surveyed;　　　　　　　　20
And many a gambol frolicked o'er the ground,
And sleights of art and feats of strength went round;
And still as each repeated pleasure tired,
Succeeding sports the mirthful band inspired;

---

l.1. Sweet Auburn: "Auburn" has many times been identified with G's native Lissoy, and various descriptive details in the poem ("the decent church" and "neighbouring hill" of l.12, and "the hawthorn bush" of l.13) have been pointed out as corresponding with the scene of his youth. But since "Auburn" has its existence in the imagination, questions of identification would seem peculiarly futile. However, whether memories of Lissoy are present or not, whether G was recalling conditions in Ireland (see R. W. Seitz's statement of "The Irish Background of G's . . . Thought," PMLA, LII [1937]), this surely is an English village, as l. 57 ("A time there was, ere England's griefs began") makes clear.

The dancing pair that simply sought renown,
By holding out to tire each other down;
The swain mistrustless of his smutted face,
While secret laughter tittered round the place;
The bashful virgin's side-long looks of love,
The matron's glance that would those looks reprove: 30
These were thy charms, sweet village; sports like these,
With sweet succession, taught e'en toil to please;
These round thy bowers their cheerful influence shed,
These were thy charms—But all these charms are fled.

    Sweet smiling village, loveliest of the lawn,
Thy sports are fled, and all thy charms withdrawn;
Amidst thy bowers the tyrant's hand is seen,
And desolation saddens all thy green:
One only master grasps the whole domain,
And half a tillage stints thy smiling plain: 40
No more thy glassy brook reflects the day,
But choked with sedges, works its weedy way.
Along thy glades, a solitary guest,
The hollow-sounding bittern guards its nest;
Amidst thy desert walks the lapwing flies,
And tires their echoes with unvaried cries.
Sunk are thy bowers, in shapeless ruin all,
And the long grass o'ertops the mouldering wall;
And, trembling, shrinking from the spoiler's hand,
Far, far away, thy children leave the land. 50

    Ill fares the land, to hastening ills a prey,
Where wealth accumulates, and men decay:
Princes and lords may flourish, or may fade;
A breath can make them, as a breath has made;

---

l.37. tyrant: Strean, who succeeded G's brother Henry at Kilkenny West, stated (see Ed. Mangin, *Essay on Light Reading* [1808]) that the tyrant was one Robt. Napper, who purchased an estate near Lissoy and had many families removed therefrom. But if the essay on "The Revolution in Low Life" (see note to l. 404 above) has direct bearing on *The D. V.*, the tyrant's hand was an English one, and it fell upon an English village.

l.52. In ch. xix of *The Vicar of W.*, the vicar holds forth at length on the accumulation of wealth in commercial states, and on some of the unfortunate consequences.

But a bold peasantry, their country's pride,
When once destroyed, can never be supplied.

A time there was, ere England's griefs began,
When every rood of ground maintained its man;
For him light labour spread her wholesome store,
Just gave what life required, but gave no more: 60
His best companions, innocence and health;
And his best riches, ignorance of wealth.

But times are altered; trade's unfeeling train
Usurp the land and dispossess the swain;
Along the lawn, where scattered hamlets rose,
Unwieldy wealth, and cumbrous pomp repose;
And every want to opulence allied,
And every pang that folly pays to pride.
Those gentle hours that plenty bade to bloom,
Those calm desires that asked but little room,   70
Those healthful sports that graced the peaceful scene,
Lived in each look, and brightened all the green;
These, far departing, seek a kinder shore,
And rural mirth and manners are no more.

Sweet AUBURN! parent of the blissful hour,
Thy glades forlorn confess the tyrant's power.
Here as I take my solitary rounds,
Amidst thy tangling walks, and ruined grounds,
And, many a year elapsed, return to view
Where once the cottage stood, the hawthorn grew,   80
Remembrance wakes with all her busy train,
Swells at my breast, and turns the past to pain.

In all my wanderings round this world of care,
In all my griefs—and GOD has given my share—
I still had hopes my latest hours to crown,
Amidst these humble bowers to lay me down;
To husband out life's taper at the close,
And keep the flame from wasting by repose.
I still had hopes, for pride attends us still,
Amidst the swains to show my book-learned skill,   90
Around my fire an evening group to draw,

And tell of all I felt, and all I saw;
And, as a hare, whom hounds and horns pursue,
Pants to the place from whence at first she flew,
I still had hopes, my long vexations passed,
Here to return—and die at home at last.

O blest retirement, friend to life's decline,
Retreats from care, that never must be mine,
How happy he who crowns in shades like these,
A youth of labour with an age of ease; 100
Who quits a world where strong temptations try
And, since 'tis hard to combat, learns to fly!
For him no wretches, born to work and weep,
Explore the mine, or tempt the dangerous deep;
No surly porter stands in guilty state
To spurn imploring famine from the gate;
But on he moves to meet his latter end,
Angels around befriending Virtue's friend;
Bends to the grave with unperceived decay,
While Resignation gently slopes the way; 110
And all his prospects brightening to the last,
His Heaven commences ere the world be passed!

Sweet was the sound, when oft at evening's close
Up yonder hill the village murmur rose;
There, as I passed with careless steps and slow,
The mingling notes came softened from below;
The swain responsive as the milk-maid sung,
The sober herd that lowed to meet their young;
The noisy geese that gabbled o'er the pool,
The playful children just let loose from school; 120
The watchdog's voice that bayed the whisp'ring wind,
And the loud laugh that spoke the vacant mind;
These all in sweet confusion sought the shade,
And filled each pause the nightingale had made.
But now the sounds of population fail,
No cheerful murmurs fluctuate in the gale,

---

l.110. Resignation: In 1771 Sir J. Reynolds exhibited a painting entitled "An Old Man." In 1772 an engraving of this appeared (by James Watson), called "Resignation," dedicated by Reynolds to G, stating that the picture was "an attempt to express a character in *The D. V.*"

No busy steps the grass-grown footway tread,
For all the bloomy flush of life is fled.
All but yon widowed, solitary thing
That feebly bends beside the plashy spring; 130
She, wretched matron, forced in age, for bread,
To strip the brook with mantling cresses spread,
To pick her wintry faggot from the thorn,
To seek her nightly shed, and weep till morn;
She only left of all the harmless train,
The sad historian of the pensive plain.

   Near yonder copse, where once the garden smiled,
And still where many a garden flower grows wild;
There, where a few torn shrubs the place disclose,
The village preacher's modest mansion rose. 140
A man he was to all the country dear,
And passing rich with forty pounds a year;
Remote from towns he ran his godly race,
Nor e'er had changed, nor wished to change his place;
Unpractised he to fawn, or seek for power,
By doctrines fashioned to the varying hour;
Far other aims his heart had learned to prize,
More skilled to raise the wretched than to rise.
His house was known to all the vagrant train,
He chid their wanderings, but relieved their pain; 150
The long remembered beggar was his guest,
Whose beard descending swept his aged breast;
The ruined spendthrift, now no longer proud,
Claimed kindred there, and had his claims allowed;
The broken soldier, kindly bade to stay,
Sat by his fire, and talked the night away;
Wept o'er his wounds, or tales of sorrow done,
Shouldered his crutch, and showed how fields were won.
Pleased with his guests, the good man learned to glow,
And quite forgot their vices in their woe; 160
Careless their merits, or their faults to scan,
His pity gave ere charity began.

---

l.136. historian: Strean (see note to l. 37 above) saw in this figure one Catherine Giraghty of Lissoy.

l.140. the village preacher: has been variously identified as G's father, his brother, and his uncle Contarine.

Thus to relieve the wretched was his pride,
And e'en his failings leaned to Virtue's side;
But in his duty prompt at every call,
He watched and wept, he prayed and felt, for all.
And, as a bird each fond endearment tries
To tempt its new-fledged offspring to the skies,
He tried each art, reproved each dull delay,
Allured to brighter worlds, and led the way. 170

Beside the bed where parting life was laid,
And sorrow, guilt, and pain, by turns dismayed,
The reverend champion stood. At his control
Despair and anguish fled the struggling soul;
Comfort came down the trembling wretch to raise,
And his last faltering accents whispered praise.

At church, with meek and unaffected grace,
His looks adorned the venerable place;
Truth from his lips prevailed with double sway,
And fools, who came to scoff, remained to pray. 180
The service passed, around the pious man,
With steady zeal, each honest rustic ran;
Even children followed with endearing wile,
And plucked his gown, to share the good man's smile.
His ready smile a parent's warmth expressed,
Their welfare pleased him, and their cares distressed,
To them his heart, his love, his griefs were given,
But all his serious thoughts had rest in Heaven.
As some tall cliff, that lifts its awful form,
Swells from the vale, and the midway leaves the storm, 190
Though round its breast the rolling clouds are spread,
Eternal sunshine settles on its head.

Beside yon straggling fence that skirts the way,
With blossomed furze unprofitably gay,
There, in his noisy mansion, skilled to rule,
The village master taught his little school;
A man severe he was, and stern to view;
I knew him well, and every truant knew;

---

l.196. master: Inevitably—and perhaps rightly—G's master at Lissoy has been seen as the original of the village master.

Well had the boding tremblers learned to trace
The day's disasters in his morning face;
Full well they laughed, with counterfeited glee,
At all his jokes, for many a joke had he;
Full well the busy whisper, circling round,
Conveyed the dismal tidings when he frowned;
Yet he was kind; or if severe in aught,
The love he bore to learning was in fault;
The village all declared how much he knew;
'Twas certain he could write, and cypher too;
Lands he could measure, terms and tides presage,
And e'en the story ran that he could gauge.
In arguing too, the parson owned his skill,
For even though vanquished, he could argue still;
While words of learned length and thund'ring sound
Amazed the gazing rustics ranged around,
And still they gazed, and still the wonder grew,
That one small head could carry all he knew.

But past is all his fame. The very spot
Where many a time he triumphed, is forgot.
Near yonder thorn, that lifts its head on high,
Where once the sign-post caught the passing eye,
Low lies that house where nut-brown draughts inspired,
Where grey-beard mirth and smiling toil retired,
Where village statesmen talked with looks profound,
And news much older than their ale went round.
Imagination fondly stoops to trace
The parlour splendours of that festive place;
The white-washed wall, the nicely sanded floor,
The varnished clock that clicked behind the door;
The chest contrived a double debt to pay,
A bed by night, a chest of drawers by day;
The pictures placed for ornament and use,
The twelve good rules, the royal game of goose;
The hearth, except when winter chilled the day,

---

l.232. twelve good rules: A favorite broadside depicted the death of Charles I and set forth twelve adages associated with this king "of Blessed Memory."

l.232. game of goose: In this a player landing, by the throw of the dice, on a square showing a goose could move forward a double number of spaces.

The Deserted Village

With aspen boughs, and flowers, and fennel gay;
While broken tea-cups, wisely kept for show,
Ranged o'er the chimney, glistened in a row.

Vain transitory splendours! Could not all
Reprieve the tottering mansion from its fall!
Obscure it sinks, nor shall it more impart
An hour's importance to the poor man's heart;   240
Thither no more the peasant shall repair
To sweet oblivion of his daily care;
No more the farmer's news, the barber's tale,
No more the wood-man's ballad shall prevail;
No more the smith his dusky brow shall clear,
Relax his ponderous strength, and lean to hear;
The host himself no longer shall be found
Careful to see the mantling bliss go round;
Nor the coy maid, half willing to be pressed,
Shall kiss the cup to pass it to the rest.   250

Yes! let the rich deride, the proud disdain,
These simple blessings of the lowly train;
To me more dear, congenial to my heart,
One native charm, than all the gloss of art;
Spontaneous joys, where Nature has its play,
The soul adopts, and owns their first-born sway;
Lightly they frolic o'er the vacant mind,
Unenvied, unmolested, unconfined:
But the long pomp, the midnight masquerade,
With all the freaks of wanton wealth arrayed,   260
In these, ere triflers half their wish obtain,
The toiling pleasure sickens into pain;
And, e'en while fashion's brightest arts decoy,
The heart distrusting asks, if this be joy.

Ye friends to truth, ye statesmen, who survey
The rich man's joys increase, the poor's decay,
'Tis yours to judge, how wide the limits stand
Between a splendid and a happy land.

1.268. Compare with the close of Letter XXV of the *Citizen of the World:* "too much commerce may injure a nation as well as too little . . ." In a preceding letter (XI) we have, to be sure, a defense of luxury, but G's

Proud swells the tide with loads of freighted ore,
And shouting Folly hails them from her shore;
Hoards, e'en beyond the miser's wish abound,
And rich men flock from all the world around.
Yet count our gains. This wealth is but a name
That leaves our useful products still the same.
Not so the loss. The man of wealth and pride
Takes up a space that many poor supplied;
Space for his lake, his park's extended bounds,
Space for his horses, equipage, and hounds;
The robe that wraps his limbs in silken sloth
Has robbed the neighbouring fields of half their growth,
His seat, where solitary sports are seen,
Indignant spurns the cottage from the green;
Around the world each needful product flies,
For all the luxuries the world supplies:
While thus the land adorned for pleasure, all
In barren splendour feebly waits the fall.

As some fair female unadorned and plain,
Secure to please while youth confirms her reign,
Slights every borrowed charm that dress supplies,
Nor shares with art the triumph of her eyes:
But when those charms are passed, for charms are frail,
When time advances, and when lovers fail,
She then shines forth, solicitous to bless,
In all the glaring impotence of dress.
Thus fares the land, by luxury betrayed,
In nature's simplest charms at first arrayed;
But verging to decline, its splendours rise,
Its vistas strike, its palaces surprise;
While scourged by famine from the smiling land,
The mournful peasant leads his humble band;
And while he sinks, without one arm to save,
The country blooms—a garden, and a grave.

Where then, ah! where, shall poverty reside,
To 'scape the pressure of contiguous pride?

---

position seems to have been that luxury is beneficial only up to a certain point, beyond which it becomes harmful to society. (See H. J. Bell, Jr., "The *D. V.* and G's Social Doctrine," *PMLA*, LIX [1944].)

The Deserted Village

If to some common's fenceless limits strayed,
He drives his flock to pick the scanty blade,
Those fenceless fields the sons of wealth divide,
And e'en the bare-worn common is denied.

If to the city sped—What waits him there?
To see profusion that he must not share; 310
To see ten thousand baneful arts combined
To pamper luxury, and thin mankind;
To see those joys the sons of pleasure know
Extorted from his fellow creature's woe.
Here, while the courtier glitters in brocade,
There the pale artist plies the sickly trade;
Here, while the proud their long-drawn pomps display,
There the black gibbet glooms beside the way.
The dome where Pleasure holds her midnight reign
Here, richly deckt, admits the gorgeous train; 320
Tumultuous grandeur crowds the blazing square,
The rattling chariots clash, the torches glare.
Sure scenes like these no troubles e'er annoy!
Sure these denote one universal joy!
Are these thy serious thoughts?—Ah, turn thine eyes
Where the poor houseless shiv'ring female lies.
She once, perhaps, in village plenty blessed,
Has wept at tales of innocence distressed,
Her modest looks the cottage might adorn,
Sweet as the primrose peeps beneath the thorn; 330
Now lost to all; her friends, her virtue fled,
Near her betrayer's door she lays her head,
And, pinched with cold, and shrinking from the shower,
With heavy heart deplores that luckless hour,
When idly first, ambitious of the town,
She left her wheel and robes of country brown.

Do thine, sweet AUBURN, thine, the loveliest train,
Do thy fair tribes participate her pain?

---

l.332. In "City Night-Piece" (*Cit. of the World*, Letter CXVII) we are given a glimpse of "poor shivering females," "prostituted to the gay luxurious villain," and now "turned out to meet the severity of winter" and "lying at the door of their betrayers," who curse but will not relieve them. There were undoubtedly as many of these poor females in the London of the 1760s as there were later on in standard English melodrama.

E'en now, perhaps, by cold and hunger led,
At proud men's doors they ask a little bread! 340

Ah, no. To distant climes, a dreary scene,
Where half the convex world intrudes between,
Through torrid tracts with fainting steps they go,
Where wild Altama murmurs to their woe.
Far different there from all that charmed before,
The various terrors of that horrid shore;
Those blazing suns that dart a downward ray,
And fiercely shed intolerable day;
Those matted woods where birds forget to sing,
But silent bats in drowsy clusters cling; 350
Those poisonous fields with rank luxuriance crowned,
Where the dark scorpion gathers death around;
Where at each step the stranger fears to wake
The rattling terrors of the vengeful snake;
Where crouching tigers wait their hapless prey,
And savage men more murderous still than they;
While oft in whirls the mad tornado flies,
Mingling the ravaged landscape with the skies.
Far different these from every former scene,
The cooling brook, the grassy-vested green, 360
The breezy covert of the warbling grove,
That only sheltered thefts of harmless love.

Good Heaven! what sorrows gloomed that parting day,
That called them from their native walks away;
When the poor exiles, every pleasure past,
Hung round their bowers, and fondly looked their last,
And took a long farewell, and wished in vain
For seats like these beyond the western main;
And shuddering still to face the distant deep,
Returned and wept, and still returned to weep. 370
The good old sire, the first prepared to go
To new-found worlds, and wept for others' woe;

---

l.344. Altama: Altamaha is a river in Georgia. Gen. Oglethorpe, founder of the colony of Georgia, was known to the Johnson circle.

l.355. tigers: G's Georgian tigers have been thoroughly investigated (see E. D. Seeber, "G's American tigers," *MLQ*, VI [1945]). G evidently meant the cougar, to which Buffon had referred under the term "tiger."

The Deserted Village

But for himself, in conscious virtue brave,
He only wished for worlds beyond the grave.
His lovely daughter, lovelier in her tears,
The fond companion of his helpless years,
Silent went next, neglectful of her charms,
And left a lover's for a father's arms.
With louder plaints the mother spoke her woes,
And blessed the cot where every pleasure rose; 380
And kissed her thoughtless babes with many a tear,
And clasped them close, in sorrow doubly dear;
Whilst her fond husband strove to lend relief
In all the silent manliness of grief.

O LUXURY! thou cursed by Heaven's decree,
How ill exchanged are things like these for thee!
How do thy potions, with insidious joy
Diffuse their pleasures only to destroy!
Kingdoms, by thee, to sickly greatness grown,
Boast of a florid vigour not their own; 390
At every draught more large and large they grow,
A bloated mass of rank unwieldy woe;
Till sapped their strength, and every part unsound,
Down, down they sink, and spread a ruin round.

E'en now the devastation is begun,
And half the business of destruction done;
E'en now, methinks, as pondering here I stand,
I see the rural virtues leave the land:
Down where yon anchoring vessel spreads the sail,
That idly waiting flaps with every gale, 400
Downward they move, a melancholy band,
Pass from the shore, and darken all the strand.
Contented toil, and hospitable care,
And kind connubial tenderness, are there;
And piety with wishes placed above,
And steady loyalty, and faithful love.
And thou, sweet Poetry, thou loveliest maid,
Still first to fly where sensual joys invade;
Unfit in these degenerate times of shame,
To catch the heart, or strike for honest fame; 410
Dear charming nymph, neglected and decried,

My shame in crowds, my solitary pride;
Thou source of all my bliss, and all my woe,
That found'st me poor at first, and keep'st me so;
Thou guide by which the nobler arts excel,
Thou nurse of every virtue, fare thee well!
Farewell, and Oh! where'er thy voice be tried,
On Torno's cliffs, or Pambamarca's side,
Whether where equinoctial fervours glow,
Or winter wraps the polar world in snow,   420
Still let thy voice, prevailing over time,
Redress the rigours of th' inclement clime;
Aid slighted truth; with thy persuasive strain
Teach erring man to spurn the rage of gain;
Teach him, that states of native strength possessed,
Though very poor, may still be very blessed;
That trade's proud empire hastes to swift decay,
As ocean sweeps the laboured mole away;
While self-dependent power can time defy,
As rocks resist the billows and the sky.   430

---

l.418. Torno: the Torne River in northern Sweden and Finland.
l.418. Pambamarca: a mountain in Ecuador.
l.427. Boswell records (*Life of J* under year 1766) that in 1783 Johnson marked "the lines which he furnished Goldsmith's 'Deserted Village,' which are only the last four. . . ."

William Cowper

1731: born 26 November at Great Berkhamsted, Hertfordshire; descended on both sides from well-connected families
1737: death of his mother, a profound emotional shock
1741: entered Westminster School, where he remained for eight years
1749: began the study of law in London; called to the bar in 1754
c. 1750: met and later fell in love with his first cousin Theadora Cowper ("Delia"); the engagement broken off in 1756 by her father who feared their degree of consanguinity and their common hereditary tendency toward melancholia
1752: first signs of mental depression
1763: first attack of insanity, probably manic depression, brought on by the strain of an approaching oral examination for a post in the House of Lords; attempted suicide; similar attacks in 1773, 1787, and 1794; never fully recovered from the last
1764: experienced an evangelical "conversion" of the Calvinist stamp
1765: moved to Huntingdon, near Cambridge, where he lived with the Reverend Morley Unwin and his wife
1767: after Unwin's death moved with Mrs. Unwin to Olney, Buckinghamshire, to be near the Reverend John Newton, the evangelical curate there
1773: had a "fatal" traumatic dream in which the voice of God announced his irrevocable damnation

1779: Olney Hymns, written in collaboration with Newton (67 by Cowper, 281 by Newton)
1781: friendship with Lady Austen, who supplied the hints for *John Gilpin* and *The Task*
1782: Poems (included *Table Talk, Progress of Error, Truth, Expostulation, Hope, Charity, Conversation*, and *Retirement*); *John Gilpin* published anonymously in *The Public Advertiser*
1785: Poems (included *The Task*, and *Tirocinium, or a Review of Schools*), which made him famous
1786: moved to nearby Weston with Mrs. Unwin
1791: *The Iliad and the Odyssey* (blank-verse translation), on which he had been working since 1786
1794: granted a pension of £300
1795: with Mrs. Unwin moved to Norfolk
1796: death of Mrs. Unwin
1798: *On the Receipt of My Mother's Picture*
1800: died 25 April
1808: *Translations of Milton's Latin and Italian Poems*

MANY TWENTIETH-CENTURY biographical and critical studies of Cowper have treated the man as a psychological battleground and his poetry as partial psychotherapy; historical studies have viewed him as the poet before Wordsworth who noticed nature and opened his heart. It is perhaps more valuable to view him as the later eighteenth century did, refreshingly new but not disturbingly revolutionary, original but not eccentric. He was didactic, although he taught Evangelical Christianity rather than Christian Stoicism; and he was descriptive, although he saw and felt familiar objects with a new detail and a finer and stronger sensibility. When fame came to him—and he was probably the most popular new poet of the last quarter of the century—it came on the basis of eighteenth, not nineteenth-century standards. Benjamin Franklin found in Cowper's 1782 volume "something so new in the manner, so easy and yet so correct—the language, so clear in the expression, yet concise, and so just in the sentiments, that I have read the whole with great pleasure, and some of the pieces more than once." Thirty-five years later, Hazlitt disparaged Cowper's "air of precaution": "He shakes hands with nature, with a pair of fashionable gloves on."

Although the two realms could never be separated in his mind,

Cowper, beginning his poetic career at the age of fifty-one with *The Olney Hymns*, was a poet of Evangelical religion before he was a poet of nature. Evangelical Christianity is emotional and subjective rather than rational and formalistic. Stressing Christ's Atonement (*There is a fountain filled with blood*), it holds by man's sinful condition and his desperate need of salvation through faith and grace, his personal relationship with his Creator (*Oh! for a closer walk with God*). Spiritual regeneration is achieved through an almost mystic moment of "conversion," a powerful and overwhelming emotional experience. The ever-present God of Cowper's hymn is not the "great Original" of Addison's or the "First Great Cause" of Pope's but a being of wonder and mystery (*God moves in a mysterious way, His wonders to perform*).

In *The Olney Hymns* Cowper sang his religion. In the eight poems of the 1782 volume he expounded it and denounced the time's numerous deviations from it. The structure and style of the pieces were usual: moral satires in the form of verse essays written in heroic couplets; the moral viewpoint, however, was more explicitly and narrowly Christian than readers accustomed to *The Essay on Man* or *The Vanity of Human Wishes* would have expected. *Table Talk* and *Conversation*, indeed, urge religious truth as a fresh subject for exhausted poetry and futile social chatter. *The Progress of Error* is a compendium of sins and sinners. In *Expostulation* Cowper weeps for England just as "The prophet wept for Israel" and for comparable reasons. *Truth* argues for justification by faith as opposed to justification by works and for humility as against pride. The Christian's *Hope* of salvation and heaven discountenances all false moral philosophies and attitudes. *Charity*—and the humanitarian note is strong throughout Cowper's work—attacks the philosophic concept of benevolence: " 'Tis truth divine, exhibited on earth, Gives Charity her being and her birth."

Retirement ("the refuge of some rural shade") brings us close to *The Task:* it provides the theory which *The Task* practices. Love of nature, Cowper says, "Is an ingredient in the compound man, Infused at the creation of the kind." But nature must not be loved and studied for itself but as the wondrous creation of God: its "every line Bears proof of an intelligence divine." "Woe to the man . . . Who studies nature with a wanton eye, Admires the work, but slips the lesson by." Viewed by the converted eye, "Nature, employed in her allotted place, Is handmaid to the purposes of grace." And since God made it all, a detailed study of nature's diversity and its individual forms should be encouraged: "To trace, in nature's most minute design, The signature and stamp of power divine." For the "Evangelical microscope" (as the Methodist devotional writer James Hervey had called it), "an atom is an ample field." The realism which these lines suggest, however, is often subtly idealized, for man longs to find in every garden that he has made "Traces of Eden."

The Task, with its six books and five-thousand lines, is a rich blending of many subjects and various styles. Cowper recognized that it contained "a variety of subjects . . . in which no particular one is predominant," although "the whole has one tendency: to discountenance the modern enthusiasm after a London life, and to recommend rural ease and leisure, as friendly to the cause of piety and virtue." Or, in his most famous aphorism: "God made the country, and man made the town."

To extract only a few themes in more or less typical order, Cowper deals with the historical deduction of seats (from the stool to the sofa), gypsies, peace among nations, Sicilian earthquakes, sacerdotal mismanagement, the want of discipline in the universities, his tame hare, the ruinous effects of gaming, a brown study, public houses, a farmer's daughter, the foddering of cattle, the Empress of Russia's palace of ice, liberty and patriotism, the Creator, the transformation of spring, cruelty to animals, Handel's *Messiah*, and the end of the world. He tells us about himself, his past and his present. And he describes with fond detail virtually every aspect and activity of his circumscribed, paradisiacal world. Of the two kinds of nature, "Wild without art, or artfully subdued," he relishes the latter: "Parks in which art preceptress nature weds."

It is the style rather than the intriguing range of subject matter that makes *The Task* a minor masterpiece. Various terms have been used to describe it, the same terms applied to Cowper's justly famous letters: familiar, confidential, conversational. Tennyson remarked that "few people could put words together with such exquisite flow and evenness." But its apparent naturalness is, of course, careful artistry. "Every man conversant with versewriting knows . . . by painful experience," Cowper wrote to Newton, "that the familiar style is of all styles the most difficult to succeed in. To make verse speak the language of prose, without being prosaic, to marshall the words of it in such an order as they might naturally take in falling from the lips of an extemporary speaker, yet without meanness, harmoniously, elegantly, and without seeming to displace a syllable for the sake of rhyme, is one of the most arduous tasks a poet can undertake."

The Task, however, contains not one style but several, ranging and shifting from "colloquial happiness" (by eighteenth-century standards) through the pathetic to the near sublime and parodies of it. To accommodate this flexibility Cowper rightly employed blank verse, largely Miltonic, but the quiet style of *Paradise Regained* rather than of *Paradise Lost*. Blank verse, admittedly "the most difficult species of poetry," "is susceptible of a much greater diversification of manner than verse in rhyme." With attention to its dramatic qualities, it can be made to catch "the various inflections of the voice."

The "winding" from subject to subject, level to level, mood to mood is co-ordinated by the modulation from answering style to answering style. And it is perfectly logical as well. *The Task* is probably the most discursive poem in the whole tradition of discursive poetry, but its discursiveness is not based on the loose logic of the verse essay but rather on the associative logic—or illogic—of a walk or a conversation with a sympathetic friend, even perhaps a "talking letter" of the "helter-skelter kind" which Cowper loved. There is constant movement of vision and thought. We walk along with the poet, seeing objects and thinking thoughts in the order and the manner in which they occurred to him, conscious always of the personality of the viewer and the thinker as well as of the scene and the thought.

How strong and how pervasive is the lyrical, subjective strain in Cowper's poetry? The Evangelical discipline certainly emphasized individual feeling as an ethical value and as the most important aspect of spiritual experience. Cowper's own psychological life was often disastrously introspective. He maintained critically that the poet's inspiration "Derived from nature's noblest part, the center of a glowing heart" and that "My delineations of the heart are from my own experience," although he never says that a poem is or should be undisciplined experience. A few of his poems, such as *To Mary* and *On the Receipt of My Mother's Picture*, are unquestionably autobiographical and even intimate in origin, although the formality and abstractness of their language act as a check to intimacy of tone and voice. But one can carry the argument too far on the basis of too few poems. *The Task* reveals a personality—that is the greater part of its charm—but a social personality rather than a psyche and one which recognizes its share in the common experience of human suffering. The often-quoted lines, "I was a stricken deer, that left the herd," are usually broken off too soon; Cowper adds, "I see that all are wanderers, gone astray Each in his own delusions. . . ." And it is worth noting that the *Lines Written during a Period of Insanity* and *The Castaway*, written out of the depths, largely make their effect not by means of intimate confession but by means of comparison and analogy: "misery still delights to trace Its semblance in another's case."

from OLNEY HYMNS

WALKING WITH GOD
(Gen. v. 24)

Oh! for a closer walk with God,
    A calm and heavenly frame;
A light to shine upon the road
    That leads me to the Lamb!

Where is the blessedness I knew
    When first I saw the Lord?
Where is the soul-refreshing view
    Of Jesus, and his word?

What peaceful hours I once enjoyed!
    How sweet their memory still!
But they have left an aching void,
    The world can never fill.

Return, O holy Dove, return,
    Sweet messenger of rest;
I hate the sins that made thee mourn,
    And drove thee from my breast.

The dearest idol I have known,
    Whate'er that idol be;
Help me to tear it from thy throne,
    And worship only thee.

So shall my walk be close with God,
    Calm and serene my frame;

So purer light shall mark the road
  That leads me to the Lamb.

LIGHT SHINING OUT OF DARKNESS

God moves in a mysterious way,
  His wonders to perform;
He plants his footsteps in the sea,
  And rides upon the storm.

Deep in unfathomable mines
  Of never-failing skill;
He treasures up his bright designs,
  And works his sovereign will.

Ye fearful saints, fresh courage take,
  The clouds ye so much dread
Are big with mercy, and shall break
  In blessings on your head.

Judge not the Lord by feeble sense,
  But trust him for his grace;
Behind a frowning providence,
  He hides a smiling face.

His purposes will ripen fast,
  Unfolding every hour;
The bud may have a bitter taste,
  But sweet will be the flower.

Blind unbelief is sure to err,
  And scan his work in vain;
God is his own interpreter,
  And he will make it plain.

from THE TASK

NOTE: The books of *The Task* are: *The Sofa, The Time-Piece, The Garden, The Winter Evening, The Winter Morning Walk,* and *The Winter Walk at Noon.* The whole of *The Task* but especially Book III is in the eighteenth-century tradition of imitation of Virgil's *Georgics:* "The loose discursiveness which was Cowper's native vein was prepared for, at least in part, by the didactic descriptive tradition which sanctioned, by ancient and modern example, a type of poem admitting moral, descriptive, narrative, scientific, preceptive, and other matter, grouped around a central theme" (D. L. Durling, *Georgic Tradition in English Poetry* [1935], p. 84). The "realistic" georgic tradition is opposed to the Arcadian pastoral eclogue. Cowper's predecessors in this vein were John Philips (*Cyder*), Thomson, Young, and Goldsmith. The most ambitious modern reading of *The Task* is Morris Golden's in *In Search of Stability* (1960): "the poem is, on the whole, an exploration of the elements of, and the possibility of, the stable balance that Cowper always despairingly sought" (p. 120); "Most conspicuously, it presents a central theme to which everything is connected and upon which everything reflects—the theme of seeking the ideal of stability, harmony, order" (p. 151); "*The Task* fulfills the final test for unity—break it where we will, its contents are discoverably arranged in their characteristic triple form: brutalism-balance-decadence (which, in view of Cowper's mental preoccupations, could also be written: God's power-harmonious and static balance-man's intolerable chaos") (p. 154).

from THE TASK

BOOK III: THE GARDEN

As one who, long in thickets and in brakes
Entangled, winds now this way and now that
His devious course uncertain, seeking home;
Or having long in miry ways been foiled
And sore discomfited, from slough to slough
Plunging, and half-despairing of escape;
If chance at length he finds a greensward smooth
And faithful to the foot, his spirits rise,
He chirrups brisk his ear-erecting steed,
And winds his way with pleasure and with ease;   10
So I, designing other themes, and called
To adorn the Sofa with eulogium due,
To tell its slumbers and to paint its dreams,
Have rambled wide. In country, city, seat
Of academic fame (howe'er deserved),
Long held, and scarcely disengaged at last.
But now, with pleasant pace, a cleanlier road
I mean to tread. I feel myself at large,
Courageous, and refreshed for future toil,
If toil await me, or if dangers new.   20
   Since pulpits fail, and sounding boards reflect
Most part an empty ineffectual sound,
What chance that I, to fame so little known,
Nor conversant with men or manners much,

---

l.12. eulogium due: A reference to the opening passage of *The Task:* "I sing the sofa." Cowper said of the genesis of the poem: "A lady [Lady Austen], fond of blank verse, demanded a poem of that kind from the author, and gave him the Sofa for a subject. He obeyed; and, having much leisure, connected another subject with it; and, pursuing the train of thought to which his situation and turn of mind led him, brought forth at length, instead of the trifle which he at first intended, a serious affair—a Volume!"

Should speak to purpose, or with better hope
Crack the satiric thong? 'Twere wiser far
For me, enamoured of sequestered scenes,
And charmed with rural beauty, to repose
Where chance may throw me, beneath elm or vine,
My languid limbs, when summer sears the plains;   30
Or when rough winter rages, on the soft
And sheltered Sofa, while the nitrous air
Feeds a blue flame, and makes a cheerful hearth;
There, undisturbed by Folly, and apprised
How great the danger of disturbing her,
To muse in silence, or at least confine
Remarks that gall so many to the few
My partners in retreat. Disgust concealed
Is ofttimes proof of wisdom, when the fault
Is obstinate, and cure beyond our reach.   40
    Domestic happiness, thou only bliss
Of Paradise that has survived the Fall!
Though few now taste thee unimpaired and pure,
Or tasting, long enjoy thee, too infirm
Or too incautious to preserve thy sweets
Unmixed with drops of bitter, which neglect
Or temper sheds into thy crystal cup.
Thou art the nurse of virtue—in thine arms
She smiles, appearing, as in truth she is,
Heaven-born, and destined to the skies again.   50
Thou art not known where pleasure is adored,
That reeling goddess with the zoneless waist
And wandering eyes, still leaning on the arm
Of novelty, her fickle frail support;
For thou art meek and constant, hating change,
And finding in the calm of truth-tried love
Joys that her stormy raptures never yield.
Forsaking thee, what shipwreck have we made
Of honour, dignity, and fair renown!
Till prostitution elbows us aside   60
In all our crowded streets, and senates seem
Convened for purposes of empire less
Than to release the adultress from her bond.
The adultress! what a theme for angry verse!
What provocation to the indignant heart

That feels for injured love! but I disdain
The nauseous task to paint her as she is,
Cruel, abandoned, glorying in her shame!
No:—let her pass, and charioted along
In guilty splendour, shake the public ways;
The frequency of crimes has washed them white!
And verse of mine shall never brand the wretch,
Whom matrons now, of character unsmirched,
And chaste themselves, are not ashamed to own.
Virtue and vice had boundaries in old time,
Not to be passed; and she, that had renounced
Her sex's honour, was renounced herself
By all that prized it; not for prudery's sake,
But dignity's, resentful of the wrong.
'Twas hard, perhaps, on here and there a waif,
Desirous to return, and not received;
But was a wholesome rigour in the main,
And taught the unblemished to preserve with care
That purity, whose loss was loss of all.
Men, too, were nice in honour in those days,
And judged offenders well. Then he that sharped,
And pocketed a prize by fraud obtained,
Was marked and shunned as odious. He that sold
His country, or was slack when she required
His every nerve in action and at stretch,
Paid with the blood that he had basely spared
The price of his default. But now, yes, now,
We are become so candid and so fair,
So liberal in construction, and so rich
In Christian charity (good-natured age!),
That they are safe, sinners of either sex,
Transgress what laws they may. Well dressed, well bred,
Well equipaged, is ticket good enough
To pass us readily through every door.
Hypocrisy, detest her as we may
(And no man's hatred ever wronged her yet),
May claim this merit still—that she admits
The worth of what she mimics with such care,
And thus gives virtue indirect applause;
But she had burned her mask, not needed here,
Where vice has such allowance, that her shifts

And specious semblances have lost their use.
  I was a stricken deer, that left the herd
Long since; with many an arrow deep infixed
My panting side was charged, when I withdrew
To seek a tranquil death in distant shades.
There was I found by one who had himself
Been hurt by the archers. In his side he bore,
And in his hands and feet, the cruel scars.
With gentle force soliciting the darts,
He drew them forth, and healed and bade me live.
Since then, with few associates, in remote
And silent woods I wander, far from those
My former partners of the peopled scene;
With few associates, and not wishing more.
Here much I ruminate, as much I may,
With other views of men and manners now
Than once, and others of a life to come.
I see that all are wanderers, gone astray
Each in his own delusions; they are lost
In chase of fancied happiness, still wooed
And never won. Dream after dream ensues,
And still they dream that they shall still succeed,
And still are disappointed. Rings the world
With the vain stir. I sum up half mankind,
And add two thirds of the remaining half,
And find the total of their hopes and fears
Dreams, empty dreams. The million flit as gay
As if created only like the fly,
That spreads his motley wings in the eye of noon,
To sport their season, and be seen no more.
The rest are sober dreamers, grave and wise,
And pregnant with discoveries new and rare.
Some write a narrative of wars, and feats
Of heroes little known, and call the rant
An history: describe the man, of whom
His own coevals took but little note;
And paint his person, character, and views,
As they had known him from his mother's womb.
They disentangle from the puzzled skein,
In which obscurity has wrapped them up,
The threads of politic and shrewd design,

That ran through all his purposes, and charge
His mind with meanings that he never had,
Or having, kept concealed. Some drill and bore   150
The solid earth, and from the strata there
Extract a register, by which we learn
That he who made it, and revealed its date
To Moses, was mistaken in its age.
Some, more acute, and more industrious still,
Contrive creation; travel nature up
To the sharp peak of her sublimest height,
And tell us whence the stars; why some are fixed,
And planetary some; what gave them first
Rotation, from what fountain flowed their light.   160
Great contest follows, and much learned dust
Involves the combatants; each claiming truth,
And truth disclaiming both. And thus they spend
The little wick of life's poor shallow lamp,
In playing tricks with nature, giving laws
To distant worlds, and trifling in their own.
Is it not a pity now, that tickling rheums
Should ever tease the lungs and blear the sight
Of oracles like these? Great pity too,
That, having wielded the elements, and built   170
A thousand systems, each in his own way,
They should go out in fume, and be forgot?
Ah! what is life thus spent? and what are they
But frantic who thus spend it? all for smoke—
Eternity for bubbles, proves at last
A senseless bargain. When I see such games
Played by the creatures of a power who swears
That he will judge the earth, and call the fool
To a sharp reckoning that has lived in vain;
And when I weigh this seeming wisdom well,   180
And prove it in the infallible result
So hollow and so false—I feel my heart

---

ll.150-51. Some . . . earth: In ll. 150-260, Cowper is attacking "unbaptized" scientists who lack the pious motive and who work in a completely mechanistic context. Newton (l. 252) and Sir Mathew Hale (l. 258) are the exemplary exceptions. Hale (1609-76), Lord Chief Justice (1671-75), author of *The Primitive Origination of Mankind* (1677), upheld the Mosaic cosmology. Compare this passage with *An Essay on Man*, ii, 1-52, and *Paradise Lost*, viii, 66ff.

Dissolve in pity, and account the learned,
If this be learning, most of all deceived.
Great crimes alarm the conscience, but it sleeps
While thoughtful man is plausibly amused.
Defend me, therefore, common sense, say I,
From reveries so airy, from the toil
Of dropping buckets into empty wells,
And growing old in drawing nothing up! 190
 " 'Twere well," says one sage erudite, profound,
Terribly arched and aquiline his nose,
And overbuilt with most impending brows,
" 'Twere well, could you permit the world to live
As the world pleases. What's the world to you?"
Much. I was born of woman, and drew milk,
As sweet as charity, from human breasts.
I think, articulate, I laugh and weep,
And exercise all functions of a man.
How then should I and any man that lives 200
Be strangers to each other? Pierce my vein,
Take of the crimson stream meandering there,
And catechise it well; apply thy glass,
Search it, and prove now if it be not blood
Congenial with thine own: and if it be,
What edge of subtlety canst thou suppose
Keen enough, wise and skilful as thou art,
To cut the link of brotherhood, by which
One common Maker bound me to the kind?
True; I am no proficient, I confess, 210
In arts like yours. I cannot call the swift
And perilous lightnings from the angry clouds,
And bid them hide themselves in earth beneath;
I cannot analyse the air, nor catch
The parallax of yonder luminous point,
That seems half quenched in the immense abyss;
Such powers I boast not—neither can I rest
A silent witness of the headlong rage
Or heedless folly by which thousands die,
Bone of my bone, and kindred souls to mine. 220
    God never meant that man should scale the heavens
By strides of human wisdom. In his works,
Though wondrous, he commands us in his word

To seek *him* rather, where his mercy shines.
The mind indeed, enlightened from above,
Views him in all; ascribes to the grand cause
The grand effect; acknowledges with joy
His manner, and with rapture tastes his style.
But never yet did philosophic tube,
That brings the planets home into the eye 230
Of observation, and discovers, else
Not visible, his family of worlds,
Discover him that rules them; such a veil
Hangs over mortal eyes, blind from the birth,
And dark in things divine. Full often, too,
Our wayward intellect, the more we learn
Of nature, overlooks her author more;
From instrumental causes proud to draw
Conclusions retrograde, and mad mistake.
But if his word once teach us, shoot a ray 240
Through all the heart's dark chambers, and reveal
Truths undiscerned but by that holy light,
Then all is plain. Philosophy, baptized
In the pure fountain of eternal love,
Has eyes indeed; and viewing all she sees
As meant to indicate a God to man,
Gives *him* his praise, and forfeits not her own.
Learning has borne such fruit in other days
On all her branches; piety has found
Friends in the friends of science, and true prayer 250
Has flowed from his lips wet with Castalian dews.
Such was thy wisdom, Newton, childlike sage!
Sagacious reader of the works of God,
And in his word sagacious. Such too thine,
Milton, whose genius had angelic wings,
And fed on manna! And such thine, in whom
Our British Themis gloried with just cause,
Immortal Hale! for deep discernment praised
And sound integrity, not more than famed
For sanctity of manners undefiled. 260
　All flesh is grass, and all its glory fades
Like the fair flower dishevelled in the wind;

---

l.251. Castalian: a spring on Mt. Parnassus, sacred to the Muses.

Riches have wings, and grandeur is a dream;
The man we celebrate must find a tomb,
And we that worship him, ignoble graves.
Nothing is proof against the general curse
Of vanity, that seizes all below.
The only amaranthine flower on earth
Is virtue; the only lasting treasure, truth.
But what is truth? 'twas Pilate's question, put
To Truth itself, that deigned him no reply.
And wherefore? will not God impart his light
To them that ask it?—Freely—'tis his joy,
His glory, and his nature, to impart.
But to the proud, uncandid, insincere,
Or negligent inquirer, not a spark.
What's that which brings contempt upon a book,
And him who writes it, though the style be neat,
The method clear, and argument exact?
That makes a minister in holy things
The joy of many, and the dread of more,
His name a theme for praise and for reproach?—
That, while it gives us worth in God's account,
Depreciates and undoes us in our own?
What pearl is it that rich men cannot buy,
That learning is too proud to gather up;
But which the poor, and the despised of all,
Seek and obtain, and often find unsought?
Tell me—and I will tell thee what is truth.

 O friendly to the best pursuits of man,
Friendly to thought, to virtue, and to peace,
Domestic life in rural leisure passed!
Few know thy value, and few taste thy sweets;
Though many boast thy favours, and affect
To understand and choose thee for their own.
But foolish man foregoes his proper bliss,
Even as his first progenitor, and quits,
Though placed in paradise (for earth has still
Some traces of her youthful beauty left),
Substantial happiness for transient joy.
Scenes formed for contemplation, and to nurse
The growing seeds of wisdom; that suggest,
By every pleasing image they present,

Reflections such as meliorate the heart,
Compose the passions, and exalt the mind;
Scenes such as these, 'tis his supreme delight
To fill with riot, and defile with blood.
Should some contagion, kind to the poor brutes
We persecute, annihilate the tribes
That draw the sportsman over hill and dale,　　　310
Fearless, and rapt away from all his cares;
Should never game-fowl hatch her eggs again,
Nor baited hook deceive the fish's eye;
Could pageantry and dance, and feast and song,
Be quelled in all our summer-months' retreat;
How many self-deluded nymphs and swains,
Who dream they have a taste for fields and groves,
Would find them hideous nurseries of the spleen,
And crowd the roads, impatient for the town!
They love the country, and none else, who seek　　　320
For their own sake, its silence and its shade.
Delights which who would leave, that has a heart
Susceptible of pity, or a mind
Cultured and capable of sober thought,
For all the savage din of the swift pack,
And clamours of the field?—Detested sport,
That owes its pleasures to another's pain;
That feeds upon the sobs and dying shrieks
Of harmless nature, dumb, but yet endued
With eloquence, that agonies inspire,　　　330
Of silent tears and heart-distending sighs!
Vain tears, alas, and sighs, that never find
A corresponding tone in jovial souls!
Well—one at least is safe. One sheltered hare
Has never heard the sanguinary yell
Of cruel man, exulting in her woes.
Innocent partner of my peaceful home,
Whom ten long years' experience of my care
Has made at last familiar; she has lost
Much of her vigilant instinctive dread,　　　340
Not needful here, beneath a roof like mine.
Yes—thou mayst eat thy bread, and lick the hand

---

l.334. hare: Cowper's pet hare, "Puss."

That feeds thee; thou mayst frolic on the floor
At evening, and at night retire secure
To thy straw couch, and slumber unalarmed;
For I have gained thy confidence, have pledged
All that is human in me to protect
Thine unsuspecting gratitude and love.
If I survive thee, I will dig thy grave;
And, when I place thee in it, sighing, say, 350
I knew at least one hare that had a friend.
    How various his employments, whom the world
Calls idle; and who justly, in return,
Esteems that busy world an idler too!
Friends, books, a garden, and perhaps his pen,
Delightful industry enjoyed at home,
And Nature in her cultivated trim
Dressed to his taste, inviting him abroad—
Can he want occupation who has these?
Will he be idle who has much to enjoy? 360
Me, therefore, studious of laborious ease,
Not slothful; happy to deceive the time,
Not waste it; and aware that human life
Is but a loan to be repaid with use,
When he shall call his debtors to account
From whom are all our blessings; business finds
Even here: while sedulous I seek to improve,
At least neglect not, or leave unemployed,
The mind he gave me; driving it, though slack
Too oft, and much impeded in its work 370
By causes not to be divulged in vain,
To its just point—the service of mankind.
He that attends to his interior self,
That has a heart, and keeps it; has a mind
That hungers, and supplies it; and who seeks
A social, not a dissipated life;
Has business; feels himself engaged to achieve
No unimportant, though a silent, task.
A life all turbulence and noise may seem,
To him that leads it, wise, and to be praised; 380
But wisdom is a pearl with most success
Sought in still water, and beneath clear skies.
He that is ever occupied in storms,

Or dives not for it, or brings up instead,
Vainly industrious, a disgraceful prize.
   The morning finds the self-sequestered man
Fresh for his task, intend what task he may.
Whether inclement seasons recommend
His warm but simple home, where he enjoys,
With her who shares his pleasures and his heart,   390
Sweet converse, sipping calm the fragrant lymph
Which neatly she prepares; then to his book,
Well chosen, and not sullenly perused
In selfish silence, but imparted oft
As ought occurs that she may smile to hear,
Or turn to nourishment, digested well.
Or, if the garden with its many cares,
All well repaid, demand him, he attends
The welcome call, conscious how much the hand
Of lubbard labour needs his watchful eye,   400
Oft loitering lazily, if not o'erseen,
Or misapplying his unskilful strength.
Nor does he govern only or direct,
But much performs himself. No works indeed
That ask robust tough sinews, bred to toil,
Servile employ; but such as may amuse,
Not tire, demanding rather skill than force.
Proud of his well-spread walls, he views his trees
That meet (no barren interval between)
With pleasure more than even their fruits afford,   410
Which, save himself who trains them, none can feel;
These, therefore, are his own peculiar charge;
No meaner hand may discipline the shoots,
None but his steel approach them. What is weak,
Distempered, or has lost prolific powers,
Impaired by age, his unrelenting hand
Dooms to the knife; nor does he spare the soft
And succulent, that feeds its giant growth,
But barren, at the expense of neighbouring twigs
Less ostentatious, and yet studded thick   420
With hopeful gems. The rest, no portion left
That may disgrace his art, or disappoint
Large expectation, he disposes neat
At measured distances, that air and sun,

Admitted freely, may afford their aid,
And ventilate and warm the swelling buds.
Hence summer has her riches, autumn hence,
And hence even winter fills his withered hand
With blushing fruits, and plenty not his own.
Fair recompense of labour well bestowed,   430
And wise precaution; which a clime so rude
Makes needful still, whose spring is but the child
Of churlish winter, in her forward moods
Discovering much the temper of her sire.
For oft, as if in her the stream of mild
Maternal nature had reversed its course,
She brings her infants forth with many smiles;
But once delivered, kills them with a frown.
He, therefore, timely warned, himself supplies
Her want of care, screening and keeping warm   440
The plenteous bloom, that no rough blast may sweep
His garlands from the boughs. Again, as oft
As the sun peeps and vernal airs breathe mild,
The fence withdrawn, he gives them every beam,
And spreads his hopes before the blaze of day.
 To raise the prickly and green-coated gourd,
So grateful to the palate, and when rare
So coveted, else base and disesteemed—
Food for the vulgar merely—is an art
That toiling ages have but just matured,   450
And at this moment unassayed in song.
Yet gnats have had, and frogs and mice, long since,
Their eulogy; those sang the Mantuan bard,
And these the Grecian, in ennobling strains;
And in thy numbers, Philips, shines for aye
The solitary shilling. Pardon then,
Ye sage dispensers of poetic fame,
The ambition of one, meaner far, whose powers,
Presuming an attempt not less sublime,
Pant for the praise of dressing to the taste   460
Of critic appetite, no sordid fare,

---

ll.452-54. strains: *Batrachomyomachia* (*The Battle of the Frogs and Mice*), a parody of an epic poem, formerly attributed to Homer; *Culex* (*The Gnat*), formerly attributed to Virgil. l.456. shilling: John Philips, *The Splendid Shilling* (1701), a burlesque of Milton.

A cucumber, while costly yet and scarce.
The stable yields a stercoraceous heap,
Impregnated with quick fermenting salts,
And potent to resist the freezing blast;
For, ere the beech and elm have cast their leaf
Deciduous, when now November dark
Checks vegetation in the torpid plant
Exposed to his cold breath, the task begins.
Warily, therefore, and with prudent heed, 470
He seeks a favoured spot; that where he builds
The agglomerated pile his frame may front
The sun's meridian disk, and at the back
Enjoy close shelter, wall, or reeds, or hedge
Impervious to the wind. First he bids spread
Dry fern or littered hay, that may imbibe
The ascending damps; then leisurely impose,
And lightly, shaking it with agile hand
From the full fork, the saturated straw.
What longest binds the closest forms secure 480
The shapely side, that as it rises takes,
By just degrees, an overhanging breadth,
Sheltering the base with its projected eaves;
The uplifted frame, compact at every joint,
And overlaid with clear translucent glass,
He settles next upon the sloping mount,
Whose sharp declivity shoots off secure
From the dashed pane the deluge as it falls.
He shuts it close, and the first labour ends.
Thrice must the voluble and restless earth 490
Spin round upon her axle, ere the warmth,
Slow gathering in the midst, through the square mass
Diffused, attain the surface; when, behold!
A pestilent and most corrosive steam,
Like a gross fog Bœotian, rising fast,
And fast condensed upon the dewy sash,
Asks egress; which obtained, the overcharged
And drenched conservatory breathes abroad,
In volumes wheeling slow, the vapour dank;
And, purified, rejoices to have lost 500
Its foul inhabitant. But to assuage
The impatient fervour which it first conceives

Within its reeking bosom, threatening death
To his young hopes, requires discreet delay.
Experience, slow preceptress, teaching oft
The way to glory by miscarriage foul,
Must prompt him, and admonish how to catch
The auspicious moment, when the tempered heat,
Friendly to vital motion, may afford
Soft fomentation, and invite the seed. 510
The seed, selected wisely, plump, and smooth,
And glossy, he commits to pots of size
Diminutive, well filled with well-prepared
And fruitful soil, that has been treasured long,
And drank no moisture from the dripping clouds;
These on the warm and genial earth, that hides
The smoking manure and o'erspreads it all,
He places lightly, and, as time subdues
The rage of fermentation, plunges deep
In the soft medium, till they stand immersed. 520
Then rise the tender germs, upstarting quick,
And spreading wide their spongy lobes; at first
Pale, wan, and livid; but assuming soon,
If fanned by balmy and nutritious air,
Strained through the friendly mats, a vivid green.
Two leaves produced, two rough indented leaves,
Cautious he pinches from the second stalk
A pimple, that portends a future sprout,
And interdicts its growth. Thence straight succeed
The branches, sturdy to his utmost wish; 530
Prolific all, and harbingers of more.
The crowded roots demand enlargement now,
And transplantation in an ampler space.
Indulged in what they wish, they soon supply
Large foliage, overshadowing golden flowers,
Blown on the summit of the apparent fruit.
These have their sexes; and when summer shines,
The bee transports the fertilizing meal
From flower to flower, and even the breathing air
Wafts the rich prize to its appointed use. 540
Not so when winter scowls. Assistant art
Then acts in nature's office, brings to pass
The glad espousals, and ensures the crop.

  Grudge not, ye rich (since luxury must have
His dainties, and the world's more numerous half
Lives by contriving delicates for you),
Grudge not the cost. Ye little know the cares,
The vigilance, the labour, and the skill,
That day and night are exercised, and hang
Upon the ticklish balance of suspense,   550
That ye may garnish your profuse regales
With summer fruits brought forth by wintry suns.
Ten thousand dangers lie in wait to thwart
The process. Heat and cold, and wind, and steam,
Moisture and drought, mice, worms, and swarming flies,
Minute as dust, and numberless, oft work
Dire disappointment that admits no cure,
And which no care can obviate. It were long,
Too long, to tell the expedients and the shifts
Which he that fights a season so severe   560
Devises, while he guards his tender trust;
And oft, at last, in vain. The learned and wise
Sarcastic would exclaim, and judge the song
Cold as its theme, and, like its theme, the fruit
Of too much labour, worthless when produced.
  Who loves a garden, loves a greenhouse too.
Unconscious of a less propitious clime,
There blooms exotic beauty, warm and snug,
While the winds whistle and the snows descend.
The spiry myrtle with unwithering leaf   570
Shines there, and flourishes. The golden boast
Of Portugal and western India there,
The ruddier orange, and the paler lime,
Peep through their polished foliage at the storm,
And seem to smile at what they need not fear.
The amomum there with intermingling flowers
And cherries hangs her twigs. Geranium boasts
Her crimson honours, and the spangled beau,
Ficoides, glitters bright the winter long.
All plants, of every leaf, that can endure   580
The winter's frown, if screened from his shrewd bite,
Live there, and prosper. Those Ausonia claims,

---

l.582. Ausonia: Italy.

Levantine regions these; the Azores send
Their jessamine, her jessamine remote
Caffraia: foreigners from many lands,
They form one social shade, as if convened
By magic summons of the Orphean lyre.
Yet just arrangement, rarely brought to pass
But by a master's hand, disposing well
The gay diversities of leaf and flower,   590
Must lend its aid to illustrate all their charms,
And dress the regular yet various scene.
Plant behind plant aspiring, in the van
The dwarfish, in the rear retired, but still
Sublime above the rest, the statelier stand.
So once were ranged the sons of ancient Rome,
A noble show! while Roscius trod the stage;
And so, while Garrick, as renowned as he,
The sons of Albion; fearing each to lose
Some note of Nature's music from his lips,   600
And covetous of Shakespeare's beauty, seen
In every flash of his far-beaming eye.
Nor taste alone and well-contrived display
Suffice to give the marshalled ranks the grace
Of their complete effect. Much yet remains
Unsung, and many cares are yet behind,
And more laborious; cares on which depends
Their vigour, injured soon, not soon restored.
The soil must be renewed, which, often washed,
Loses its treasure of salubrious salts,   610
And disappoints the roots; the slender roots
Close interwoven, where they meet the vase,
Must smooth be shorn away; the sapless branch
Must fly before the knife; the withered leaf
Must be detached, and where it strews the floor
Swept with a woman's neatness, breeding else
Contagion, and disseminating death.
Discharge but these kind offices (and who
Would spare, that loves them, offices like these?).
Well they reward the toil. The sight is pleased,   620
The scent regaled, each odoriferous leaf,

---

l.585. Caffraia: Kaffraria, in southern Africa.   l.597. Roscius: famed actor of ancient Rome.

Each opening blossom, freely breathes abroad
Its gratitude, and thanks him with its sweets.
So manifold, all pleasing in their kind,
All healthful, are the employs of rural life,
Reiterated as the wheel of time
Runs round; still ending, and beginning still.
Nor are these all. To deck the shapely knoll
That, softly swelled and gaily dressed, appears
A flowery island, from the dark green lawn   630
Emerging, must be deemed a labour due
To no mean hand, and asks the touch of taste.
Here also grateful mixture of well-matched
And sorted hues (each giving each relief,
And by contrasted beauty shining more)
Is needful. Strength may wield the ponderous spade,
May turn the clod, and wheel the compost home;
But elegance, chief grace the garden shows,
And most attractive, is the fair result
Of thought, the creature of a polished mind.   640
Without it, all is gothic as the scene
To which the insipid citizen resorts
Near yonder heath; where industry misspent,
But proud of his uncouth ill-chosen task,
Has made a heaven on earth; with suns and moons
Of close rammed stones has charged the encumbered soil,
And fairly laid the zodiac in the dust.
He, therefore, who would see his flowers disposed
Sightly and in just order, ere he gives
The beds the trusted treasure of their seeds,   650
Forecasts the future whole; that, when the scene
Shall break into its preconceived display,
Each for itself, and all as with one voice
Conspiring, may attest his bright design.
Nor even then, dismissing as performed
His pleasant work, may he suppose it done.
Few self-supported flowers endure the wind
Uninjured, but expect the upholding aid
Of the smooth-shaven prop, and, neatly tied,

---

l.641. gothic: Cowper disliked the growing fashion of the Gothic in architecture and landscape, especially the building of sham ruins to enhance the picturesque effects of a scene.

The Task

  Are wedded thus, like beauty to old age,   660
For interest sake, the living to the dead.
Some clothe the soil that feeds them, far diffused
And lowly creeping, modest and yet fair,
Like virtue, thriving most where little seen;
Some, more aspiring, catch the neighbour shrub
With clasping tendrils, and invest his branch,
Else unadorned, with many a gay festoon
And fragrant chaplet, recompensing well
The strength they borrow with the grace they lend.
All hate the rank society of weeds,   670
Noisome, and ever greedy to exhaust
The impoverished earth; an overbearing race,
That, like the multitude made faction-mad,
Disturb good order, and degrade true worth.
  Oh, blest seclusion from a jarring world,
Which he, thus occupied, enjoys! Retreat
Cannot indeed to guilty man restore
Lost innocence, or cancel follies past;
But it has peace, and much secures the mind
From all assaults of evil; proving still   680
A faithful barrier, not o'erleaped with ease
By vicious custom, raging uncontrolled
Abroad, and desolating public life.
When fierce temptation, seconded within
By traitor appetite, and armed with darts
Tempered in hell, invades the throbbing breast,
To combat may be glorious, and success
Perhaps may crown us; but to fly is safe.
Had I the choice of sublunary good,
What could I wish that I possess not here?   690
Health, leisure, means to improve it, friendship, peace,
No loose or wanton, though a wandering, muse,
And constant occupation without care.
Thus blest, I draw a picture of that bliss;
Hopeless, indeed, that dissipated minds,
And profligate abusers of a world
Created fair so much in vain for them,
Should seek the guiltless joys that I describe,

---

l.675. Compare ll. 675-88 with *The Deserted Village*, ll. 97-112.

Allured by my report; but sure no less,
That, self-condemned, they must neglect the prize, 700
And what they will not taste must yet approve.
What we admire, we praise; and, when we praise,
Advance it into notice, that, its worth
Acknowledged, others may admire it too.
I therefore recommend, though at the risk
Of popular disgust, yet boldly still,
The cause of piety and sacred truth,
And virtue, and those scenes which God ordained
Should best secure them and promote them most;
Scenes that I love, and with regret perceive 710
Forsaken, or through folly not enjoyed.
Pure is the nymph, though liberal of her smiles,
And chaste, though unconfined, whom I extol.
Not as the prince in Shushan, when he called,
Vainglorious of her charms, his Vashti forth
To grace the full pavilion. His design
Was but to boast his own peculiar good,
Which all might view with envy, none partake.
My charmer is not mine alone; my sweets,
And she that sweetens all my bitters too, 720
Nature, enchanting Nature, in whose form
And lineaments divine I trace a hand
That errs not, and find raptures still renewed,
Is free to all men—universal prize.
Strange that so fair a creature should yet want
Admirers, and be destined to divide
With meaner objects even the few she finds!
Stripped of her ornaments, her leaves and flowers,
She loses all her influence. Cities then
Attract us, and neglected Nature pines, 730
Abandoned, as unworthy of our love.
But are not wholesome airs, though unperfumed
By roses; and clear suns, though scarcely felt;
And groves, if unharmonious, yet secure
From clamour, and whose very silence charms;
To be preferred to smoke, to the eclipse

---

l.714. Shushan: the capital city of King Ahasuerus of Persia. He summoned Vashti, his queen, to present herself to his guests. When she refused, he repudiated her. See Esther: I.

That metropolitan volcanos make,
Whose Stygian throats breathe darkness all day long;
And to the stir of commerce, driving slow,
And thundering loud, with his ten thousand wheels? 740
They would be, were not madness in the head,
And folly in the heart; were England now
What England was: plain, hospitable, kind,
And undebauched. But we have bid farewell
To all the virtues of those better days,
And all their honest pleasures. Mansions once
Knew their own masters; and laborious hinds
That had survived the father, served the son.
Now the legitimate and rightful lord
Is but a transient guest, newly arrived, 750
And soon to be supplanted. He that saw
His patrimonial timber cast its leaf,
Sells the last scantling, and transfers the price
To some shrewd sharper, ere it buds again.
Estates are landscapes, gazed upon awhile,
Then advertised, and auctioneered away.
The country starves, and they that feed the o'ercharged
And surfeited lewd town with her fair dues,
By a just judgment strip and starve themselves.
The wings that waft our riches out of sight 760
Grow on the gamester's elbows; and the alert
And nimble motion of those restless joints,
That never tire, soon fans them all away.
Improvement too, the idol of the age,
Is fed with many a victim. Lo, he comes!
The omnipotent magician, Brown, appears!
Down falls the venerable pile, the abode
Of our forefathers—a grave whiskered race,
But tasteless. Springs a palace in its stead,
But in a distant spot; where, more exposed, 770
It may enjoy the advantage of the north,
And aguish east, till time shall have transformed
Those naked acres to a sheltering grove.
He speaks. The lake in front becomes a lawn;

---

l.766. Brown: Lancelot Brown, known as "Capability" Brown, the most fashionable and (Cowper thought) elaborate of contemporary landscape gardeners.

Woods vanish, hills subside, and valleys rise;
And streams, as if created for his use,
Pursue the track of his directing wand,
Sinuous or straight, now rapid and now slow,
Now murmuring soft, now roaring in cascades—
Even as he bids! The enraptured owner smiles. 780
'Tis finished, and yet, finished as it seems,
Still wants a grace, the loveliest it could show,
A mine to satisfy the enormous cost.
Drained to the last poor item of his wealth,
He sighs, departs, and leaves the accomplished plan
That he has touched, retouched, many a long day
Laboured, and many a night pursued in dreams,
Just when it meets his hopes, and proves the heaven
He wanted, for a wealthier to enjoy!
And now perhaps the glorious hour is come, 790
When, having no stake left, no pledge to endear
Her interests, or that gives her sacred cause
A moment's operation on his love,
He burns with most intense and flagrant zeal
To serve his country. Ministerial grace
Deals him out money from the public chest;
Or if that mine be shut, some private purse
Supplies his need with an usurious loan,
To be refunded duly when his vote,
Well managed, shall have earned its worthy price. 800
Oh innocent, compared with arts like these,
Crape, and cocked pistol, and the whistling ball
Sent through the traveller's temples! He that finds
One drop of heaven's sweet mercy in his cup,
Can dig, beg, rot, and perish, well content,
So he may wrap himself in honest rags
At his last gasp; but could not for a world
Fish up his dirty and dependent bread
From pools and ditches of the commonwealth,
Sordid and sickening at his own success. 810
 Ambition, avarice, penury incurred
By endless riot, vanity, the lust
Of pleasure and variety, dispatch,
As duly as the swallows disappear,
The world of wandering knights and squires to town.

London ingulfs them all! The shark is there,
And the shark's prey; the spendthrift, and the leech
That sucks him. There the sycophant, and he
Who, with bareheaded and obsequious bows,
Begs a warm office, doomed to a cold jail   820
And groat per diem, if his patron frown.
The levee swarms, as if, in golden pomp,
Were charactered on every statesman's door:
BATTERED AND BANKRUPT FORTUNES MENDED HERE.
These are the charms that sully and eclipse
The charms of nature. 'Tis the cruel gripe
That lean hard-handed poverty inflicts,
The hope of better things, the chance to win,
The wish to shine, the thirst to be amused,
That at the sound of winter's hoary wing   830
Unpeople all our counties of such herds
Of fluttering, loitering, cringing, begging, loose
And wanton vagrants, as make London, vast
And boundless as it is, a crowded coop.
  Oh thou, resort and mart of all the earth,
Checkered with all complexions of mankind,
And spotted with all crimes; in whom I see
Much that I love, and more that I admire,
And all that I abhor; thou freckled fair,
That pleasest and yet shock'st me, I can laugh   840
And I can weep, can hope, and can despond,
Feel wrath and pity, when I think on thee!
Ten righteous would have saved a city once,
And thou hast many righteous.—Well for thee!
That salt preserves thee; more corrupted else,
And therefore more obnoxious at this hour
Than Sodom in her day had power to be,
For whom God heard his Abraham plead in vain.

ON THE RECEIPT OF
MY MOTHER'S PICTURE
OUT OF NORFOLK

THE GIFT OF MY COUSIN ANN BODHAM

Oh that those lips had language! Life has passed
With me but roughly since I heard thee last.
Those lips are thine—thy own sweet smiles I see,
The same that oft in childhood solaced me;
Voice only fails, else, how distinct they say,
"Grieve not, my child, chase all thy fears away!"
The meek intelligence of those dear eyes
(Blest be the art that can immortalize
The art that baffles time's tyrannic claim
To quench it) here shines on me still the same.   10
    Faithful remembrancer of one so dear,
O welcome guest, though unexpected, here!
Who biddest me honour with an artless song,
Affectionate, a mother lost so long,
I will obey, not willingly alone,
But gladly, as the precept were her own;
And, while that face renews my filial grief,
Fancy shall weave a charm for my relief—
Shall steep me in Elysian reverie,
A momentary dream, that thou art she.   20
    My mother! when I learned that thou wast dead,
Say, wast thou conscious of the tears I shed?
Hovered thy spirit o'er thy sorrowing son,
Wretch even then, life's journey just begun?
Perhaps thou gavest me, though unseen, a kiss;
Perhaps a tear, if souls can weep in bliss—

On the Receipt . . . : Written in 1790; Cowper's mother had died in 1737.

Ah, that maternal smile! it answers—Yes.
I heard the bell tolled on thy burial day,
I saw the hearse that bore thee slow away,
And, turning from my nursery window, drew
A long, long sigh, and wept a last adieu!
But was it such?—It was.—Where thou art gone
Adieus and farewells are a sound unknown.
May I but meet thee on that peaceful shore,
The parting sound shall pass my lips no more!
Thy maidens grieved themselves at my concern,
Oft gave me promise of a quick return.
What ardently I wished, I long believed,
And, disappointed still, was still deceived;
By disappointment every day beguiled,
Dupe of *tomorrow* even from a child.
Thus many a sad tomorrow came and went,
Till, all my stock of infant sorrow spent,
I learned at last submission to my lot;
But, though I less deplored thee, ne'er forgot.
    Where once we dwelt our name is heard no more,
Children not thine have trod my nursery floor;
And where the gardener Robin, day by day,
Drew me to school along the public way,
Delighted with my bauble coach, and wrapped
In scarlet mantle warm, and velvet capped,
'Tis now become a history little known,
That once we called the pastoral house our own.
Short-lived possession! but the record fair,
That memory keeps of all thy kindness there,
Still outlives many a storm that has effaced
A thousand other themes less deeply traced.
Thy nightly visits to my chamber made,
That thou mightst know me safe and warmly laid;
Thy morning bounties ere I left my home,
The biscuit, or confectionary plum;
The fragrant waters on my cheeks bestowed
By thy own hand, till fresh they shone and glowed;
All this, and more endearing still than all,
Thy constant flow of love, that knew no fall,
Ne'er roughened by those cataracts and brakes,
That humour interposed too often makes;

All this still legible in memory's page,
And still to be so, to my latest age,
Adds joy to duty, makes me glad to pay 70
Such honours to thee as my numbers may;
Perhaps a frail memorial, but sincere,
Not scorned in heaven, though little noticed here.
 Could Time, his flight reversed, restore the hours,
When, playing with thy vesture's tissued flowers,
The violet, the pink, and jessamine,
I pricked them into paper with a pin
(And thou wast happier than myself the while,
Would'st softly speak, and stroke my head and smile),
Could those few pleasant hours again appear, 80
Might one wish bring them, would I wish them here?
I would not trust my heart—the dear delight
Seems so to be desired, perhaps I might.—
But no—what here we call our life is such,
So little to be loved, and thou so much,
That I should ill requite thee to constrain
Thy unbound spirit into bonds again.
 Thou, as a gallant bark from Albion's coast
(The storms all weathered and the ocean crossed)
Shoots into port at some well-havened isle, 90
Where spices breathe and brighter seasons smile,
There sits quiescent on the floods that show
Her beauteous form reflected clear below,
While airs impregnated with incense play
Around her, fanning light her streamers gay;
So thou, with sails how swift! hast reached the shore,
"Where tempests never beat nor billows roar,"
And thy loved consort on the dangerous tide
Of life, long since, has anchored at thy side.
But me, scarce hoping to attain that rest, 100
Always from port withheld, always distressed—
Me howling winds drive devious, tempest tossed,
Sails ripped, seams opening wide, and compass lost,
And day by day some current's thwarting force
Sets me more distant from a prosperous course.
But oh the thought, that thou art safe, and he!

---

l.97: Misquoted from Samuel Garth, *The Dispensary*, iii, 226: "Where billows never break, nor tempests roar."

That thought is joy, arrive what may to me.
My boast is not that I deduce my birth
From loins enthroned, and rulers of the earth;
But higher far my proud pretensions rise— 110
The son of parents passed into the skies.
And now, farewell—time, unrevoked, has run
His wonted course, yet what I wished is done.
By contemplation's help, not sought in vain,
I seem to have lived my childhood o'er again;
To have renewed the joys that once were mine,
Without the sin of violating thine;
And, while the wings of fancy still are free,
And I can view this mimic show of thee,
Time has but half succeeded in his theft— 120
Thyself removed, thy power to soothe me left.

THE CASTAWAY

Obscurest night involved the sky,
    The Atlantic billows roared,
When such a destined wretch as I,
    Washed headlong from on board,
Of friends, of hope, of all bereft,
His floating home for ever left.

No braver chief could Albion boast
    Than he with whom he went,
Nor ever ship left Albion's coast,
    With warmer wishes sent.   10
He loved them both, but both in vain,
Nor him beheld, nor her again.

Not long beneath the whelming brine
    Expert to swim, he lay;
Nor soon he felt his strength decline,
    Or courage die away;
But waged with death a lasting strife,
Supported by despair of life.

He shouted; nor his friends had failed
    To check the vessel's course,
But so the furious blast prevailed,   20
    That, pitiless perforce,
They left their outcast mate behind,
And scudded still before the wind.

The Castaway: Cowper's last written poem (20 March 1799). The analogy to his despair at being spiritually lost is from Admiral George Anson's *Voyage round the World* (1748). The images of the storm at sea and of the castaway (in part derived from I Corinthians ix. 25-27) are constant in Cowper's poetry (see *On the Receipt of My Mother's Picture*, ll. 88 ff.). He referred to one of his attacks of insanity as "the storm."

Some succour yet they could afford;
   And, such as storms allow,
The cask, the coop, the floated cord,
   Delayed not to bestow.
But so the furious blast prevailed,
Whater'er they gave, should visit more.

Nor, cruel as it seemed, could he
   Their haste himself condemn,
Aware that flight, in such a sea,
   Alone could rescue them;
Yet bitter felt it still to die
Deserted, and his friends so nigh.

He long survives, who lives an hour
   In ocean, self-upheld;
And so long he, with unspent power,
   His destiny repelled;
And ever, as the minutes flew,
Entreated help, or cried—"Adieu!"

At length, his transient respite past,
   His comrades, who before
Had heard his voice in every blast,
   Could catch the sound no more.
For then, by toil subdued, he drank
The stifling wave, and then he sank.

No poet wept him; but the page
   Of narrative sincere,
That tells his name, his worth, his age,
   Is wet with Anson's tear.
And tears by bards or heroes shed
Alike immortalize the dead.

I therefore purpose not, or dream,
   Descanting on his fate,
To give the melancholy theme
   A more enduring date;
But misery still delights to trace
Its semblance in another's case.

> No voice divine the storm allayed,
>   No light propitious shone,
> When, snatched from all effectual aid,
>   We perished, each alone:
> But I beneath a rougher sea,
> And whelmed in deeper gulfs than he.

James Beattie

1735: born 25 October near Laurencekirk, Kincardineshire, the son of a tenant farmer who also kept a small shop; attended the parish school
1749-53: at Marischal College, Aberdeen, on a scholarship; M. A., 1753
1753-58: taught school at Fordoun while studying for the ministry; began to publish verse in the *Scots Magazine*
1758-60: taught at the Aberdeen Grammar School
1760: through the influence of friends appointed Professor of Moral Philosophy at Marischal College
1761: *Original Poems and Translations* (dated 1760; 2nd enlarged ed., 1766)
1765: *The Judgment of Paris*
1767: married Mary Dun, daughter of the head of the Aberdeen Grammar School
1770: *An Essay on the Nature and Immutability of Truth in opposition to Sophistry and Scepticism,* an attack on Hume, enthusiastically received; LL. D., King's College, Aberdeen
1771: *The Minstrel, or The Progress of Genius,* Book I
1773: at the height of his fame, made one of several triumphant visits to London; granted a pension of £200; D. C. L., Oxford; painted by Reynolds
1774: *The Minstrel,* Book II
1776: *Essays: on Poetry and Music . . . , on Laughter and Ludicrous Composition, on the Utility of Classical Learning*
1783: *Dissertations Moral and Critical: on Memory and Imag-*

ination, on Dreaming, on the Theory of Language, on Fable and Romance, on the Attachments of Kindred, Illustrations on Sublimity
1786: Evidences of the Christian Religion
1790: Elements of Moral Science (vol. ii, 1793)
1803: died 18 August, his middle and late age darkened by the inherited insanity of his wife, his own ill health, and the early death of both of his sons

JAMES BEATTIE was one Scotsman writing in English who had no reason to complain of his reception in London. His admirers included Johnson, Burke, Mrs. Montagu (the Queen of the Blues), and George III. His fame was due not so much to his poetry as to his defense of orthodoxy against the enlightened thought of his time. Reynolds was moved to paint him allegorically and without charge in "The Triumph of Truth": Beattie sits dressed in a doctor's gown and holding a copy of his *Essay on Truth* as an angel thrusts down the figures of Prejudice, Scepticism, and Folly, one of which represents Voltaire and one, possibly, Hume.

Beattie's only important poem is *The Minstrel, or The Progress of Genius*. He regarded his other verses as "juvenile and incorrect," "miscarriages of my youth." *The Minstrel* is, in his own words, "a moral and descriptive poem," a loose form which could be "either droll or pathetic, descriptive or sentimental, tender or satirical, as the humour strikes me; for, if I mistake not, the manner which I have adopted admits equally of all these kinds of composition." "The hint of the subject was taken from Percy's *Essay on the Ancient Minstrels in England*" (included in his *Reliques of Ancient English Poetry*, 1765), although Beattie confused, as Percy did not, the earlier bards with the later minstrels; the hint of the name of the hero and of some details of setting and mood may have come from Goldsmith's ballad *Edwin and Angelina* (included in *The Vicar of Wakefield*, 1766).

The Minstrel was "written in the stanza of Spenser, but not much in his style" because Beattie "was always fond of it"—"I think it the most harmonious that ever was contrived. It admits of more variety and pauses than either the couplet or the alternate rhyme, and it concludes with a pomp and majesty of sound which to my ear is wonderfully delightful"—and because Thomson had utilized it in *The Castle of Indolence* (1748). The scene is set

"On Scotia's mountains" "in Gothic days," and Macpherson helped him draw it.

"The design was to trace the progress of a Poetical Genius, born in a rude age, from the first dawning of fancy and reason, till that period at which he may be supposed capable of appearing in the world as a Minstrel." Book I shows Edwin ("a picture of myself, as I was in my younger days") in the solitary state of childhood, "When Fancy roamed through Nature's works at will." (Resemblances, often noted, between *The Minstrel* and *The Prelude* are accidental and superficial.) In Book II Edwin undergoes an education in virtue and wisdom from the lips of that favorite eighteenth-century oracle, the hermit who, having made the journey of experience, dispenses in retirement what he has learned. Rational virtue and simplicity in art and life are recommended and their rise and fall traced through the progress of human history. The usual vices, follies, and vanities are condemned, especially luxury and wealth. Hope for man is based on Christian liberty, "sacred Freedom, when by law restrained." The logic and sometimes the very phrases are those of Thomson's *Liberty* (1735-36). A projected third book of *The Minstrel* was never written, and the poem stops rather than ends.

Some of the descriptive passages of *The Minstrel* have a certain naive charm, but the passages of abstract moralizing, especially in the second book, both outnumber and overweight them. The two strains do not blend as they do in the best eighteenth-century reflective and descriptive verse, such as *The Deserted Village*. Hence the poem is uneven, a danger Beattie thought inherent "in poems of a sentimental cast." He agreed, too, with Gray and other friendly critics that "Its great fault is want of fable [plot], but that is a fault in the plan, and now irremediable. My intention from the beginning was to give a philosophical or didactic rather than a narrative poem. Whether I did right in this I know not; but were it in my power, I believe I should alter my design."

from THE MINSTREL, OR THE PROGRESS OF GENIUS

BOOK I

Ah! who can tell how hard it is to climb
The steep where Fame's proud temple shines afar!
Ah! who can tell how many a soul sublime
Hath felt the influence of malignant star,
And waged with Fortune an eternal war!
Checked by the scoff of Pride, by Envy's frown,
And Poverty's unconquerable bar,
In life's low vale remote hath pined alone,
Then dropped into the grave, unpitied and unknown!

And yet, the languor of inglorious days   10
Not equally oppressive is to all.
Him who ne'er listened to the voice of praise
The silence of neglect can ne'er appall.
There are, who, deaf to mad Ambition's call,
Would shrink to hear the obstreperous trump of Fame;
Supremely blessed if to their portion fall
Health, competence, and peace. Nor higher aim
Had he whose simple tale these artless lines proclaim.

This sapient age disclaims all classic lore;
Else I should here in cunning phrase display,   20
How forth the Minstrel fared in days of yore,
Right glad of heart, though homely in array,
His waving locks and beard all hoary grey;
And from his bending shoulder decent hung

The Minstrel . . . : The present text gives thirty-three of the sixty stanzas, selected to represent the main descriptive features and moral themes of the first book.
ll.5-9. Compare Gray's *Elegy* (1751), ll. 49ff.

The Minstrel, or The Progress of Genius

His harp, the sole companion of his way,
Which to the whistling wind responsive rung;
And ever as he went some merry lay he sung.

Fret not yourselves, ye silken sons of pride,
That a poor Wanderer should inspire my strain.
The Muses fortune's fickle smile deride, 30
Nor ever bow the knee in Mammon's fane;
For their delights are with the village train,
Whom Nature's laws engage, and Nature's charms:
They hate the sensual, and scorn the vain;
The parasite their influence never warms,
Nor him whose sordid soul the love of wealth alarms.

Though richest hues the peacock's plumes adorn,
Yet horror screams from his discordant throat.
Rise, sons of harmony, and hail the morn,
While warbling larks on russet pinions float; 40
Or seek at noon the woodland scene remote,
Where the grey linnets carol from the hill.
Oh, let them ne'er with artificial note,
To please a tyrant, strain the little bill,
But sing what Heaven inspires, and wander where they will.

Liberal, not lavish, is kind Nature's hand;
Nor was perfection made for man below;
Yet all her schemes with nicest art are planned,
Good counteracting ill, and gladness woe.
With gold and gems if Chilian mountains glow, 50
If bleak and barren Scotia's hills arise,
There plague and poison, lust and rapine grow;
Here peaceful are the vales and pure the skies,
And freedom fires the soul, and sparkles in the eyes.

Then grieve not, thou to whom the indulgent Muse
Vouchsafes a portion of celestial fire;
Nor blame the partial Fates, if they refuse
The imperial banquet and the rich attire.
Known thine own worth, and reverence the lyre.

---

ll.22-27. Compare Gray's *Bard* (1757), ll. 15-22.

Wilt thou debase the heart which God refined? 60
No; let thy heaven-taught soul to Heaven aspire,
To fancy, freedom, harmony, resigned;
Ambition's groveling crew forever left behind.

Canst thou forego the pure ethereal soul
In each fine sense so exquisitely keen,
On the dull couch of Luxury to loll,
Stung with disease, and stupefied with spleen;
Fain to implore the aid of Flattery's screen,
Even from thyself thy loathsome heart to hide,
(The mansion then no more of joy serene), 70
Where fear, distrust, malevolence, abide,
And impotent desire, and disappointed pride?

Oh, how canst thou renounce the boundless store
Of charms which Nature to her votary yields?
The warbling woodland, the resounding shore,
The pomp of groves, and garniture of fields;
All that the genial ray of morning gilds,
And all that echoes to the song of even,
And that the mountain's sheltering bosom shields,
And all the dread magnificence of heaven, 80
Oh, how canst thou renounce, and hope to be forgiven?

* * *

The wight whose tale these artless lines unfold 127
Was all the offspring of this simple pair.
His birth no oracle or seer foretold:
No prodigy appeared in earth or air, 130
Nor aught that might a strange event declare.
You guess each circumstance of Edwin's birth;
The parent's transport and the parent's care;
The gossip's prayer for wealth and wit and worth;
And one long summer day of indolence and mirth.

And yet poor Edwin was no vulgar boy;
Deep thought oft seemed to fix his infant eye;

---

l.128. Omitted lines describe Edwin's parents, a "shepherd swain . . . of the north countrie" and his "blameless Phoebe."

The Minstrel, or The Progress of Genius

    Dainties he heeded not, nor gaud, nor toy,
Save one short pipe of rudest minstrelsy.
Silent when glad; affectionate, though shy;   140
And now his look was most demurely sad,
And now he laughed aloud, yet none knew why.
The neighbours stared and sighed, yet blessed the lad;
Some deemed him wondrous wise, and some believed him
    mad.

    But why should I his childish feats display?
Concourse and noise and toil he ever fled;
Nor cared to mingle in the clamorous fray
Of squabbling imps; but to the forest sped,
Or roamed at large the lonely mountain's head;
Or, where the maze of some bewildered stream   150
To deep untrodden groves his footsteps led,
  There would he wander wild, till Phœbus' beam,
Shot from the western cliff, released the weary team.

    The exploit of strength, dexterity, or speed
To him nor vanity nor joy could bring.
His heart, from cruel sport estranged, would bleed
To work the woe of any living thing,
By trap or net, by arrow or by sling;
These he detested, those he scorned to wield;
He wished to be the guardian, not the king,   160
  Tyrant far less, or traitor of the field.
And sure the sylvan reign unbloody joy might yield.

    *   *   *

    In truth he was a strange and wayward wight,   190
Fond of each gentle and each dreadful scene.
In darkness and in storm he found delight;
Nor less than when on ocean-wave serene
The southern sun diffused his dazzling sheen.
Even sad vicissitude amused his soul;
And if a sigh would sometimes intervene,
  And down his cheek a tear of pity roll,
A sigh, a tear, so sweet, he wished not to control.

* * *

    See, in the rear of the warm sunny shower,
The visionary boy from shelter fly!
For now the storm of summer rain is o'er,
And cool and fresh and fragrant is the sky.
And, lo! in the dark east, expanded high,
The rainbow brightens to the setting sun!
Fond fool, that deemest the streaming glory nigh,
How vain the case thine ardour has begun!
'Tis fled afar, ere half thy purposed race be run.

    Yet couldst thou learn that thus it fares with age,
When pleasure, wealth, or power, the bosom warm,
This baffled hope might tame thy manhood's rage,
And Disappointment of her sting disarm.
But why should foresight thy fond heart alarm?
Perish the lore that deadens young desire!
Pursue, poor imp, the imaginary charm,
Indulge gay Hope, and Fancy's pleasing fire:
Fancy and Hope too soon shall of themselves expire.

    When the long-sounding curfew from afar
Loaded with loud lament the lonely gale,
Young Edwin, lighted by the evening star,
Lingering and listening, wandered down the vale.
There would he dream of graves, and corses pale,
And ghosts that to the charnel-dungeon throng,
And drag a length of clanking chain, and wail,
Till silenced by the owl's terrific song,
Or blast that shrieks by fits the shuddering isles along.

    Or, when the setting moon, in crimson dyed,
Hung o'er the dark and melancholy deep,
To haunted stream, remote from man, he hied,
Where fays of yore their revels wont to keep;
And there let Fancy roam at large, till sleep
A vision brought to his entrancèd sight.
And first, a wildly murmuring wind 'gan creep
Shrill to his ringing ear; then tapers bright,
With instantaneous gleam, illumed the vault of night.

The Minstrel, or The Progress of Genius

* * *

But who the melodies of morn can tell? 334
The wild brook babbling down the mountainside;
The lowing herd; the sheepfold's simple bell;
The pipe of early shepherd dim descried
In the lone valley; echoing far and wide
The clamorous horn along the cliffs above;
The hollow murmur of the ocean tide; 340
The hum of bees, and linnet's lay of love,
And the full choir that wakes the universal grove.

The cottage curs at early pilgrim bark;
Crowned with her pail the tripping milkmaid sings;
The whistling plowman stalks afield; and, hark!
Down the rough slope the ponderous wagon rings;
Through rustling corn the hare astonished springs;
Slow tolls the village clock the drowsy hour;
The partridge bursts away on whirring wings;
Deep mourns the turtle in sequestered bower, 350
And shrill lark carols clear from her aerial tower.

O Nature, how in every charm supreme!
Whose votaries feast on raptures ever new!
Oh, for the voice and fire of seraphim,
To sing thy glories with devotion due!
Blessed be the day I 'scaped the wrangling crew,
From Pyrrho's maze, and Epicurus' sty;
And held high converse with the godlike few
Who to the enraptured heart and ear and eye
Teach beauty, virtue, truth, and love, and melody. 360

Hence! ye, who snare and stupefy the mind,
Sophists, of beauty, virtue, joy, the bane!
Greedy and fell, though impotent and blind,
Who spread your filthy nets in Truth's fair fane,
And ever ply your venomed fangs amain!

---

l.357. Pyrrho: A sceptic of the fourth century B.C.
l.357: "Epicuri de grege porcum" (Horace, *Epistles*, I.iv.16), a phrase which misrepresents Epicurus as an advocate of sensualism. The entire line refers to Hume and Beattie's attack on him in the *Essay on Truth*.

Hence to dark Error's den, whose rankling slime
First gave you form! hence! lest the Muse should deign,
(Though loth on theme so mean to waste a rhyme),
With vengeance to pursue your sacrilegious crime.

But hail, ye mighty masters of the lay, 370
Nature's true sons, the friends of man and truth,
Whose song, sublimely sweet, serenely gay,
Amused my childhood, and informed my youth!
Oh, let your spirit still my bosom soothe,
Inspire my dreams, and my wild wanderings guide.
Your voice each rugged path of life can smooth;
For well I know, wherever ye reside,
There harmony and peace and innocence abide.

Ah me! abandoned on the lonesome plain,
As yet poor Edwin never knew your lore, 380
Save when against the winter's drenching rain
And driving snow the cottage shut the door.
Then, as instructed by tradition hoar,
Her legends when the beldam 'gan impart,
Or chant the old heroic ditty o'er,
Wonder and joy ran thrilling to his heart;
Much he the tale admired, but more the tuneful art.

Various and strange was the long-winded tale;
And halls and knights and feats of arms displayed;
Or merry swains, who quaff the nut-brown ale, 390
And sing enamoured of the nut-brown maid;
The moonlight revel of the fairy glade;
Or hags that suckle an infernal brood,
And ply in caves the unutterable trade,
'Midst fiends and spectres, quench the moon in blood,
Yell in the midnight storm, or ride the infuriate flood.

* * *

Thus Heaven enlarged his soul in riper years. 451
For Nature gave him strength and fire to soar
On Fancy's wing, above this vale of tears;
Where dark cold-hearted sceptics, creeping, pore

Through microscope of metaphysic lore;
And much they grope for truth, but never hit.
For why? Their powers, inadequate before,
This art preposterous renders more unfit;
Yet deem they darkness light, and their vain blunders wit.

Nor was this ancient dame a foe to mirth.　　460
Her ballad, jest, and riddle's quaint device
Oft cheered the shepherds round their social hearth;
Whom levity or spleen could ne'er entice
To purchase chat or laughter at the price
Of decency. Nor let it faith exceed,
That Nature forms a rustic taste so nice.
Ah! had they been of court or city breed,
Such delicacy were right marvelous indeed.

Oft, when the winter storm had ceased to rave,
He roamed the snowy waste at even, to view　　470
The cloud stupendous, from the Atlantic wave
High-towering, sail along the horizon blue;
Where midst the changeful scenery ever new
Fancy a thousand wondrous forms descries
More wildly great than ever pencil drew,
Rocks, torrents, gulfs, and shapes of giant size,
And glittering cliffs on cliffs, and fiery ramparts rise.

Thence musing onward to the sounding shore,
The lone enthusiast oft would take his way,
Listening with pleasing dread to the deep roar　　480
Of the wide-weltering waves. In black array
When sulphurous clouds rolled on the vernal day,
Even then he hastened from the haunt of man,
Along the darkening wilderness to stray,
What time the lightning's fierce career began,
And o'er heaven's rending arch the rattling thunder ran.

Responsive to the sprightly pipe when all
In sprightly dance the village youth were joined,
Edwin, of melody aye held in thrall,
From the rude gambol far remote reclined,　　490
Soothed with the soft notes warbling in the wind.

Ah, then all jollity seemed noise and folly.
To the pure soul by Fancy's fire refined
Ah, what is mirth, but turbulence unholy,
When with the charm compared of heavenly melancholy?

Is there a heart that music cannot melt?
Ah me! how is that rugged heart forlorn!
Is there who ne'er those mystic transports felt
Of solitude and melancholy born?
He needs not woo the Muse; he is her scorn.   500
The sophist's rope of cobweb he shall twine;
Mope o'er the schoolman's peevish page; or mourn,
And delve for life, in Mammon's dirty mine;
Sneak with the scoundrel fox, or grunt with glutton swine.

For Edwin, Fate a nobler doom had planned;
Song was his favourite and first pursuit.
The wild harp rang to his adventurous hand,
And languished to his breath the plaintive flute.
His infant Muse, though artless, was not mute;
Of elegance as yet he took no care;   510
For this of time and culture is the fruit;
And Edwin gained at last this fruit so rare,
As in some future verse I purpose to declare.

Meanwhile, whate'er of beautiful or new,
Sublime or dreadful, in earth, sea, or sky,
By chance or search, was offered to his view,
He scanned with curious and romantic eye.
Whate'er of lore tradition could supply
From Gothic tale, or song, or fable old,
Roused him, still keen to listen and to pry.   520
At last, though long by penury controlled,
And solitude, his soul her graces 'gan unfold.

* * *

James Macpherson

1736: born 27 October at Ruthven, Inverness, in the Highlands, the son of a poor farmer; educated at home and at the district school at Badenoch
1752-56: at King's College and at Marischal College, Aberdeen; the University of Edinburgh; probably studied for the ministry
1756-57: taught school at Ruthven
1758-60: employed as a private tutor in the Graham family
1758: *The Highlander: An Heroic Poem in Six Cantos* published in Edinburgh
1760: at the instance of John Home, Alexander Carlyle, and Hugh Blair, published anonymously in Edinburgh *Fragments of Ancient Poetry Collected in the Highlands of Scotland and Translated from the Gaelic or Erse Language;* with funds subscribed by Scottish patrons made a tour of the Highlands and the Western Islands to collect more Gaelic poetry
1761: went to London at the invitation of Lord Bute, whose political influence was often used in favor of his fellow Scots
1762: *Fingal: An Ancient Epic Poem in Six Books with Several Other Poems Translated from the Gaelic Language* published (December 1761, dated 1762) over his own name in London; the authenticity of the work strongly questioned
1763: *Temora: An Ancient Epic Poem in Eight Books . . . Composed by Ossian, the Son of Fingal,* dedicated to Lord Bute; even stronger charges of counterfeit

1764-66: to the newly acquired colony of Florida as secretary to Governor Johnstone, Surveyor-General and President of the Council

C. 1769: engaged by the government as a political propagandist to combat the *Letters of Junius*

1771: *An Introduction to the History of Great Britain and Ireland*, much attacked for its Celtic bias

1773: *The Iliad of Homer*, a prose translation

1775: *Original Papers Containing the Secret History of Great Britain from the Restoration to the Accession of the House of Hanover; A History of Great Britain from the Restoration to the Accession of the House of Hanover*, commissioned as a "continuation" of Hume's *History*, written from a Jacobite point of view; Johnson's attack on Macpherson in his *Journey to the Western Islands of Scotland* revived the Ossian controversy

1776: engaged by Lord North's ministry to supervise the government newspapers and to defend their American policy; *The Rights of Great Britain Asserted against the Claims of America*, an answer to the Declaration of Independence

1777: began to represent the interests of Mohammed Ali, nabob of Arcot, against the East India Company

1780: Member of Parliament for Camelford, Cornwall; retained the seat until his death

1786: now wealthy, began to purchase an estate and build a mansion at Badenoch for his retirement

1796: died 17 February at Badenoch; buried in Westminster Abbey, near the Poets' Corner

1797-1805: investigation by a committee of the Highland Society of Scotland into the authenticity of the Ossian poems

WHILE STILL a young man, James Macpherson astonished Europe and set England and Scotland quarreling with his alleged translations from the Gaelic of a cache of ancient literature, miraculously preserved through fifteen hundred years of oral tradition. These were the poems of Ossian, who, in the third century A.D., had sung the deeds of his father Fingal and mourned the passing of the glories of the Celtic kingdom of Morven in the western Highlands. Partly by luck and partly by design, Macpherson catered to several predilections of his period: the interest in non-Graeco-Roman mythologies and cultures, in noble primitive men and untaught primitive bards, in the melancholy pleasures of ruins, in a poetry of more refined sentiment. Other writers had explored the way. Gray was an amateur of Celtic studies; in his *Ode* Collins had repeated John Home's advice to consider the superstitions of the Highlands as a subject of poetry, but none had Macpherson's bold originality or his popular success. Macpherson may have been, as David Hume said, a "strange and heteroclite . . . mortal, than whom I have scarce ever known a man more perverse and unamiable," but he was as accomplished an opportunist in literature as he was to be in politics.

The poems of Ossian are highly fanciful, but their basis is not entirely imaginary. The Fenian or Ossianic cycle of heroic tales, one of the two main branches of Irish saga literature, is widespread in the Gaelic folklore common to Ireland and Scotland. Macpherson knew enough Gaelic to utilize ballads of the late fifteenth and early sixteenth centuries (both those still current in the Highlands and gathered by him or his associates and those preserved in manuscript collections) and histories of ancient Ireland. He treated his sources with a very free hand, especially as success made him bolder. He claimed that Fingal and his men, and hence the bard who sang them, were of Scottish not Irish origin, thus appealing to Scottish pride (sunk low since the failure of the Jacobite uprising of 1745) and arousing English prejudice. He bowdlerized and refined; he added atmosphere and themes which were patently modern. Later scholarship has, on the whole, confirmed Johnson's intuitive judgment: "He has found names, and stories, and phrases, nay, passages in old songs, and with them has blended his own compositions, and so made what he gives to the world as the translation of an ancient poem."

Macpherson was alternately canny and silent about his methods and sources. He threw investigators off his track by denouncing ballads that were his very sources as "disgustful to true taste," "spurious pieces," "inconsistent and notoriously fabulous." But as one investigator has remarked, "while the learned exhausted their arguments, the poems were everywhere read." In England and, in translation, in Germany, Italy, France, and Spain, they became a part of the literary and popular consciousness of two generations. Macpherson, in defending his works, always appealed to their sales at home and their popularity abroad.

Contemporary critical theory or overreaching ambition led Macpherson to display most of his work in the guise of the epic, the highest and noblest genre. (It was inevitable that Macpherson should translate the *Iliad* into Ossianic prose, "trying to prove," as Horace Walpole remarked, "how easy it is to make a *Fingal* out of Homer, after having tried to prove that *Fingal* was an original poem.") Perceptive readers, however, noticed at once that the poems of Ossian were not epic either in form or effect. Both Beattie and Gray admired "particular beauties" and "detached pieces" but found the poems deficient in construction. In all the fuss over the possibility of the survival of a Gaelic epic and in all the comparisons of Homer and Ossian, a few noticed that the success of the works was due to their lyric cast and atmosphere.

The narrative line of the Ossian poems is diffuse and important only as an excuse for lyric effusions. The lyric note is one of retrospective melancholy, the lament for happier and more glorious days by one who has alone survived them. They have the eternal appeal of the lost cause. The backdrop and imagery are appropriate but vague and repetitious: a world of trees, crags, torrents, caves, and tombs in mist, shadow, and night, populated by innumerable ghosts. The effect is cumulative rather than striking, quantitative rather than qualitative. Wordsworth perfectly caught the Ossianic mood as he speculated about the Gaelic song of his Solitary Reaper:

> Perhaps the plaintive numbers flow
> For old, unhappy, far-off things,
> And battles long ago.

Macpherson wisely chose as his medium an incantory "measured" prose, clearly Biblical in origin. His prose-poems, he said,

> are more calculated to please persons of exquisite feelings of heart, than those who receive all their impressions by the ear. The novelty of cadence, in what is called a prose version, though not destitute of harmony, will not to common readers supply the absence of the frequent returns of rhyme. This was the opinion of the writer himself, though he yielded to the judgment of others, in a mode which presented freedom and dignity of expression, instead of fetters which cramp the thought, whilst the harmony of language is preserved.

Contemporary admirers judged his style to be simple, pathetic, and sublime.

Macpherson was a borrower as well as an inventor. Turns of phrase come from the Bible, Milton, and Pope's *Homer*, coincidences which Macpherson pointed out in his own notes as proof of Ossian's talent and his scholarship. Tricks of style, like the apostrophe and the exclamatory statement, were common in contemporary poetic practice. Macpherson had been touched by Young's moods and settings, though he largely avoided his moralizing; it was no less than fitting that the *Night Thoughts* and Ossian were famous in Europe together. The great original of Ossian himself is surely Gray's *Bard*, the last of the poets in a desolated land, "Robed in the sable garb of woe."

The poems of Ossian interest us now only because they interested the later eighteenth century. "The melody of our verse," Shenstone wrote in 1761,

> has been perhaps carried to its utmost perfection; that of prose seems to have been more neglected, and to be capable of greater than it has yet attained. It seems to be a very favorable era for the appearance of such irregular poetry. The taste of the age, so far as it regards plan and style, seems to have been carried to its utmost height. . . . The public has seen all that art can do, and they want the more striking efforts of wild, original, enthusiastic genius. It seems to exclaim aloud with the chorus in *Julius Caesar:*
>
> > Oh rather than be slaves to these deep learned men,
> > Give us our wilderness and our woods, our huts and caves again!

from CARTHON

..."King of Morven," Carthon said, "I fall in the midst of my course. A foreign tomb receives, in youth, the last of Reuthámir's race. Darkness dwells in Balclutha: the shadows of grief in Crathmo. But raise my remembrance on the banks of Lora, where my fathers dwelt. Perhaps the husband of Moina will mourn over his fallen Carthon." His words reached the heart of Clessámmor; he fell, in silence, on his son. The host stood darkened around; no voice is on the plain. Night came, the moon, from the east, looked on the mournful field; but still they stood, like a silent grove that lifts its head on Gormal, when the loud winds are laid, and dark autumn is on the plain.

Three days they mourned above Carthon; on the fourth his father died. In the narrow plain of the rock they lie; a dim ghost defends their tomb. There lovely Moina is often seen; when the sun-beam darts on the rock, and all around is dark. There she is seen, Malvina! but not like the daughters of the hill. Her robes are from the stranger's land; and she is still alone!

Fingal was sad for Carthon; he commanded his bards to mark the day, when shadowy autumn returned. And often did they mark the day and sing the hero's praise. "Who comes so dark from ocean's roar, like autumn's shadowy cloud? Death is trembling in his hand! his eyes are flames of fire! Who roars along dark Lora's heath? Who but Carthon, king of swords! The people fall! see how he strides, like the sullen ghost of Morven! But there he lies

---

Carthon: one of the shorter poems in the *Fingal* volume. The "subject of it, as of most of Ossian's compositions, [is] tragical": Clessámmor unknowingly kills his son Carthon in single combat and dies of grief. Fingal, in whose kingdom of Morven the fight occurred, orders his bards to commemorate the event. Ossian does so in retrospect ("A tale of the times of old! The deeds of days of other years!"), addressing himself to Malvina. The final four paragraphs are given here. The concluding apostrophe to the sun was perhaps the most famous single passage in all the Ossianic poems. Macpherson disingenuously pointed out that it "is something similar to Satan's address to the sun in the fourth book of *Paradise Lost*" (11.32ff.).

a goodly oak, which sudden blasts overturned! When shalt thou rise, Balclutha's joy? When, Carthon, shalt thou arise? Who comes so dark from ocean's roar, like autumn's shadowy cloud?" Such were the words of the bards, in the day of their mourning; Ossian often joined their voice, and added to their song. My soul has been mournful for Carthon; he fell in the days of his youth; and thou, O Clessámmor! where is thy dwelling in the wind? Has the youth forgot his wound? Flies he, on clouds, with thee? I feel the sun, O Malvina! leave me to my rest. Perhaps they may come to my dreams; I think I hear a feeble voice! The beam of heaven delights to shine on the grave of Carthon; I feel it warm around!

O thou that rollest above, round as the shield of my fathers! Whence are thy beams, O sun! thy everlasting light? Thou comest forth, in thy awful beauty; the stars hide themselves in the sky; the moon, cold and pale, sinks in the western wave. But thou thyself movest alone; who can be a companion of thy course? The oaks of the mountains fall: the mountains themselves decay with years; the ocean shrinks and grows again: the moon herself is lost in heaven; but thou art for ever the same, rejoicing in the brightness of thy course. When the world is dark with tempests; when thunder rolls, and lightning flies; thou lookest in thy beauty from the clouds, and laughest at the storm. But to Ossian, thou lookest in vain; for he beholds thy beams no more; whether thy yellow hair flows on the eastern clouds, or thou tremblest at the gates of the west. But thou art perhaps, like me, for a season; thy years will have an end. Thou shalt sleep in the clouds, careless of the voice of the morning. Exult then, O sun! in the strength of thy youth: Age is dark and unlovely; it is like the glimmering light of the moon, when it shines through broken clouds, and the mist is on the hills;* the blast of the north is on the plain, the traveller shrinks in the midst of his journey.

---

* Compare Ecclesiastes xi.9 and xii.
1-2.

Thomas Chatterton

1752: born 20 November in Bristol, the posthumous son of a schoolmaster; the Chatterton family had for generations been workmen and sextons at the church of St. Mary Redcliffe, where the boy spent much of his time looking at neglected medieval legal documents

1760-67: at Colston's Hospital, a charity school, which prepared boys for business

1763: published his first poem, On the Last Epiphany, in Felix Farley's Bristol Journal

1767: apprenticed for seven years to John Lambert, a lawyer

1768: in March, the earliest trustworthy mention by Chatterton of the existence of some of the Rowley poems; in October, published his first "forgery," a Description of the Mayor's First Passing over the Old Bridge, taken from an old Manuscript, a topical article since the new bridge had just been opened; when questioned, he claimed the original was one of many manuscripts found in the muniment room of St. Mary's; in December, he unsuccessfully offered to the printer James Dodsley "copies of several ancient Poems; and an Interlude, perhaps the oldest dramatic piece extant; wrote by one Rowley, a Priest in Bristol, who lived in the reigns of Henry VIth and Edward IVth"

1769: began contributing modern prose and verse to the Town and Country Magazine (London); in March, "Being versed a little in antiquitys," offered "Curious Manuscripts" to Horace Walpole, hoping to secure his patronage; Walpole was at first interested but consulted William Mason and Gray, who declared them forgeries; in May, *Elinoure and Juga* appeared in *Town and Country*, the only Rowley poem published in Chatterton's lifetime

1770: contributed satiric political verse and prose, in the manner of Churchill and Junius, to the *Middlesex Journal* and other papers which supported "Wilkes and Liberty" and inveighed against George III's ministers; in April, frightened Lambert into dismissing him by threatening suicide; went to London, where he had a moderate though brief success as a political satirist and a writer of songs and libretti for comic operas; 24 August, committed suicide by drinking poison

1777: *Poems, Supposed to Have Been Written at Bristol, by Thomas Rowley, and Others* edited by Thomas Tyrwhitt

1778: 3rd edition of the above with an appendix "tending to prove that they were written, not by any ancient author, but entirely by Thomas Chatterton"; Tyrwhitt's edition sparked a controversy of several years over the authenticity of the Rowley poems

THOMAS CHATTERTON became even more of a romantic hero than Burns. Coleridge thought his *Monody on the Death of Chatterton* worth many revisions. Wordsworth celebrated him as "the marvellous Boy, The sleepless Soul that perished in his pride," in *Resolution and Independence*, a poem perhaps patterned after the *Balade of Charitie*. Keats dedicated *Endymion* to the memory of this "most English of poets except Shakespeare." Shelley, in *Adonais*, linked Chatterton with "The inheritors of unfulfilled renown." Vigny wrote a play about him in 1835 ("La cause, c'est le martyre perpétuel et la perpétuelle immolation du Poète"); Hans Jahnn, another in German in 1955. In all this idolization there is not only compassion and self-recognition but a different way of reading poetry as well. When Blake wrote in 1826 "I believe both Macpherson and Chatterton that what they say is ancient, is so," he was perhaps believing in a new way: are not a poet's "forgeries" imaginative truth, a seer's visions true?

For Chatterton's contemporaries the problem, though complicated, was simpler: were the Rowley poems genuine or not? Chatterton as a figure was admired in the eighteenth century, but he was admired in humanistic terms. "It was owing to his pride,"

Thomas Warton wrote in 1782, "which has been construed into veracity, that he so inflexibly persisted to the last, that these poems were by Rowley. To this secret of his bosom he had vowed eternal fidelity, and there is a degree of heroism in his obstinacy."

Chatterton was indeed a marvellous boy, or, as Johnson put it, "This is the most extraordinary young man that has encountered my knowledge. It is wonderful how the whelp has written such things." Dead before his eighteenth birthday, he left work enough to fill three volumes. The variety is remarkable: occasional, lyric, dramatic, narrative, and satiric poetry, prose in the form of story, antiquarian note, political letter, and topical essay. But except for the three exotic *African Eclogues*, attention has always centered on his medieval poems, which he claimed not to have written but only to have discovered and transcribed.

He created—or forged—not only medieval poems but, supplying documents and letters, the fifteenth-century world out of which they came. Taking hints from tombstones and records, he imagined William Canynge, whom he described to Walpole as "Founder of that noble Gothic Pile, Saint Mary Redclift Church. . . . : the Maecenas of his time: one who could happily blend the Poet, the Painter, the Priest, and the Christian—perfect in each: a Friend to all in distress, an honor to Bristol, and a Glory to the Church." His boldest invention was, first among a group of poets, Thomas Rowley, "a Secular Priest of St. John's. . . . His Merit as a Biographer, Historiographer is great, as a Poet still greater: Some of his Pieces would do honor to Pope." "Rowley was employ'd by Canynge to go to the Principal Monasterys in the Kingdom to Collect Drawings, Paintings & all MSS relating to Architecture" and was liberally rewarded by his patron for his own poems and plays. Cleric-poets like Alexander Barclay and John Lydgate have been suggested as models for Rowley, but models cannot account for the figure who stands revealed, as Browning said, "a Man, a Time, a Language, all at once."

Chatterton did not create Rowley out of nothing. His own natural taste for history was encouraged by his period's awakening interest in the art and architecture, if not the life, of the past—Gray, Collins, and Thomas Warton, for instance. Collections like Elizabeth Cooper's *Muses' Library* (1737, etc.) and Thomas Percy's *Reliques of Ancient English Poetry* (1765) gave him knowledge as well as inspiration, and to his daring mind it may have seemed only a step from works like James Macpherson's

"Ossian" (1760, etc.) and Horace Walpole's *Castle of Otranto* (1765), both of which pretended to be translations of older originals, to fabrications of Rowley's poems and Canynge's world.

Chatterton did not know much medieval literature aside from a little Chaucer, but he had read to his profit Spenser, Shakespeare, Dryden, Pope, and Gray. ("I wish I knew the classics, I could then do anything.") His "ancient" language was, as modern scholars have shown, a "farrago of old words of all periods and dialects." He seems to have written, or to have conceived, his poems in modern English and then to have translated them into his "ghost English" with the aid of an ancient-modern, modern-ancient lexicon which he compiled himself out of the glossary to Thomas Speght's edition of Chaucer (1598), John Kersey's *Dictionarium Anglo-Britannicum* (1708), and Nathan Bailey's *Universal Etymological Dictionary* (1721, etc.). He made many careless errors and took many deliberate liberties with words, a fair risk, since his contemporaries were far more ignorant of the history of their language than he.

But contemporary trends cannot explain nor his relative ignorance minimize the fact that Chatterton had, more than anyone else in his time, a true historic sense, both aesthetic and antiquarian. As Frances Miller has shown, he had "the awareness, sympathetic rather than superior, of the 'differentness' of the past." "Nor does Chatterton sigh for the good old days. Bygone times are presented with neither a brief for the past nor propaganda for the present." His "verse does not look back *to* the fifteenth century; it is *of* the fifteenth century, where the consciousness of succeeding ages cannot exist." Surely it is mistaken, or irrelevant, to read the Rowley poems primarily as a projection of some inner or other self or as a wishful escape from the mercenary "Bristollish" souls which Chatterton hated. To realize in art an almost unknown world of three hundred years ago is to be as objective as it is possible to be.

AN EXCELENTE BALADE OF CHARITIE

AS WROTEN BIE THE GODE PRIESTE THOMAS ROWLEY 1464

In Virginè the sweltry sun 'gan sheene,
  And hot upon the mees did cast his ray;
The apple rodded from its paly green,
  And the mole pear did bend the leafy spray;
  The peed chelàndre sung the livelong day;
'Twas now the pride, the manhood of the year,
And eke the ground was dight in its mose deft aumere.

The sun was gleaming in the mid of day,
  Dead still the air, and eke the welkin blue,
When from the sea arist in drear array   10
  A heap of clouds of sable sullen hue,
  The which full fast unto the woodland drew
Hiltring attenes the sunnìs fetive face,
And the black tempest swol'n, and gathered up apace.

Beneath an holm, fast by a pathway side,
  Which did unto Saint Godwin's covent led,
A hapless pilgrim moaning did abide,
  Poor in his view, ungentle in his weed,
  Long bretful of the miseries of need.

Balade: Chatterton unsuccessfully submitted the *Balade* to the *Town and Country* 4 July 1770, observing that "the Sentiment, Description, and Versification are highly deserving the attention of the Literati." It may be his last poem. The stanzaic form is rime royal with a final Alexandrine, imitated from Spenser. The subject was doubtless taken from the parable of the Good Samaritan.

It is now usual to modernize Chatterton's decoratively antique spelling. This has been done here except for the title. No sound values have been changed. A glossary follows the text; the glosses are Chatterton's own.
l.17: Compare the following lines with Spenser, *Faerie Queene*, I.ix.35.

An Excelente Balade of Charitie

  Where from the hailstone could the almer fly?   20
  He had no housen there, ne any convent nigh.

    Look in his glommèd face, his sprite there scan;
      How woe-begone, how withered, forwind, dead!
    Haste to thy church-glebe-house, ashrewèd man!
      Haste to thy kiste, thy only dortour bed.
    Cale as the clay which will gree on thy head
  Is charity and love aming high elves;
  Knightìs and barons live for pleasure and themselves.

    The gathered storm is ripe; the big drops fall,
      The forswat meadows smethe, and drench the rain;   30
    The coming ghastness do the cattle 'pall,
      And the full flocks are driving o'er the plain;
    Dashed from the clouds, the waters flott again;
  The welkin opes; the yellow levin flies,
  And the hot fiery smothe in the wide lowings dies.

    List! now the thunder's rattling climming sound
      Cheves slowly on, and then embollen clangs,
    Shakes the high spire, and lost, dispended, drowned,
      Still on the gallard ear of terror hangs;
    The winds are up; the lofty elmen swangs;   40
  Again the levin and the thunder pours,
  And the full clouds are brast attenes in stonen showers.

    Spurring his palfrey o'er the watery plain,
      The Abbot of Saint Godwin's convent came;
    His chapournette was drentèd with the rain,
      And his pencte girdle met with mickle shame;
    He ayneward told his bead-roll at the same
  The storm increasen, and he drew aside,
  With the mist alms craver near to the holm to bide.

    His cope was all of Lincoln cloth so fine,   50
      With a gold button fastened near his chin,
    His autremete was edged with goldeñ twine,
      And his shoon pike a loverd's might have been;

---

l.24. church-glebe-house: the grave.   cursed.
l.47. ayneward . . . bead-role:

Full well it shewn he thoughten cost no sin.
The trammels of his palfrey pleased his sight,
For the horse-milliner his head with roses dight.

    "An alms, sir priest!" the dropping pilgrim said,
      "Oh! let me wait within your covent door,
    Till the sun shineth high above our head,
      And the loud tempest of the air is o'er.   60
    Helpless and old am I, alas! and poor.
Ne house, ne friend, ne money in my pouch,
All that I call my own is this my silver crouche."

    "Varlet!" replied the Abbot, "cease your din;
      This is no season alms and prayers to give,
    My porter never lets a faitour in;
      None touch my ring who not in honour live."
    And now the sun with the black clouds did strive,
And shetting on the ground his glary ray;
The abbot spurred his steed, and eftsoons rode away.   70

    Once moe the sky was black, the thunder rolled,
      Fast reining o'er the plain a priest was seen;
    Ne dight full proud, ne buttoned up in gold,
      His cope and jape were grey, and eke were clean;
    A limitour he was of order seen;
And from the pathway side then turnèd he,
Where the poor almer lay beneath the holmen tree.

    "An alms, sir priest!" the dropping pilgrim said,
      "For sweet Saint Mary and your order sake."
    The limitour then loosened his pouch thread,   80
      And did thereout a groat of silver take:
    The mister pilgrim did for halline shake,
"Here, take this silver, it may eathe thy care,
We are God's stewards all, nete of our own we bear.

    "But ah! unhaily pilgrim, learn of me.
      Scathe any give a rent-roll to their Lord;
    Here, take my semi-cope, thou'rt bare, I see,
      'Tis thine; the saints will give me my reward."
    He left the pilgrim, and his way aborde.

Virgin and holy saint, who sit in gloure, 90
Or give the mighty will, or give the good man power.

GLOSSARY

aborde, went on
almer, beggar
arist, arose
ashrewed, accursed
attenes, at once
aumere, a loose robe or mantle
autremete, a loose white robe
ayneward, backwards
brast, burst
bretful of, filled with
cale, cold
chapournette, a small round hat
chelandre, goldfinch
cheves, moves
climming, noisy
crouche, crucifix
deft, neat, ornamental
dight, dressed, arrayed
dortour, a sleeping room
drench, drink
drented, drained, (drenched?)
eathe, ease
eftsoons, quickly
eke, also
elmen, elms
embollen, swelled, strengthened
faitour, beggar or vagabond
fetive, beauteous
flott, fly
forswat, sunburnt
forwind, dry, sapless

gallard, frighted
glommed, clouded, dejected
gloure, glory
gree, grow
halline, joy
hiltring, hiding, shrouding
holm, a holm oak
jape, a short surplice
kiste, coffin
levin, lightning
limitour, a licensed begging friar
loverd, lord
lowings, flames
mees, meads
mist, mister, poor, needy
mole, soft
mose, most
nete, nought
'pall, appall, frighten
peed, pied
pencte, painted
reining, running
rodded, reddened
scathe, scarce
shetting, shooting
smethe, smoke
smothe, steam, vapors
sprite, spirit, soul
swol'n, swelled
ungentle, beggarly
unhaily, unhappy

George Crabbe

1754: born 24 December, the son of a minor revenue official, at Aldeburgh, Suffolk, the setting of much of his poetry
1768: left school to be apprenticed to an apothecary-surgeon
1775: *Inebriety*
1780-81: went to London to become a writer; after much disappointment appealed to Burke, who responded generously, introducing him to his circle and arranging for the publication of *The Library* (1781)
1781: ordained in the Church of England; held various country livings throughout his life; known for his sermons against Methodism
1783: after a long engagement married Sarah Elmy (died 1813); *The Village*
1785: *The Newspaper*
1807: *Poems* (contains *The Parish Register* and *Sir Eustace Grey*)
1810: *The Borough*
1812: *Tales in Verse*
1819: *Tales of the Hall*
1832: died 3 February at Trowbridge, Wiltshire
1834: *Posthumous Tales* (vol. viii of *The Works*, edited by his son)

ALTHOUGH CRABBE lived two fifths of his life and published four fifths of his poetry in the nineteenth century, he is, in his way of seeing, judging, and putting things, an eighteenth-century mind and artist. This is not to say that he was not original—both Johnson and Byron thought so, generations apart—or that there is no development in his art. *Inebriety, The Library,* and *The Newspaper* are, to be sure, conventional moral essays in the tradition and manner of Pope and Johnson. *The Village,* too, is based on a popular model, the discursive "topographical" poem with its combination of descriptive and didactic elements. But the bluntness of Crabbe's attack on the idealized pastoral and the acuteness of his verse "characters" with their "ruling passions" proclaimed a new eye reviewing a familiar landscape. *The Parish Register* and *The Borough* recreate more particular and more comprehensive social worlds, primarily by means of a conducted tour of a gallery of poetic portraits. The portraits grow increasingly more subtle and detailed until, in some of the latter books of *The Borough,* they have been transformed into Crabbe's mature and unique achievement—the narratives which reveal the individual inner man rather than the generic social being. His remaining volumes are all entitled *Tales.*

Crabbe was as detached and clearsighted about the strength and the limitation of his poetry as he was about the people and the world he described. His lengthy prefaces remain the best key to his work and its place. "I have," he wrote, "no peculiar notion to defend, no poetical heterodoxy to support, nor theory of any kind to vindicate or oppose." He agrees with tradition that "The first intention of the poet must be to please; for, if he means to instruct, he must render the instruction which he hopes to convey palatable and pleasant." He is not convinced, however, that poetry can "make any material impression on the mind" or that the "pain caused by sympathy" in representations of distress "should serve for more than a stimulus to benevolence." The effect of a serious poetic imitation of life is less a simple question of moral reason and more a complex of moral emotion and aesthetic psychology, similar to our reaction to tragedy: such poems "will excite in some minds that mingled pity and abhorrence, which, while it is not unpleasant to the feelings, is useful in its operation: it ties and binds us to all mankind by sensations common to us all, and in some degree connects us, without degradation, even to the most miserable and guilty of our fellow-men."

Crabbe concedes that the poetry of "imagination" and "inspiration" is a "higher and more dignified kind of composition," but this ranking must not "exclude those who address their productions to the plain sense and sober judgment of their readers, rather than to their fancy and imagination." Otherwise, much of Chaucer, Dryden, and Pope would have to go, all poems, indeed, which are "adapted and addressed to the common sense of the reader and prevail by the strong language of truth and nature." Are not the ends of poetry well served "by a fair representation of existing character," "by a faithful delineation of those painful realities, those every-day concerns, and those perpetually-occurring vexations"?

As to his own works, which, like Pope's, have "no small portion of this actuality of relation, this nudity of description, and poetry without an atmosphere," "it is manifest that while much is lost for want of unity of subject and grandeur of design, something is gained by greater variety of incident and more minute display of character, by accuracy of description and diversity of scene."

There is great variety in Crabbe's tales, but *Peter Grimes* displays most of the facets of his mature narrative art. Crabbe is concerned with the psychology of moral experience and particularly with the steps in the tragic process of human degradation. The narrative line becomes inevitably slower, more intense. The scenes are progressively realized more dramatically and with a greater dependence on dialogue. The outer world of land and sea and men reciprocates the inner world of the "mind's delusion and the passions' storm." Crabbe's viewpoint is detached and unsentimental and his style neutral and controlled. Crabbe rarely abandoned the heroic couplet, the "common measure" of his century. Nor did he abandon its presuppositions of art. He drew on his own distressing experience in the hard world of Aldeburgh, but it was experience completed and objectively reviewed by a rational man of letters.

from THE VILLAGE

from BOOK I

The Village Life, and every care that reigns
O'er youthful peasants and declining swains;
What labour yields, and what, that labour past,
Age, in its hour of languor, finds at last;
What form the real picture of the poor,
Demand a song—the Muse can give no more.
   Fled are those times, when, in harmonious strains,
The rustic poet praised his native plains;
No shepherds now, in smooth alternate verse,
Their country's beauty or their nymphs' rehearse;   10
Yet still for these we frame the tender strain,
Still in our lays fond Corydons complain,
And shepherds' boys their amorous pains reveal,
The only pains, alas! they never feel.
   On Mincio's banks, in Caesar's bounteous reign,
If Tityrus found the Golden Age again,
Must sleepy bards the flattering dream prolong,
Mechanic echoes of the Mantuan song?
From Truth and Nature shall we widely stray,
Where Virgil, not where Fancy, leads the way?   20
   Yes, thus the Muses sing of happy swains,
Because the Muses never knew their pains.
They boast their peasants' pipes; but peasants now
Resign their pipes and plod behind the plough;
And few, amid the rural-tribe, have time
To number syllables, and play with rhyme;

The Village: The opening lines of *The Village* are Crabbe's best statement and justification of his realism in opposition to the sentimental and idealized pastoral.
l.16. Tityrus: a shepherd in the first *Eclogue* of Virgil (the "Mantuan").

Save honest Duck, what son of verse could share
The poet's rapture, and the peasant's care?
Or the great labours of the field degrade,
With the new peril of a poorer trade? 30
  From this chief cause these idle praises spring,
That themes so easy few forbear to sing;
For no deep thought the trifling subjects ask;
To sing of shepherds is an easy task:
The happy youth assumes the common strain,
A nymph his mistress, and himself a swain;
With no sad scenes he clouds his tuneful prayer,
But all, to look like her, is painted fair.
  I grant indeed that fields and flocks have charms
For him that grazes or for him that farms; 40
But when amid such pleasing scenes I trace
The poor laborious natives of the place,
And see the mid-day sun, with fervid ray,
On their bare heads and dewy temples play;
While some, with feebler heads and fainter hearts,
Deplore their fortune, yet sustain their parts;
Then shall I dare these real ills to hide
In tinsel trappings of poetic pride?
  No; cast by Fortune on a frowning coast,
Which neither groves nor happy valleys boast; 50
Where other cares than those the Muse relates,
And other shepherds dwell with other mates;
By such examples taught, I paint the Cot,
As Truth will paint it, and as Bards will not;
Nor you, ye poor, of lettered scorn complain,
To you the smoothest song is smooth in vain;
O'ercome by labour, and bowed down by time,
Feel you the barren flattery of a rhyme?
Can poets soothe you, when you pine for bread,
By winding myrtles round your ruined shed? 60
Can their light tales your weighty griefs o'erpower,
Or glad with airy mirth the toilsome hour?

* * *

---

l.27. honest Duck: Stephen Duck (1705-56), a self-educated "peasant poet," made famous by his *Poems on Several Subjects* (1730).
l.49. coast: Aldeburgh, Suffolk, Crabbe's birthplace.

from THE PARISH REGISTER

from PART III: BURIALS

* * *

    Next died the Widow Goe, an active dame,   125
Famed ten miles round, and worthy all her fame;
She lost her husband when their loves were young,
But kept her farm, her credit, and her tongue;
Full thirty years she ruled, with matchless skill,
With guiding judgment and resistless will;   130
Advice she scorned, rebellions she suppressed,
And sons and servants bowed at her behest.
Like that great man's, who to his Saviour came,
Were the strong words of this commanding dame;—
"Come," if she said, they came; if "go," were gone;
And if "do this,"—that instant it was done.
Her maidens told she was all eye and ear,
In darkness saw and could at distance hear;—
No parish-business in the place could stir,
Without direction or assent from her;   140
In turn she took each office as it fell,
Knew all their duties, and discharged them well;
The lazy vagrants in her presence shook,
And pregnant damsels feared her stern rebuke;
She looked on want with judgment clear and cool,
And felt with reason and bestowed by rule;
She matched both sons and daughters to her mind,
And lent them eyes, for Love, she heard, was blind;

The Parish Register: A country parson recounts the memories awakened in him as he leafs through the entries in his registers of birth (Book i), marriages (ii), and burials (iii). The poem consists of both general reflections and "characters" such as that of the Widow Goe.

Yet ceaseless still she throve, alert, alive,
The working bee, in full or empty hive;   150
Busy and careful, like that working bee,
No time for love nor tender cares had she;
But when our farmers made their amorous vows,
She talked of market-steeds and patent-ploughs.
Not unemployed her evenings passed away,
Amusement closed, as business waked the day;
When to her toilet's brief concern she ran,
And conversation with her friends began,
Who all were welcome, what they saw, to share;
And joyous neighbours praised her Christmas fare,   160
That none around might, in their scorn, complain
Of Gossip Goe as greedy in her gain.
   Thus long she reigned, admired, if not approved;
Praised, if not honoured; feared, if not beloved;—
When, as the busy days of Spring drew near,
That called for all the forecast of the year;
When lively hope the rising crops surveyed,
And April promised what September paid;
When strayed her lambs where gorse and greenweed grow;
When rose her grass in richer vales below;   170
When pleased she looked on all the smiling land,
And viewed the hinds, who wrought at her command;
(Poultry in groups still followed where she went);
Then dread o'ercame her—that her days were spent.
   "Bless me! I die, and not a warning given,—
With *much* to do on Earth, and *all* for Heaven!—
No reparation for my soul's affairs,
No leave petitioned for the barn's repairs;
Accounts perplexed, my interest yet unpaid,
My mind unsettled, and my will unmade;—   180
A lawyer haste, and, in your way, a priest;
And let me die in one good work at least."
She spake, and, trembling, dropped upon her knees,
Heaven in her eye and in her hand her keys;
And still the more she found her life decay,
With greater force she grasped those signs of sway;

Then fell and died!—In haste her sons drew near,
And dropped, in haste, the tributary tear,
Then from the adhering clasp the keys unbound,
And consolation for their sorrow found.   190

* * *

from THE BOROUGH

NOTE: *The Borough* consists of twenty-four "Letters" describing life and men in Aldeburgh. Of *Peter Grimes* Crabbe said in his Preface:

> The character of Grimes, his obduracy and apparent want of feeling, his gloomy kind of misanthropy, the progress of his madness, and the horrors of his imagination, I must leave to the judgment and observation of my readers. The mind here exhibited is one untouched by pity, unstung by remorse, and uncorrected by shame: yet is this hardihood of temper and spirit broken by want, disease, solitude, and disappointment; and he becomes the victim of a distempered and horror-stricken fancy. It is evident, therefore, that no feeble vision, no half-visible ghost, not the momentary glance of an unbodied being, nor the half-audible voice of an invisible one, would be created by the continual workings of distress on a mind so depraved and flinty. The ruffian of Mr. Scott [in *Marmion*] has a mind of this nature: he has no shame or remorse: but the corrosion of hopeless want, the wasting of unabating disease, and the gloom of unvaried solitude, will have their effect on every nature; and the harder that nature is, and the longer time required to work upon it, so much the more strong and indelible is the impression. This is all the reason I am able to give, why a man of feeling so dull should yet become insane, should be of so horrible a nature.

from **THE BOROUGH**

LETTER XXII, THE POOR OF THE BOROUGH:
PETER GRIMES

Old Peter Grimes made fishing his employ;
His wife he cabined with him and his boy,
And seemed that life laborious to enjoy;
To town came quiet Peter with his fish,
And had of all a civil word and wish.
He left his trade upon the sabbath-day,
And took young Peter in his hand to pray;
But soon the stubborn boy from care broke loose,
At first refused, then added his abuse;
His father's love he scorned, his power defied,
But being drunk, wept sorely when he died.
    Yes! then he wept, and to his mind there came
Much of his conduct, and he felt the shame—
How he had oft the good old man reviled,
And never paid the duty of a child;
How, when the father in his Bible read,
He in contempt and anger left the shed;
"It is the word of life," the parent cried;
—"This is the life itself," the boy replied;
And while old Peter in amazement stood,
Gave the hot spirit to his boiling blood;—
How he, with oath and furious speech, began
To prove his freedom and assert the man;
And when the parent checked his impious rage,
How he had cursed the tyranny of age—
Nay, once had dealt the sacrilegious blow
On his bare head, and laid his parent low;
The father groaned—"If thou art old," said he,
"And hast a son—thou wilt remember me;
Thy mother left me in a happy time,

Thou kill'dst not her—Heaven spares the double crime."
  On an inn-settle, in his maudlin grief,
This he revolved, and drank for his relief.
  Now lived the youth in freedom, but debarred
From constant pleasure, and he thought it hard;
Hard that he could not every wish obey,
But must awhile relinquish ale and play;
Hard! that he could not to his cards attend,
But must acquire the money he would spend.
  With greedy eye he looked on all he saw,   40
He knew not justice, and he laughed at law;
On all he marked he stretched his ready hand;
He fished by water, and he filched by land;
Oft in the night has Peter dropped his oar,
Fled from his boat and sought for prey on shore;
Oft up the hedge-row glided, on his back
Bearing the orchard's produce in a sack,
Or farm-yard load, tugged fiercely from the stack;
And as these wrongs to greater numbers rose,
The more he looked on all men as his foes.   50
  He built a mud-walled hovel, where he kept
His various wealth, and there he oft-times slept;
But no success could please his cruel soul,
He wished for one to trouble and control;
He wanted some obedient boy to stand
And bear the blow of his outrageous hand;
And hoped to find in some propitious hour
A feeling creature subject to his power.
  Peter had heard there were in London then—
Still have they being!—workhouse-clearing men,   60
Who, undisturbed by feelings just or kind,
Would parish-boys to needy tradesmen bind;
They in their want a trifling sum would take,
And toiling slaves of piteous orphans make.
  Such Peter sought, and when a lad was found,
The sum was dealt him, and the slave was bound.
Some few in town observed in Peter's trap
A boy, with jacket blue and woollen cap;
But none inquired how Peter used the rope,
Or what the bruise, that made the stripling stoop;   70
None could the ridges on his back behold,

None sought him shivering in the winter's cold;
None put the question—"Peter, dost thou give
The boy his food?—What, man! the lad must live;
Consider, Peter, let the child have bread,
He'll serve thee better if he's stroked and fed."
None reasoned thus—and some, on hearing cries,
Said calmly, "Grimes is at his exercise."
   Pinned, beaten, cold, pinched, threatened, and abused—
His efforts punished and his food refused— 80
Awake tormented—soon aroused from sleep—
Struck if he wept, and yet compelled to weep,
The trembling boy dropped down and strove to pray,
Received a blow, and trembling turned away,
Or sobbed and hid his piteous face;—while he,
The savage master, grinned in horrid glee;
He'd now the power he ever loved to show,
A feeling being subject to his blow.
   Thus lived the lad, in hunger, peril, pain,
His tears despised, his supplications vain; 90
Compelled by fear to lie, by need to steal,
His bed uneasy and unblessed his meal,
For three sad years the boy his tortures bore,
And then his pains and trials were no more.
   "How died he, Peter?" when the people said,
He growled—"I found him lifeless in his bed";
Then tried for softer tone, and sighed, "Poor Sam is dead."
Yet murmurs were there, and some questions asked—
How he was fed, how punished, and how tasked?
Much they suspected, but they little proved, 100
And Peter passed untroubled and unmoved.
   Another boy with equal ease was found,
The money granted, and the victim bound;
And what his fate?—One night it chanced he fell
From the boat's mast and perished in her well,
Where fish were living kept, and where the boy
(So reasoned men) could not himself destroy.—
   "Yes! so it was," said Peter, "in his play
(For he was idle both by night and day),
He climbed the main-mast and then fell below";— 110
Then showed his corpse and pointed to the blow;
"What said the jury?"—They were long in doubt,

But sturdy Peter faced the matter out;
So they dismissed him, saying at the time,
"Keep fast your hatchway when you've boys who climb."
This hit the conscience, and he coloured more
Than for the closest questions put before.
Thus all his fears the verdict set aside,
And at the slave-shop Peter still applied.
 Then came a boy, of manners soft and mild—
Our seamen's wives with grief beheld the child;
All thought (the poor themselves) that he was one
Of gentle blood, some noble sinner's son,
Who had, belike, deceived some humble maid,
Whom he had first seduced and then betrayed;—
However this, he seemed a gracious lad,
In grief submissive and with patience sad.
 Passive he laboured, till his slender frame
Bent with his loads, and he at length was lame;
Strange that a frame so weak could bear so long
The grossest insult and the foulest wrong;
But there were causes—in the town they gave
Fire, food, and comfort, to the gentle slave;
And though stern Peter, with a cruel hand,
And knotted rope, enforced the rude command,
Yet he considered what he'd lately felt,
And his vile blows with selfish pity dealt.
 One day such draughts the cruel fisher made,
He could not vend them in his borough-trade,
But sailed for London-mart; the boy was ill,
But ever humbled to his master's will;
And on the river, where they smoothly sailed,
He strove with terror and awhile prevailed;
But new to danger on the angry sea,
He clung affrightened to his master's knee;
The boat grew leaky and the wind was strong,
Rough was the passage and the time was long;
His liquor failed, and Peter's wrath arose—
No more is known—the rest we must suppose,
Or learn of Peter;—Peter says, he "spied
The stripling's danger and for harbour tried;
Meantime the fish, and then th' apprentice died."
 The pitying women raised a clamour round,

And weeping said, "Thou hast thy 'prentice drowned."
   Now the stern man was summoned to the hall,
To tell his tale before the burghers all;
He gave th' account; professed the lad he loved,
And kept his brazen features all unmoved.
   The mayor himself with tone severe replied,—
"Henceforth with thee shall never boy abide;
Hire thee a freeman, whom thou durst not beat,
But who, in thy despite, will sleep and eat;
Free thou art now!—again shouldst thou appear,
Thou'lt find thy sentence, like thy soul, severe."
   Alas! for Peter not a helping hand,
So was he hated, could he now command;
Alone he rowed his boat, alone he cast
His nets beside, or made his anchor fast;
To hold a rope or hear a curse was none—
He toiled and railed; he groaned and swore alone.
   Thus by himself compelled to live each day,
To wait for certain hours the tide's delay;
At the same times the same dull views to see,
The bounding marsh-bank and the blighted tree;
The water only, when the tides were high,
When low, the mud half-covered and half-dry;
The sun-burnt tar that blisters on the planks,
And bank-side stakes in their uneven ranks;
Heaps of entangled weeds that slowly float,
As the tide rolls by the impeded boat.
   When tides were neap, and, in the sultry day,
Through the tall bounding mud-banks made their way,
Which on each side rose swelling, and below
The dark warm flood ran silently and slow;
There anchoring, Peter chose from man to hide,
There hang his head, and view the lazy tide
In its hot slimy channel slowly glide;
Where the small eels that left the deeper way
For the warm shore, within the shallows play;
Where gaping mussels, left upon the mud,
Slope their slow passage to the fallen flood;—
Here dull and hopeless he'd lie down and trace
How sidelong crabs had scrawled their crooked race;
Or sadly listen to the tuneless cry

Of fishing gull or clanging golden-eye;
What time the sea-birds to the marsh would come,
And the loud bittern, from the bull-rush home,
Gave from the salt-ditch side the bellowing boom;
He nursed the feelings these dull scenes produce,
And loved to stop beside the opening sluice; 200
Where the small stream, confined in narrow bound,
Ran with a dull, unvaried, saddening sound;
Where all, presented to the eye or ear,
Oppressed the soul with misery, grief, and fear.

  Besides these objects, there were places three,
Which Peter seemed with certain dread to see;
When he drew near them he would turn from each,
And loudly whistle till he passed the reach.

  A change of scene to him brought no relief;
In town, 'twas plain, men took him for a thief; 210
The sailors' wives would stop him in the street,
And say, "Now, Peter, thou'st no boy to beat";
Infants at play, when they perceived him, ran,
Warning each other—"That's the wicked man";
He growled an oath, and in an angry tone
Cursed the whole place and wished to be alone.

  Alone he was, the same dull scenes in view,
And still more gloomy in his sight they grew;
Though man he hated, yet employed alone
At bootless labour, he would swear and groan, 220
Cursing the shoals that glided by the spot,
And gulls that caught them when his arts could not.

  Cold nervous tremblings shook his sturdy frame,
And strange disease—he couldn't say the name;
Wild were his dreams, and oft he rose in fright,
Waked by his view of horrors in the night—
Horrors that would the sternest minds amaze,
Horrors that demons might be proud to raise;
And though he felt forsaken, grieved at heart,
To think he lived from all mankind apart; 230
Yet, if a man approached, in terrors he would start.

  A winter passed since Peter saw the town,
And summer-lodgers were again come down;
These, idly curious, with their glasses spied
The ships in bay as anchored for the tide—

The river's craft—the bustle of the quay—
And sea-port views, which landmen love to see.
　One, up the river, had a man and boat
Seen day by day, now anchored, now afloat;
Fisher he seemed, yet used no net nor hook; 240
Of sea-fowl swimming by no heed he took,
But on the gliding waves still fixed his lazy look;
At certain stations he would view the stream,
As if he stood bewildered in a dream,
Or that some power had chained him for a time,
To feel a curse or meditate on crime.
　This known, some curious, some in pity went,
And others questioned—"Wretch, dost thou repent?"
He heard, he trembled, and in fear resigned
His boat; new terror filled his restless mind; 250
Furious he grew, and up on the country ran,
And there they seized him—a distempered man.—
Him we received, and to a parish-bed,
Followed and cursed, the groaning man was led.
　Here when they saw him, whom they used to shun,
A lost, lone man, so harassed and undone;
Our gentle females, ever prompt to feel,
Perceived compassion on their anger steal;
His crimes they could not from their memories blot,
But they were grieved, and trembled at his lot. 260
　A priest too came, to whom his words are told;
And all the signs they shuddered to behold.
"Look! look!" they cried; "his limbs with horror shake.
And as he grinds his teeth, what noise they make!
How glare his angry eyes, and yet he's not awake;
See! what cold drops upon his forehead stand,
And how he clenches that broad bony hand."
　The priest attending, found he spoke at times
As one alluding to his fears and crimes;
"It was the fall," he muttered; "I can show 270
The manner how—I never struck a blow";—
And then aloud—"Unhand me, free my chain;
On oath, he fell—it struck him to the brain;—
Why ask my father?—that old man will swear
Against my life; besides, he wasn't there;—
What, all agreed?—Am I to die today?—

My Lord, in mercy, give me time to pray."
　　Then, as they watched him, calmer he became,
And grew so weak he couldn't move his frame,
But murmuring spake—while they could see and hear　　280
The start of terror and the groan of fear;
See the large dew-beads on his forehead rise,
And the cold death-drop glaze his sunken eyes;
Nor yet he died, but with unwonted force
Seemed with some fancied being to discourse;
He knew not us, or with accustomed art
He hid the knowledge, yet exposed his heart;
'Twas part confession and the rest defence,
A madman's tale, with gleams of waking sense.
　　"I'll tell you all," he said, "the very day　　290
When the old man first placed them in my way;
My father's spirit—he who always tried
To give me trouble, when he lived and died—
When he was gone, he could not be content
To see my days in painful labour spent,
But would appoint his meetings, and he made
Me watch at these, and so neglect my trade.
　　" 'Twas one hot noon, all silent, still, serene,
No living being had I lately seen;
I paddled up and down and dipped my net,　　300
But (such his pleasure) I could nothing get,—
A father's pleasure, when his toil was done,
To plague and torture thus an only son!
And so I sat and looked upon the stream,
How it ran on, and felt as in a dream;
But dream it was not; no!—I fixed my eyes
On the mid stream and saw the spirits rise;
I saw my father on the water stand,
And hold a thin pale boy in either hand;
And there they glided ghastly on the top　　310
Of the salt flood, and never touched a drop;
I would have struck them, but they knew th' intent,
And smiled upon the oar, and down they went.
　　"Now, from that day, whenever I began
To dip my net, there stood the hard old man—
He and those boys, I humbled me and prayed
They would be gone;—they heeded not, but stayed;

Nor could I turn, nor would the boat go by,
But gazing on the spirits, there was I;
They bade me leap to death, but I was loth to die;
And every day, as sure as day arose,
Would these three spirits meet me ere the close;
To hear and mark them daily was my doom,
And 'Come,' they said, with weak, sad voices, 'come.'
To row away with all my strength I tried,
But there were they, hard by me in the tide,
The three unbodied forms—and 'Come,' still 'come,' they cried.

"Fathers should pity—but this old man shook
His hoary locks, and froze me by a look;
Thrice, when I struck them, through the water came
A hollow groan, that weakened all my frame;
'Father!' said I, 'have mercy!'—He replied,
I know not what—the angry spirit lied;—
'Didst thou not draw thy knife?' said he;—'Twas true,
But I had pity and my arm withdrew;
He cried for mercy which I kindly gave.
But he has no compassion in his grave.

"There were three places, where they ever rose—
The whole long river has not such as those—
Places accursed, where, if a man remain,
He'll see the things which strike him to the brain;
And there they made me on my paddle lean,
And look at them for hours—accursed scene!
When they would glide to that smooth eddy-space,
Then bid me leap and join them in the place;
And at my groans each little villain sprite
Enjoyed my pains and vanished in delight.

"In one fierce summer-day, when my poor brain
Was burning hot and cruel was my pain,
Then came this father-foe, and there he stood
With his two boys again upon the flood;
There was more mischief in their eyes, more glee
In their pale faces when they glared at me;
Still did they force me on the oar to rest,
And when they saw me fainting and oppressed,
He, with his hand, the old man, scooped the flood,
And there came flame about him mixed with blood;

He bade me stoop and look upon the place,
Then flung the hot-red liquor in my face;
Burning it blazed, and then I roared for pain,   360
I thought the demons would have turned my brain.
    "Still there they stood, and forced me to behold
A place of horrors—they cannot be told—
Where the flood opened, there I heard the shriek
Of tortured guilt—no earthly tongue can speak;
'All days alike! for ever!' did they say,
'And unremitted torments every day!'—
Yes, so they said."—But here he ceased and gazed
On all around, affrightened and amazed;
And still he tried to speak, and looked in dread   370
Of frightened females gathering round his bed;
Then dropped exhausted and appeared at rest,
Till the strong foe the vital powers possessed;
Then with an inward, broken voice he cried,
"Again they come," and muttered as he died.

William Blake

1757: born 28 November, his father a London hosier and lower-middle-class Nonconformist
1768: sent to a drawing school in the Strand
1772: apprenticed to James Basire, an engraver
1779: finished apprenticeship; set up for himself as engraver for booksellers
1782: married Catherine Boucher, daughter of a Battersea market-gardener, beautiful, intelligent though uneducated, who seems to have made Blake an almost perfect wife
1783: *Poetical Sketches*
1789: *Songs of Innocence* etched*
  Early mythic narratives:
  The Book of Thel (1789)
  Tiriel (1789; left in ms.)
  The Marriage of Heaven and Hell (c. 1790-93)
  The French Revolution (printed 1791 but never published)
1793-94: *Songs of Experience*†
  Earlier prophetic works:

---

* From this time forward, with the single exception of *The French Revolution* as noted in the biographical table, all Blake's books were published in his original manner, which he called "illuminated printing": the words and accompanying designs and illustrations were etched, the pulled sheets then being colored individually by hand. Save where otherwise noted, the dates assigned in the table to the works of verse indicate when the book was etched.
† These present bibliographical problems. In a Prospectus which he issued in 1793 Blake referred to a *Songs of*

Visions of the Daughters of Albion (1793)
America (1793)
The First Book of Urizen (1784)
Europe (1794)
Song of Los (1795)
The Book of Ahania (1795)
The Book of Los (1795)

1800: 18 September moved to Felpham, on the Sussex coast, where he served as a kind of artist assistant to the well-meaning but limited William Hayley, Cowper's friend and biographer

Later prophecies:

Vala, or the Four Zoas (written and revised 1795-1804; not printed in Blake's lifetime)
Milton (written and etched 1804-08)
Jerusalem (written and etched 1804-20)
The Everlasting Gospel (c. 1818; left unfinished in ms.)

1803: returned to London, living at 17 Moulton street
1821: moved to 2 Fountain Court, the Strand; during his closing years, recognized by a group of young artists who gathered round him
1827: died 12 August; one of his friends, present at his death, recorded that just before he died "His countenance became fair—His eyes Brighten'd and He burst out in singing of the things he saw in Heaven"

BLAKE'S LIFE presents the sharpest contrast between his career in terms of ordinary, everyday events and his inner, imaginative history. He worked at his profession of engraver when necessity required, but his and his wife's needs were spare. The better part of his energy went into his creative work. We can truthfully say that Blake lived fully only in the world created by his imagination.

He has a curious place in literary history. The *Songs of Innocence and Experience* is startlingly unlike what we commonly think of as eighteenth-century poetry, and Blake's violent revolt

---

Innocence and a *Songs of Experience* as though there were two separate books. But the extant copies of the latter poems all include the verse previously issued in the *Innocence* volume of 1791; and about 1794 Blake added a general title-page, *Songs of Innocence and of Experience. Shewing the Two Contrary States of the Human Soul*, thus emphasizing the organic character of the entire body of poems.

against the empiricism and rationalism of the Enlightenment does indeed place him among the Romantics. Yet he does not wholly conform to typical Romanticism. If he made much of the creative imagination, he did not exalt the self in the way characteristic of many of the Romantics. Rather, he thought in terms of a cosmic myth according to which it is man's destiny to transcend his self through creative energy. In fact, there was still much of the eighteenth-century in him. For instance, his admiration for Ossian and for the Ossianic style he adopted in the mythic narratives and prophecies. Yet he was also dominated, in the *Songs* at least, by an almost post-nineteenth-century aversion to poetic imagery that is not concrete, particular, overwhelmingly immediate.

Blake was familiar with the tradition of mysticism through the writings of Swedenborg, certain of the neo-Platonists, and Boehme. He was indebted to them in various ways and at various periods, but the full story is never likely to be worked out. So far as the average reader of Blake is concerned, it scarcely needs to be. The essential contours of the system he developed emerge plainly enough from his writings. The universe he envisaged is the realm within which the destiny of Man is acted out. In the beginning is a primal unity. This is shattered, the angels fall, and out of the chaos two contrary and warring forces—one imagination, the other reason or selfhood—produce a fallen world. The ensuing conflict between these opposed principles leads ultimately to the triumph of the imagination, to the union of imagination with reason and selfhood. This is the return to primal unity, to Eden, to Christ.

The spiritual history of man in terms of a fall and a return is one of the central myths of our cultural tradition, accessible to all of us. Though Blake's amplifications of this central myth often bewilder us, his essential meaning is never wholly clouded. Blake sought only to elucidate, never to confuse, nor does he confuse in regard to the great and simple things he sets forth: love, forgiveness, the realization of self through the annihilation of narrow selfhood; the death-wish expressed as jealousy and a desire to exert power over others; the imaginative and creative reality which we find within ourselves and which is Christ. Blake stands in the tradition of Christian humanism, linking the mythic visions of the past with the insights of recent psychology.

The *Poetical Sketches*, the *Songs of Innocence*, and the *Songs of Experience* are likely to remain his best-known verse. The earliest volume embodies little of his cosmic system, but it is already present, though in its simplest form, in the *Songs of Innocence,* where the condition of being is that of innocence preceding the fall and, we should add, of innocence as yet unrefined in the fires of experience. Between this second volume and the *Songs of Experience* the early mythic narratives intervene. Here Blake was beginning to come to grips with the problem of the fallen state. *Songs of Experience* everywhere reflects a new grimness but at the same time a more intense concept of the ultimate victory for the creative imagination.

In the *Poetical Sketches, Songs of Innocence,* and *Songs of Experience,* Blake uses the simpler lyric forms, suggestive of the fairy tale, the legend, the ballad. His language is easy, often colloquial; his phrasing is concise, epigrammatic. This poetic style resembles the Gothic sharpness of outline which he insisted upon as artist. "Nature," he once asserted, "has no outline, but imagination has." Unfortunately Blake was beguiled into using a quite different style—bardic, Ossianic, "sublime"—in the later prophetic books, and many feel that in consequence his undeniably first-rate poetry ended with the *Songs of Experience.*

from SONGS OF INNOCENCE

INTRODUCTION

Piping down the valleys wild,
Piping songs of pleasant glee,
On a cloud I saw a child,
And he laughing said to me,

"Pipe a song about a Lamb!"
So I piped with merry cheer.
"Piper, pipe that song again!"
So I piped. He wept to hear.

"Drop thy pipe, thy happy pipe;
"Sing thy songs of happy cheer."
So I sung the same again,   10
While he wept with joy to hear.

"Piper, sit thee down and write
"In a book, that all may read."
So he vanished from my sight,
And I plucked a hollow reed,

Introduction: This and the following notes on the *Songs* are intended merely as suggestions to alert the reader. Sometimes it is folly to give exact interpretations (multiple layers of statement and meaning may be involved); sometimes the best informed readers of Blake differ as to his intentions. The notes and observations given by Gleckner and Bateson are interesting and helpful (see bibliography).

In the *Introduction* the Piper may be thought of as the poet, the creative artist. The scene in the opening lines is that of pastoral poetry and, simultaneously, of the state of innocence, of the child's world, of the world of gentle animals and the child Jesus. Stanzas 2, 3, 4, 5 progress from song without words, to song with words, to the written word (and "stained with water clear" may carry some reference to Blake's new process of illuminated printing).

And I made a rural pen,
And I stained the water clear,
And I wrote my happy songs
Every child may joy to hear.   20

THE LAMB

Little Lamb, who made thee?
Dost thou know who made thee?
Gave thee life, and bid thee feed,
By the stream and o'er the mead?
Gave thee clothing of delight,
Softest clothing, woolly, bright?
Gave thee such a tender voice,
Making all the vales rejoice?
Little Lamb, who made thee?
Dost thou know who made thee?   10

Little Lamb, I'll tell thee,
Little Lamb, I'll tell thee:
He is callèd by thy name,
For he calls Himself a Lamb.
He is meek, and He is mild;
He became a little child.
I a child and thou a lamb,
We are callèd by His name.
Little Lamb, God bless thee!
Little Lamb, God bless thee!   20

THE LITTLE BLACK BOY

My mother bore me in the southern wild,
And I am black, but O! my soul is white;
White as an angel is the English child,
But I am black, as if bereaved of light.

The Little Black Boy: This is naturally taken as a poem of protest against social evils. That element is unquestionably present, but the black boy and the white boy seem also to be symbols operating in another system of meanings, where the relation between the two as disclosed in this dramatic address has reference not so much to a world in which slavery is permitted as to a state of the soul and the soul's awareness of the Divine. The black boy has felt the full beams of God's light; as yet the white boy has not, but he too will learn in time "the heat to bear."

Songs of Innocence

My mother taught me underneath a tree,
And, sitting down before the heat of day,
She took me on her lap and kissèd me,
And, pointing to the east, began to say:

"Look on the rising sun. There God does live,
"And gives His light, and gives His heat away;　　10
"And flowers and trees and beasts and men receive
"Comfort in morning, joy in the noonday.

"And we are put on earth a little space,
"That we may learn to bear the beams of love;
"And these black bodies and this sunburnt face
"Is but a cloud, and like a shady grove.

"For when our souls have learned the heat to bear,
"The cloud will vanish; we shall hear His voice,
"Saying, 'Come out from the grove, My love and care,
"And round My golden tent like lambs rejoice.' "　　20

Thus did my mother say, and kissèd me,
And thus I say to little English boy.
When I from black and he from white cloud free,
And round the tent of God like lambs we joy,

I'll shade him from the heat, till he can bear
To lean in joy upon our Father's knee.
And then I'll stand and stroke his silver hair,
And be like him, and he will then love me.

THE CHIMNEY SWEEPER

When my mother died I was very young,
And my father sold me while yet my tongue
Could scarcely cry " 'weep! 'weep! 'weep! 'weep!"
So your chimneys I sweep, and in soot I sleep.

The Chimney Sweeper: The poem carries two simultaneous sets of meanings. It can be read as a poignant statement of social evil in Blake's London. It also takes place in Blake's imaginary world of innocence, into which each of the *Songs of I.* gives us a dramatic glimpse. The central figure in this world is the child, who can never be lost for long because of the protecting influence of an all-loving mother (the loving father plays almost no part in the drama of Innocence). *The Chimney Sweeper* is

There's little Tom Dacre, who cried when his head,
That curled like a lamb's back, was shaved; so I said
"Hush, Tom! never mind it, for when your head's bare
"You know that the soot cannot spoil your white hair."

And so he was quiet, and that very night,
As Tom was a-sleeping, he had such a sight!—   10
That thousands of sweepers, Dick, Joe, Ned, and Jack,
Were all of them locked up in coffins of black;

And by came an Angel who had a bright key,
And he opened the coffins and set them all free.
Then down a green plain leaping, laughing, they run,
And wash in a river, and shine in the sun.

Then naked and white, all their bags left behind,
They rise upon clouds and sport in the wind;
And the Angel told Tom, if he'd be a good boy,
He'd have God for his father, and never want joy.   20

And so Tom awoke, and we rose in the dark,
And got with our bags and our brushes to work.
Tho' the morning was cold, Tom was happy and warm;
So if all do their duty, they need not fear harm.

HOLY THURSDAY

'Twas on a Holy Thursday, their innocent faces clean,
The children walking two and two, in red and blue and green;

---

unusual in that the child who is speaking has indeed lost both his parents. But as always in Innocence, no matter how imminently the cruel world of Experience seems, as here, to threaten, there is a protecting influence, in this instance the Angel of Tom Dacre's dream, who seems to free the sweeps. *Holy Thursday:* The scene is historical enough, describing the annual services in London for Charity School children.

Tension is introduced by the contrast between the innocent children on the one hand and the grey-bearded beadles and aged men who govern them. "Wise guardians of the poor" is ironic: they may seem so to the children and to those who accept the unimaginative condition of the experienced world, but to Blake they are symbols of that rational authority which seeks to destroy the spirit.

Grey-headed beadles walked before, with wands as white as
   snow,
Till into the high dome of Paul's they like Thames' waters
   flow.

O what a multitude they seemed, these flowers of London
   town!
Seated in companies they sit with radiance all their own.
The hum of multitudes was there, but multitudes of lambs,
Thousands of little boys and girls raising their innocent hands.

Now like a mighty wind they raise to Heaven the voice of song,
Or like harmonious thunderings the seats of Heaven among;   10
Beneath them sit the agèd men, wise guardians of the poor.
Then cherish pity, lest you drive an angel from your door.

THE DIVINE IMAGE

> To Mercy, Pity, Peace, and Love
> All pray in their distress;
> And to these virtues of delight
> Return their thankfulness.
>
> For Mercy, Pity, Peace, and Love
> Is God, our Father dear;
> And Mercy, Pity, Peace, and Love
> Is man, His child and care.
>
> For Mercy has a human heart,
> Pity a human face,   10
> And Love, the human form divine,
> And Peace, the human dress.
>
> Then every man, of every clime,
> That prays in his distress,
> Prays to the human form divine,
> Love, Mercy, Pity, Peace.

The Divine Image: A direct and burning statement of Blake's positive faith. God, "our Father dear," is Blake's true God, the God we know in Innocence, the God all of whose aspects are indwelling in us.

All must love the human form,
In heathen, Turk, or Jew.
Where Mercy, Love, and Pity dwell
There God is dwelling too.

from SONGS OF EXPERIENCE

INTRODUCTION

Hear the voice of the Bard!
Who Present, Past, and Future sees;
Whose ears have heard
The Holy Word,
That walked among the ancient trees,

Calling the lapsèd soul
And weeping in the evening dew,
That might control
The starry pole,
And fallen, fallen light renew: 10

Introduction: As the corresponding Introduction to *Songs of I.* takes us dramatically into one state of being, so this *Introduction* plunges us into the fallen world of experience. The protecting mother has vanished. In her stead we have a tyrant father (if any mother appears, she is a weak reflection of father), often sensed as the avenging God of the Old Testament (not "our Father dear" of *The Divine Image*). Yet the Fall is necessary, marking the limit of our departure from true Being and the beginning of our return. Thus Experience presents an ambiguous appearance, for if it is cruel like the tiger, it engenders the tiger's terrific energy whereby we repudiate and so transcend experience.

"The voice of the Bard": the Bard of Experience is the Piper of Innocence, and we can take both as Blake, the imagination, creative art.

"The Holy Word": stanza 2 describes and stanzas 3 and 4 give the utterance of the Holy Word. Which of Blake's gods is intended here? According to one interpretation, the Holy Word represents the evil and restrictive God of the Old Testament and of Experience. In this case, stanza 2 means that this God could, if only he would, reverse the condition of the Fall: he could renew the shattered light; he could reorder the fallen stars. His call to Earth in stanzas 3 and 4 would then be interpreted as embodying either blind rationalism or complete hypocrisy: Earth or Man is to return wholly to bondage; the evil conditions—"starry floor," "watery shore"—will last only until the break of day (when your hopes of betterment will be realized). Such a set of primary meanings seems borne out in the linked poem *Earth's Answer*, though it should be added that Miss Raine has a different reading (see bibliography).

"O Earth, O Earth, return!
"Arise from out the dewy grass;
"Night is worn,
"And the morn
"Rises from the slumberous mass.

"Turn away no more!
"Why wilt thou turn away?
"The starry floor,
"The watery shore,
"Is given thee till the break of day."   20

EARTH'S ANSWER

Earth raised up her head
From the darkness dread and drear.
Her light fled,
Stony dread!
And her locks covered with grey despair.

"Prisoned on watery shore,
"Starry Jealousy does keep my den:
"Cold and hoar,
"Weeping o'er,
"I hear the Father of the Ancient Men.   10

"Selfish Father of Men!
"Cruel, jealous, selfish Fear!
"Can delight,
"Chained in night,
"The virgins of youth and morning bear?

"Does spring hide its joy
"When buds and blossoms grow?
"Does the sower
"Sow by night,
"Or the ploughman in darkness plow?   20

"Break this heavy chain
"That does freeze my bones around.
"Selfish! vain!

"Eternal bane!
"That free Love with bondage bound."

HOLY THURSDAY

Is this a holy thing to see
In a rich and fruitful land,
Babes reduced to misery,
Fed with cold and usurous hand?

Is that trembling cry a song?
Can it be a song of joy?
And so many children poor?
It is a land of poverty!

And their sun does never shine,
And their fields are bleak and bare,
And their ways are filled with thorns.
It is eternal winter there.

For where'er the sun does shine,
And where'er the rain does fall,
Babe can never hunger there,
Nor poverty the mind appal.

THE CHIMNEY SWEEPER

A little black thing among the snow,
Crying " 'weep! 'weep!" in notes of woe!
"Where are thy father and mother, say?"—
"They are both gone up to the Church to pray.

"Because I was happy upon the heath,
"And smiled among the winter's snow,
"They clothed me in the clothes of death,
"And taught me to sing the notes of woe.

"And because I am happy and dance and sing,
"They think they have done me no injury,
"And are gone to praise God and His Priest and King,
"Who make up a Heaven of our misery."

THE TIGER

Tiger! Tiger! burning bright
In the forests of the night,
What immortal hand or eye
Could frame thy fearful symmetry?

In what distant deeps or skies
Burnt the fire of thine eyes?
On what wings dare he aspire?
What the hand dare seize the fire?

And what shoulder, and what art,
Could twist the sinews of thy heart?
And when thy heart began to beat,
What dread hand? and what dread feet?

What the hammer? what the chain?
In what furnace was thy brain?
What the anvil? what dread grasp
Dare its deadly terrors clasp?

When the stars threw down their spears,
And watered heaven with their tears,
Did he smile his work to see?
Did he who made the Lamb make thee?

Tiger! Tiger! burning bright
In the forests of the night,
What immortal hand or eye,
Dare frame thy fearful symmetry?

The Tiger: The night-darkened forests are the fallen state of experience. Stanzas 2, 3, 4: the scene is of a workman at his forge, fashioning the dread tiger. Stanza 5: at the Fall, when the fallen Angels, or stars, were defeated, the creation of Man's world took place (so that Man could fall no further; so that the return might begin).

What does the question at the close of stanza 5 convey? If we can find no answer, it is because the contrary states, lamb and tiger, defy reconciliation. But we do answer: Yes!; the contrary states are in us, and it must be through the Divine Image in us that we create an imaginative unity.

LONDON

I wander thro' each chartered street,
Near where the chartered Thames does flow,
And mark in every face I meet
Marks of weakness, marks of woe.

In every cry of every man,
In every infant's cry of fear,
In every voice, in every ban,
The mind-forged manacles I hear.

How the chimney-sweeper's cry
Every blackening church appals;
And the hapless soldier's sigh
Runs in blood down palace walls.

But most thro' midnight streets I hear
How the youthful harlot's curse
Blasts the new-born infant's tear,
And blights with plagues the marriage hearse.

Robert Burns

1759: born 25 January at Alloway, Ayrshire, the eldest son of a tenant farmer ("This kind of life, the cheerless gloom of a hermit with the unceasing moil of a galley-slave")
1765-68: sporadic schooling
1773: wrote his first poem, a love song ("Thus with me began Love and Poesy")
1781: went to Irvine to learn flax-dressing
1784: death of his father, leaving Burns the responsible head of the family; they move to a farm at Mossgiel
1786: considered emigrating to Jamaica; legal and other troubles attending his binding but "private" marriage to Jean Armour; *Poems, Chiefly in the Scottish Dialect*, published in Kilmarnock, which brought him instant fame; went to Edinburgh
1787: in Edinburgh, where he was lionized as "Caledonia's Bard"; revised edition of *Poems* published there and in London; toured the Border Country and the Highlands; began work for James Johnson's *Scots Musical Museum* (vol. i, published this year, contained two songs by Burns)
1788: vol. ii of *Museum* published, containing many songs by Burns; acknowledged Jean Armour as his wife; undertook lease of a farm at Ellisland, Dumfriesshire
1789: began work as an Excise officer
1790: *Museum*, vol. iii
1791: *Tam o' Shanter* published; gave up Ellisland lease and moved into Dumfries

1792: *Museum*, vol. iv; began collecting and writing songs for George Thomson's *A Select Collection of Original Scottish Airs;* his political loyalty investigated
1793: *Poems,* 3rd ed.; *Select Collection,* vol. i
1796: died 21 July of rheumatic endocarditis, contracted when a boy and aggravated by heavy manual labor; *Museum,* vol. v
1799: *Select Collection,* vol. ii

IT HAS TAKEN almost a century and a half, but Burns—outside of Scotland at least—has finally been disentangled from the sentimental image of the poet and peasant, the patriot and lover, from the toasts to his "Immortal Memory" by the Burns Clubs, who have, as G. M. Thomson said, "made Burns safe for hypocrisy." We can see him now more plainly as man and artist in his time, his place, and his tradition.

His literary tradition is a long and complex one, but it is not fundamentally English. In the late fifteenth and early sixteenth centuries the Scottish "Makars," less justly known as the Scottish Chaucerians—Robert Henryson, William Dunbar, and Gavin Douglas—produced a sophisticated poetic literature equal to any in Europe. But it did not last. The Reformation, harsher on the arts in Scotland than elsewhere, the union of the Scottish and English crowns and the removal of the court to London in 1603, the strife of the seventeenth century, all worked against the continuance or even the survival of a native literary culture and turned Scottish thought and expression toward England and English. In the eighteenth century, however, partly because patriotic sentiments were aroused in reaction against the Act of Union, the "treason" of 1707, there was a new Golden Age—or an Indian Summer.

The revival took two directions. The "literati," such as David Hume, William Robertson, Adam Smith, and Hugh Blair, made Edinburgh one of the intellectual and educational centers of Europe in philosophy, history, criticism, and economics, but they worked in prose and in deliberate English. Anglo-Scots who wrote poetry in English are somewhat less impressive to the modern eye, although James Thomson, James Beattie, and Robert Blair were much admired throughout Britain, and Thomson has some notes of observation of nature and reactions to it which were new in England but not in Scotland.

The second direction was a revival of interest in native Scots literature. Collectors started it, moved by antiquarian zeal, nationalistic pride, and imaginative taste. James Watson's *Choice Collection of Comic and Serious Poems Both Ancient and Modern* (1706-11), Allan Ramsay's *Ever Green: A Collection of Scots Poems Wrote by the Ingenious before 1600* (1724) and *Tea-Table Miscellany: A Collection of Choice Songs, Scots and English* (1724-37), David Herd's *Ancient and Modern Scots Songs* (1769, 1776)—edited, bowdlerized, improved, and fabricated as they sometimes were—made available a fascinating body of the finished products and the raw material of Scots poetry from the works of the Makars, old folk songs and ballads, and modern art songs by "ingenious young gentlemen." (To the collecting and enriching of Scots songs Burns, in collaboration with James Johnson and George Thomson, was to devote the last nine years of his life.)

Out of this matrix grew two young poets. The first was Robert Fergusson (1750-74), who showed how a once proud literary language, now sunk to a vernacular, could serve as the living language of an original, modern poetry. The second, and until the twentieth century the last, was Burns, who acknowledged his debt: "meeting with Fergusson's Scotch Poems, I strung anew my wildly-sounding rustic lyre with emulating vigour."

Not all of Burns's knowledge of vernacular literature came from printed pages. "I owed much," he recalled, "to an old Maid of my Mother's, remarkable for her ignorance, credulity and superstition.—She had, I suppose, the largest collection in the county of tales and songs concerning devils, ghosts, fairies, brownies, witches, warlocks, spunkies, kelpies, elf-candles, deadlights, wraiths, apparitions, cantraips, giants, inchanted towers, dragons and other trumpery.—This cultivated the latent seeds of Poesy." Nor were his literary sympathies confined to Scotland. All of his formal schooling and much of his reading was in English authors of the eighteenth century or in those writers admired by the eighteenth century. In *The Cotter's Saturday Night* alone one scholar had detected echoes of Gray, Goldsmith, Pope, Gay, Thomson, Milton, Shenstone, Beattie, Fergusson, Thomas Warton, Collins, Young, Rochester, Sterne, Shakespeare—and others. The Edinburgh intellectuals did not need to urge Burns to imitate Shenstone and Homer; the danger was that he would do so.

David Daiches has best summed up Burns's literary obligations and his cultural focus:

Burns only re-established contact with the Scots literary tradition by looking at it through the spectacles provided by folk-song and other kinds of popular art, and as a result the tradition as he uses it is a composite one, in which the satiric boisterousness of Lindsay's *Satyre of the Thrie Estaits*, the happy artifice of [Alexander] Montgomerie, the stark clarity of the ballads, the richness and warmth and earthiness of folk-song, the pious beat of Scottish psalmody, combine to produce a precarious but—while it lasted—a brilliant unity. It was Burns's predecessors who made that synthesis possible; it was his own genius that made it brilliant; it was the cultural context of his time that made it precarious.

The later eighteenth century had a passion, partly faddish and partly theoretical, for original, untaught genius. In 1787 Burns became the chief idol of this cult. Henry Mackenzie, the author of *The Man of Feeling* and a leading sentimentalist, while preferring Burns's "almost English" poems in "the grave style," hailed the "uncommon penetration and sagacity" with which "this heaven-taught ploughman, from his humble and unlettered station, has looked upon men and manners." Burns was sometimes willing to assume the role, although it was largely a false one and he knew it. Dr. Robert Anderson reported the following conversation with him:

It was, I know, a part of the machinery, as he called it, of his poetical character to pass for an illiterate ploughman who wrote from pure inspiration. When I pointed out some evident traces of poetical imitation in his verses, privately, he readily acknowledged his obligations, and even admitted the advantages he enjoyed in poetical composition from the *copia verborum*, the command of phraseology, which the knowledge and use of the English and Scottish dialects afforded him; but in company he did not suffer his pretensions to pure inspiration to be challenged, and it was seldom done where it might be supposed to affect the success of the subscription for his *Poems*.

The *Epistle to John Lepraik* gives a distinctly one-sided view of his art; it does not do justice to his "critic-craft."
The complexities of Burns's cultural tradition and the subtleties of his poetic role offer fewer obstacles than the difficulties of lan-

guage.* We can translate Burns into English, but we cannot catch the connotations of words, the levels and tone of language, or even the different kinds of language. Sometimes Burns writes in pure Scots, sometimes in pure, Augustan English that is meant to be read and pronounced as if written by an English author. The greater number of his poems and the best of them, however, are written in an organic blend of Scots and English, a compromise idiom which was one of his greatest achievements. The proportions of the two languages may vary, but the whole is linguistically unified by being pronounced with a Scottish accent.

Or Burns will alternate Scots and English—a kind of shift of key—at times to exploit the richer concreteness of Scots and the greater power of abstraction of English, at other times for ironic modulations. (Kurt Willig notes that "This linguistic stratification is curiously reminiscent of the different levels of style so characteristic of the poetry of the Makars, with its power of effortless transition from one to the other.") Scottish accent and pronunciation account for effects strange to the English ear. Scots has different vowel timbres, different intonation patterns, stronger consonants and accentuation, a firmer articulation due to fewer diphthongs, and some sounds unknown in English (the [ç] sound in li*ch*t, the [x] sound in lo*ch*, the tongue-tip trilled *r*). One has not heard Burns until he has heard Burns read or sung by a Scotsman.

While Burns was a Scotsman writing in Scots-English, he was not intellectually provincial. Although he was not an abstract or a deep thinker, his poetry as a whole does express certain basic themes and attitudes which were not confined to the British Isles or even to Europe. He was a passionate individualist. Avoiding the trap of sentimentality but sharing some of the tenets of eighteenth-century sentimentalism, he believed that the confusing complex of desire, instinct, emotion, and thought was basically good both as experience and as value. How could Love be separated from desire, or any abstract value from individual human feeling? "Feelings and sentiments," he wrote, are "original and component parts of the human soul"; he spoke not of mind and sense but of the *"senses of the mind."* He meant it when he wrote the lines which shocked so many:

---

* See glossary at the end of the selections.

> But yet the light that led astray
> Was light from Heaven.

He believed in right feeling and the good heart. From these premises, which must by definition be both felt and believed, most of his likes and dislikes follow: his faith in the sanctity of the individual human being and the free honest man, his trust in the bonds of affection and loyalty between a man and woman in love and between men in comradeship or political action, his hatred of men or forces who oppose these goods with repression or restraint.

Burns's political and social views are, as a contemporary said, "abundantly motley"; they tended to be emotional rather than reasoned. He could recognize the futility of the Stuart kings, while at the same time his contempt for the Hanoverian dynasty and his Scottish patriotism made him lament their exile like any sentimental Jacobite. He believed in liberty, equality, and fraternity, but *The Jolly Beggars* is the greatest hymn to freedom as anarchy that we have until Yeats took up the same figure. In his period Burns may be classed as a radical Whig. He admired the "able," "enlightened," and "honest" American Congress of 1776; he once toasted George Washington as a "better man" than William Pitt. His devotion to the ideals of the French Revolution is well known: *For A' That* was inspired by Paine's *Rights of Man*, and *Scots Wha Hae* concerns itself less with Scotland in 1314 than with Europe in 1793. Burns's Jacobin sympathies prompted an investigation into his reliability as a government officer in 1793, and to protect his livelihood and his family he was forced to recant. His own experience from first to last had taught him to hate the brutal alliance of money and power encased, more often than not, in unctuous self-righteousness.

Burns's religious convictions are usually known by their opposites, that is through his attacks on false and hypocritical religious attitudes as they manifest themselves in men and society. He rejected the fundamentalist Calvinism of the "Auld Licht," still powerful in the countryside, with its rigid moral discipline, its fear of all human instincts, the sensitive nose for others' sins of the flesh on the part of its Holy Willies and "holy beagles." His was a "Religion of Sentiment and Reason," and he sided with the "New Licht" party which, heavily influenced by the doctrines of Shaftesbury and Francis Hutcheson, took its stand on man's common, "moral sense" and dismissed original sin in favor of innate virtue. But Burns did not really belong to any religious sect. His was "an enthusiastic, incoherent Benevolence" shared by all the humanitarian deists of England, France, and America.

It is, of course, what Burns the poet did with his tradition, his language, and his beliefs that matters. The variety of forms and moods in which they found expression is astonishing. He renewed virtually every literary type that Scottish literature could provide: the satires, the mock elegies, the animal poems, the verse epistles, the tales of folklore, the descriptions and recreations of country life, the song.* He wrote narratively, lyrically, and dramatically; he encompassed a wide range of the poetic voice from passion to wit. The hallmark of all his best verse is his directness and immediacy, his skillful manipulation of language, style, and point of view in order to realize the here and now of human experience. In David Daiches' words, this was his "passionate acceptance of the reality and validity of the given situation." Burns does not recall experience, or even recapture it, but gives the illusion of reproducing it. No one else in his time could do this, except for Crabbe in his strictly narrative poems. Almost no one else tried.

Burns often thought about the nature of his own poetry, as his letters and journals show. Some of his statements have seemed romantic. Burns's "skinless sensibility" sounds Keatsian. "My Passions when once they were lighted up, raged like so many devils, till they got vent in rhyme; and then conning over my verses, like a spell, soothed all into quiet" sounds like Wordsworth's "Poetry is the spontaneous overflow of powerful feelings: it takes its origin from emotion recollected in tranquillity." But the two worlds are not the same. Burns knew nothing of the awful power of imagination or the transcendant vision.

---

* Burns's songs usually attract the English reader most strongly, for they constitute a genre in which the English tradition is weak. Burns wrote about 350 songs, three quarters of them love songs, the rest largely treating some facet of social life or voicing a patriotic or political sentiment. "Wrote" is perhaps the wrong term. Sometimes he merely transcribed a traditional song, or he altered an existing, integral text to improve it or to expurgate it. Some songs are based on and inspired by only the chorus or a few lines of an older text; others are mosaics of phrases gathered from several traditional sources. Some are entirely original. Burns always wrote to a pre-existing melody: "until I am complete master of a tune, in my own singing (such as it is), I never can compose for it. My way is: I consider the poetic Sentiment, correspondent to my idea of the musical expression, then choose my theme."

ADDRESS TO THE DEIL

*"O Prince! O chief of many thronèd powers
That led the embattled seraphim to war—"*
                                        MILTON

O thou! whatever title suit thee,
Auld Hornie, Satan, Nick, or Clootie,
Wha in yon cavern grim an' sootie,
    Closed under hatches,
Spairges about the brunstane cootie,
    To scaud poor wretches!

Hear me, auld Hangie, for a wee,
An' let poor damnèd bodies be;
I'm sure sma' pleasure it can gie,
    Ev'n to a deil,   10
To skelp an' scaud poor dogs like me,
    An' hear us squeal!

Great is thy pow'r, an' great thy fame;
Far kenned an' noted is thy name;
An', tho' yon lowin heugh's thy hame,
    Thou travels far;
An' faith! thou's neither lag nor lame,
    Nor blate nor scaur.

Whyles rangin' like a roarin' lion
For prey, a' holes an' corners tryin';   20

Address to the Deil: Burns always professed admiration for "the dauntless magnanimity, the intrepid unyielding independence, the desperate daring and noble defiance of hardship in that great personage, [Milton's] Satan." But the portrait in the *Address* is the devil of popular folklore and superstition, who is almost a friendly imp rather than Milton's grand character or the insidious tempter of hell-fire sermons.

Whyles on the strong-winged tempest flyin',
    Tirlin' the kirks;
Whyles, in the human bosom pryin',
    Unseen thou lurks.

I've heard my reverend grannie say,
In lanely glens ye like to stray;
Or, where auld ruined castles gray
    Nod to the moon,
Ye fright the nightly wand'rer's way,
    Wi' eldritch croon.

When twilight did my grannie summon
To say her pray'rs, douce, honest woman!
Aft yont the dyke she's heard you bummin',
    Wi' eerie drone;
Or, rustlin', thro' the boortrees comin',
    Wi' heavy groan.

Ae dreary windy winter night
The stars shot down wi' sklentin' light,
Wi' you mysel I gat a fright
    Ayont the lough;
Ye like a rash-buss stood in sight
    Wi' waving sough.

The cudgel in my nieve did shake,
Each bristled hair stood like a stake,
When wi' an eldritch stoor "quaick, quaick,"
    Amang the springs,
Awa ye squattered like a drake
    On whistlin' wings.

Let warlocks grim an' withered hags
Tell how wi' you on ragweed nags
They skim the muirs, an' dizzy crags
    Wi' wicked speed;
And in kirk-yards renew their leagues
    Owre howkit dead.

Thence country wives, wi' toil an' pain,
May plunge an' plunge the kirn in vain;
For oh! the yellow treasure's taen
    By witchin' skill;
An' dawtit twal-pint Hawkie's gane
    As yell's the bill.   60

Thence mystic knots mak great abuse
On young guidmen, fond, keen, an' crouse;
When the best wark-lume i' the house,
    By cantrip wit,
Is instant made no worth a louse,
    Just at the bit.

When thowes dissolve the snawy hoord,
An' float the jinglin' icy-boord,
Then water-kelpies haunt the foord,
    By your direction,   70
An' 'nighted trav'llers are allured
    To their destruction.

An' aft your moss-traversing spunkies
Decoy the wight that late an' drunk is:
The bleezin, curst, mischievous monkies
    Delude his eyes,
Till in some miry slough he sunk is,
    Ne'er mair to rise.

When masons' mystic word an' grip
In storms an' tempests raise you up,   80
Some cock or cat your rage maun stop,
    Or, strange to tell!
The youngest brither ye wad whip
    Aff straught to hell.

Lang syne, in Eden's bonnie yard,
When youthfu' lovers first were paired,
And all the soul of love they shared,
    The raptured hour,

Sweet on the fragrant flow'ry swaird,
    In shady bow'r;

Then you, ye auld snick-drawing dog!
Ye cam to Paradise incog.
An' played on man a cursèd brogue,
    (Black be your fa'!)
An' gied the infant warld a shog,
    'Maist ruined a'.

D'ye mind that day, when in a bizz,
Wi' reekit duds, an' reestit gizz,
Ye did present your smoutie phiz
    'Mang better folk,
An' sklented on the man of Uz
    Your spitefu' joke?

An' how ye gat him i' your thrall,
An' brak him out o' house an' hal',
While scabs an' blotches did him gall
    Wi' bitter claw,
An' lowsed his ill-tongued wicked scawl,
    Was warst ava?

But a' your doings to rehearse,
Your wily snares an' fechtin' fierce,
Sin' that day Michael did you pierce,
    Down to this time,
Wad ding a' Lallan tongue, or Erse,
    In prose or rhyme.

An' now, auld Cloots, I ken ye're thinkin',
A certain Bardie's rantin', drinkin',
Some luckless hour will send him linkin',
    To your black pit;
But faith! he'll turn a corner jinkin',
    An' cheat you yet.

But fare you weel, auld Nickie-ben!
O wad ye tak a thought an' men'!

Ye aiblins might—I dinna ken—
 Still hae a stake:
I'm wae to think upo' yon den,
 Ev'n for your sake!

EPISTLE TO JOHN LAPRAIK,
AN OLD SCOTTISH BARD

APRIL 1, 1785

While briers an' woodbines budding green,
An' paitricks scraichin' loud at e'en,
An' morning poussie whiddin' seen,
 Inspire my Muse,
This freedom, in an unknown frien',
 I pray excuse.

On Fasten-een we had a rockin',
To ca' the crack and weave our stockin';
And there was muckle fun and jokin',
 Ye need na doubt;   10
At length we had a hearty yokin'
 At sang about.

There was ae sang, amang the rest,
Aboon them a' it pleased me best,
That some kind husband had addrest
 To some sweet wife:
It thirl'd the heart-strings thro' the breast,
 A' to the life.

I've scarce heard ought described sae weel,
What gen'rous, manly bosoms feel;   20
Thought I "Can this be Pope, or Steele,
 Or Beattie's wark?"

Epistle to John Lapraik: John Lapraik (1727-1807) was an untaught rustic poet whose poem, perhaps plagiarized, *When I upon Thy Bosom Lean,* had caught Burns's eye. The *Epistle* is written in the Standard Habbie measure, a favorite with Burns: aaa$_4$b$_2$a$_4$b$_2$.

They tauld me 'twas an odd kind chiel
    About Muirkirk.

It pat me fidgin' fain to hear't,
And sae about him there I spiered;
Then a' that kenned him round declared
    He had ingine,
That nane excelled it, few cam near't,
    It was sae fine.   30

That, set him to a pint of ale,
An' either douce or merry tale,
Or rhymes an' sangs he'd made himsel,
    Or witty catches,
'Tween Inverness and Teviotdale,
    He had few matches.

Then up I gat, an' swoor an aith,
Tho' I should pawn my pleugh and graith,
Or die a cadger pownie's death,
    At some dyke-back,   40
A pint an' gill I'd gie them baith
    To hear your crack.

But, first an' foremost, I should tell,
Amaist as soon as I could spell,
I to the crambo-jingle fell;
    Tho' rude an' rough,
Yet crooning to a body's sel,
    Does weel eneugh.

I am nae poet, in a sense,
But just a rhymer, like, by chance,   50
An' hae to learning nae pretence,
    Yet what the matter?
Whene'er my Muse does on me glance,
    I jingle at her.

Your critic-folk may cock their nose,
And say "How can you e'er propose,

You wha ken hardly verse frae prose,
    To mak a sang?"
But, by your leaves, my learnèd foes,
    Ye're maybe wrang.

What's a' your jargon o' your schools,
Your Latin names for horns an' stools;
If honest nature made you fools,
    What sairs your grammars?
Ye'd better ta'en up spades and shools,
    Or knappin'-hammers.

A set o' dull conceited hashes
Confuse their brains in college classes!
They gang in stirks, and come out asses,
    Plain truth to speak;
An' syne they think to climb Parnassus
    By dint o' Greek!

Gie me ae spark o' Nature's fire,
That's a' the learning I desire;
Then tho' I drudge thro' dub an' mire
    At pleugh or cart,
My Muse, though hamely in attire,
    May touch the heart.

O for a spunk o' Allan's glee,
Or Fergusson's, the bauld an' slee,
Or bright Lapraik's, my friend to be,
    If I can hit it!
That would be lear eneugh for me,
    If I could get it.

Now, sir, if ye hae friends enow,
Tho' real friends, I b'lieve, are few,
Yet, if your catalogue be fou,
    I'se no insist,
But gif ye want ae friend that's true,
    I'm on your list.

---

l.79. Allan: Allan Ramsay.

I winna blaw about mysel,
As ill I like my fauts to tell;
But friends, an' folks that wish me well,
    They sometimes roose me;
Tho' I maun own, as mony still
    As far abuse me.

There's ae wee faut they whiles lay to me,
I like the lasses—Gude forgie me!
For mony a plack they wheedle frae me,
    At dance or fair;   100
Maybe some ither thing they gie me
    They weel can spare.

But Mauchline race, or Mauchline fair,
I should be proud to meet you there;
We'se gie ae night's discharge to care,
    If we forgather,
An' hae a swap o' rhymin'-ware
    Wi' ane anither.

The four-gill chap, we'se gar him clatter,
An' kirsen him wi' reekin water;   110
Syne we'll sit down an' tak our whitter,
    To cheer our heart;
An' faith, we'se be acquainted better
    Before we part.

Awa, ye selfish warly race,
Wha think that havins, sense, an' grace,
Ev'n love an' friendship, should give place
    To catch-the-plack!
I dinna like to see your face,
    Nor hear your crack.   120

But ye whom social pleasure charms,
Whose hearts the tide of kindness warms,
Who hold your being on the terms,
    "Each aid the others,"
Come to my bowl, come to my arms,
    My friends, my brothers!

But to conclude my lang epistle,
As my auld pen's worn to the gristle;
Twa lines frae you wad gar me fissle,
　　Who am, most fervent,
While I can either sing, or whistle,
　　Your friend and servant.

HOLY WILLIE'S PRAYER

"And send the godly in a pet to pray."
                                POPE

O Thou, wha in the Heavens dost dwell,
Wha, as it pleases best thysel',
Sends ane to heaven and ten to hell,
    A' for thy glory,
And no for ony guid or ill
    They've done afore thee!

I bless and praise thy matchless might,
Whan thousands thou hast left in night,
That I am here afore thy sight,
    For gifts an' grace   10
A burnin' an' a shinin' light,
    To a' this place.

Holy Willie's Prayer: A dramatic monologue through which Willie, an "Auld Licht" Calvinist, stands revealed not so much as a natural hypocrite as a hypocrite by consequence of his beliefs. He is not an imaginary character. Burns himself explained: "Holy Willie was a rather oldish bachelor elder, in the parish of Mauchline, and much and justly famed for that polemical chattering, which ends in tippling orthodoxy, and for that spiritualized bawdry which refines to liquorish devotion. In a sessional process with a gentleman in Mauchline—a Mr. Gavin Hamilton [l.67]—Holy Willie and his priest, Fauther Auld [l.89], after full hearing in the presbytery of Ayr, came off but second best; owing partly to the oratorical powers of Mr. Robert Aiken [l.85], Mr. Hamilton's counsel; but chiefly to Mr. Hamilton's being one of the most irreproachable and truly respectable characters in the county. On losing his process, the muse overheard [Holy Willie] at his devotions." Hamilton and Aiken, both friends of Burns, adhered to the more liberal "New Licht." In the "sessional process" Hamilton was under threat of excommunication for missing church five times, traveling on Sunday, and having potatoes dug on Sunday (ll.77-78). The poem was not published by Burns in his lifetime. It is written in the Standard Habbie measure.

What was I, or my generation,
That I should get sic exaltation?
I, wha deserve most just damnation,
    For broken laws,
Sax thousand years 'fore my creation,
    Thro' Adam's cause.

When frae my mither's womb I fell,
Thou might hae plungèd me in hell,
To gnash my gums, to weep and wail,
    In burnin' lakes,
Where damnèd devils roar and yell,
    Chained to their stakes;

Yet I am here a chosen sample,
To show thy grace is great and ample;
I'm here a pillar in thy temple,
    Strong as a rock,
A guide, a buckler, an example
    To a' thy flock.

O Lord, thou kens what zeal I bear,
When drinkers drink, and swearers swear,
And singin' there and dancin' here,
    Wi' great an' sma';
For I am keepit by thy fear
    Free frae them a'.

But yet, O Lord! confess I must
At times I'm fashed wi' fleshy lust;
An' sometimes too, in warldly trust,
    Vile self gets in;
But thou remembers we are dust,
    Defiled in sin.

O Lord! yestreen, thou kens, wi' Meg—
Thy pardon I sincerely beg;
O! may't ne'er be a livin' plague
    To my dishonour,
An' I'll ne'er lift a lawless leg
    Again upon her.

Besides I farther maun allow,
Wi' Lizzie's lass, three times I trow—
But, Lord, that Friday I was fou,
    When I cam near her,
Or else thou kens thy servant true
    Wad never steer her.

May be thou lets this fleshly thorn
Beset thy servant e'en and morn
Lest he owre high and proud should turn,
    That he's sae gifted;
If sae, thy hand maun e'en be borne,
    Until thou lift it.

Lord, bless thy chosen in this place,
For here thou hast a chosen race;
But God confound their stubborn face,
    And blast their name,
Wha bring thy elders to disgrace
    An' public shame.

Lord, mind Gawn Hamilton's deserts,
He drinks, an' swears, an' plays at cartes,
Yet has sae mony takin' arts
    Wi' grit an' sma',
Frae God's ain priest the people's hearts
    He steals awa'.

An' when we chastened him therefor,
Thou kens how he bred sic a splore
As set the warld in a roar
    O' laughin' at us;
Curse thou his basket and his store,
    Kail and potatoes.

Lord, hear my earnest cry an' pray'r,
Against that presbyt'ry o' Ayr;
Thy strong right hand, Lord, make it bare
    Upo' their heads;
Lord, weigh it down, and dinna spare,
    For their misdeeds.

O Lord my God, that glib-tongued Aiken,
My very heart and soul are quakin',
To think how we stood sweatin', shakin',
   An pissed wi' dread,
While he, wi' hingin' lips and snakin',
   Held up his head.   90

Lord, in the day of vengeance try him;
Lord, visit them wha did employ him,
And pass not in thy mercy by them,
   Nor hear their pray'r;
But, for thy people's sake, destroy them,
   And dinna spare.

But, Lord, remember me and mine
Wi' mercies temp'ral and divine,
That I for gear and grace may shine
   Excelled by nane,   100
And a' the glory shall be thine,
   Amen, Amen!

ADDRESS TO THE UNCO GUID, OR THE RIGIDLY RIGHTEOUS

O Ye wha are sae guid yoursel,
    Sae pious and sae holy,
Ye've nought to do but mark and tell
    Your neibour's fauts and folly!
Whase life is like a weel-gaun mill,
    Supplied wi' store o' water;
The heapèd happer's ebbing still,
    And still the clap plays clatter.

Hear me, ye venerable core,
    As counsel for poor mortals,   10
That frequent pass douce Wisdom's door,
    For glaikit Folly's portals;
I, for their thoughtless careless sakes,
    Would here propone defences—
Their donsie tricks, their black mistakes,
    Their failings and mischances.

Ye see your state wi' their's compared,
    And shudder at the niffer;
But cast a moment's fair regard—
    What maks the mighty differ?   20
Discount what scant occasion gave,
    That purity ye pride in;
And (what's aft mair than a' the lave)
    Your better art o' hidin'.

Think, when your castigated pulse
    Gies now and then a wallop!

What ragings must his veins convulse,
   That still eternal gallop!
Wi' wind and tide fair i' your tail,
   Right on ye scud your sea-way;
But in the teeth o' baith to sail,
   It maks an unco leeway.

See Social Life and Glee sit down,
   All joyous and unthinking,
Till, quite transmogrified, they're grown
   Debauchery and Drinking:
O would they stay to calculate
   Th' eternal consequences;
Or your more dreaded hell to state,
   Damnation of expenses!

Ye high, exalted, virtuous Dames,
   Tied up in godly laces,
Before ye gie poor Frailty names,
   Suppose a change o' cases;
A dear loved lad, convenience snug,
   A treacherous inclination—
But, let me whisper i' your lug,
   Ye're aiblins nae temptation.

Then gently scan your brother man,
   Still gentler sister woman;
Tho' they may gang a kennin wrang,
   To step aside is human.
One point must still be greatly dark,
   The moving *why* they do it;
And just as lamely can ye mark
   How far perhaps they rue it.

Who made the heart, 'tis He alone
   Decidedly can try us;
He knows each chord, its various tone,
   Each spring, its various bias.
Then at the balance let's be mute,
   We never can adjust it;
What's done we partly may compute,
   But know not what's resisted.

GREEN GROW THE RASHES

CHORUS

Green grow the rashes O,
Green grow the rashes O;
The sweetest hours that e'er I spend,
Are spent amang the lasses O!

There's nought but care on ev'ry han',
    In ev'ry hour that passes O;
What signifies the life o' man,
    An' 'twere na for the lasses O.

The warly race may riches chase,
    An' riches still may fly them O; 10
An' tho' at last they catch them fast,
    Their hearts can ne'er enjoy them O.

But gie me a canny hour at e'en,
    My arms about my dearie O;
An' warly cares, an' warly men,
    May a' gae tapsalteerie O!

For you sae douce, ye sneer at this;
    Ye're nought but senseless asses O;
The wisest man the warl' e'er saw,
    He dearly loved the lasses O. 20

Auld nature swears, the lovely dears
    Her noblest work she classes O;
Her prentice han' she tried on man,
    An' then she made the lasses O.

Green Grow the Rashes: Set to an old tune of the same name. The traditional versions of the lyrics are bawdy.

JOHN ANDERSON MY JO

John Anderson my jo, John,
    When we were first acquent,
Your locks were like the raven,
    Your bonnie brow was brent;
But now your brow is beld, John,
    Your locks are like the snaw;
But blessings on your frosty pow,
    John Anderson, my jo.

John Anderson my jo, John,
    We clamb the hill thegither;
And mony a canty day, John,
    We've had wi' ane anither:
Now we maun totter down, John,
    And hand in hand we'll go,
And sleep thegither at the foot,
    John Anderson, my jo.

John Anderson My Jo: Adapted from an old bawdy song of the same title, tune, and stanzaic form. Burns has retained only the first line.

AULD LANG SYNE

Should auld acquaintance be forgot,
   And never brought to mind?
Should auld acquaintance be forgot,
   And auld lang syne?

CHORUS

For auld lang syne, my dear,
   For auld lang syne,
We'll tak a cup o' kindness yet,
   For auld lang syne.

We twa hae run about the braes,
   And pu'd the gowans fine;
But we've wandered mony a weary foot
   Sin' auld lang syne.

We twa hae paidled i' the burn,
   From morning sun till dine;
But seas between us braid hae roared
   Sin' auld lang syne.

And there's a hand, my trusty fiere,
   And gie's a hand o' thine;
And we'll tak a right guid-willie waught,
   For auld lang syne.

And surely ye'll be your pint-stowp,
   And surely I'll be mine;
And we'll tak a cup o' kindness yet
   For auld lang syne.

Auld Lang Syne: Set to a tune of the same name. Burns never claimed the authorship of this song, but it is undoubtedly his reworking of several earlier versions.

A MAN'S A MAN FOR A' THAT

Is there, for honest poverty
 That hings his head, and a' that?
The coward-slave, we pass him by;
 We dare be poor for a' that!
  For a' that, and a' that,
   Our toils obscure, and a' that;
  The rank is but the guinea's stamp;
   The man's the gowd for a' that.

What tho' on hamely fare we dine,
 Wear hoddin-gray, and a' that; 10
Gie fools their silks, and knaves their wine,
 A man's a man for a' that.
  For a' that, and a' that,
   Their tinsel show, and a' that;
  The honest man, tho' e'er sae poor,
   Is king o' men for a' that.

Ye see yon birkie, ca'd a lord,
 Wha struts, and stares, and a' that;
Tho' hundreds worship at his word,
 He's but a coof for a' that. 20
  For a' that, and a' that,
   His riband, star, and a' that;
  The man of independent mind,
   He looks and laughs at a' that.

A prince can mak a belted knight,
 A marquis, duke, and a' that;

A Man's a Man for A' That: To the tune of *For A' That.* Earlier traditional lyrics to the same tune belong both to popular bawdry and to Jacobite sentiment.

… But an honest man's aboon his might,
  Guid faith he mauna fa' that!
    For a' that, and a' that,
      Their dignities, and a' that;
    The pith o' sense, and pride o' worth,
      Are higher rank than a' that.

Then let us pray that come it may,
  As come it will for a' that;
That sense and worth, o'er a' the earth,
  Shall bear the gree, and a' that.
    For a' that and a' that,
      It's coming yet, for a' that,
    That man to man the world o'er
      Shall brothers be for a' that.

SCOTS WHA HAE

ROBERT BRUCE'S ADDRESS TO HIS ARMY BEFORE
THE BATTLE OF BANNOCKBURN

Scots, wha hae wi' Wallace bled,
Scots, wham Bruce has aften led,
Welcome to your gory bed,
    Or to victorie!

Now's the day, and now's the hour;
See the front o' battle lour!
See approach proud Edward's power—
    Chains and slaverie!

Wha will be a traitor knave?
Wha can fill a coward's grave?   10
Wha sae base as be a slave?
    Let him turn and flee!

Wha for Scotland's King and law
Freedom's sword will strongly draw,
Freeman stand, or freeman fa'?
    Let him follow me!

By Oppression's woes and pains,
By your sons in servile chains,
We will drain our dearest veins,
    But they shall be free!   20

Scots Wha Hae: To the tune of *Hey, Tutti Taitie,* supposedly Bruce's march at the battle of Bannockburn, where he defeated the English in 1314. Burns admitted the contemporary relevance (1793) of the poem: "the accidental recollection of that glorious struggle for Freedom, associated with the glowing ideas of some other struggles of the same nature, *not quite so ancient,* roused my rhyming mania."

Lay the proud usurpers low!
Tyrants fall in every foe!
Liberty's in every blow!
  Let us do or die!

O, WERT THOU IN THE CAULD BLAST

O, wert thou in the cauld blast,
    On yonder lea, on yonder lea,
My plaidie to the angry airt,
    I'd shelter thee, I'd shelter thee.
Or did misfortune's bitter storms
    Around thee blaw, around thee blaw,
Thy bield should be my bosom,
    To share it a', to share it a'.

Or were I in the wildest waste,
    Sae black and bare, sae black and bare,
The desert were a paradise,
    If thou wert there, if thou wert there.
Or were I monarch o' the globe,
    Wi' thee to reign, wi' thee to reign,
The brightest jewel in my crown
    Wad be my queen, wad be my queen.

GLOSSARY

aboon, above
aiblins, perhaps
airt, direction
ava, at all, of all
ayont, beyond

bauld, bold
be, stand (a drink)
beld, bald

bield, shelter
bill, bull
birkie, conceited fellow
bit, nick of time
bizz, flurry
blate, shy
bleeze, blaze
boord, board, surface
boortrees, shrub-elder

O, *Wert Thou in the Cauld Blast:* Written a few weeks before Burns's death, addressed to Jessie Lewars, the young sister of one of Burns's fellow excisemen, who nursed him in his last illness. It is set to the tune of *Lenox Love to Blantyre,* her favorite air.

Glossary

brent, straight
brogue, trick
bum, hum
burn, brook

ca' the crack, have a chat
cadger, hawker
cantrip, magic
canty, lively, merry
catch-the-plack, hunt for coin
chiel, fellow
clatter, rattle
coof, dolt
cootie, wooden dish
core, corps
crack, tale, talk
crambo-jingle, rhyming
crouse, cocksure

dawtit, fondled, petted
ding, beat, surpass
donsie, unlucky
douce, sedate, sober, prudent
dub, puddle
dyke-back, back of a fence

eldritch, unearthly
Erse, Gaelic

fa', lot, portion; claim; fall
fash, to trouble oneself
Fasten-e'en, evening before Lent
fecht, fight
fiere, comrade
fissle, tingle
fitt, foot
fou, full, drunk

gar, cause, make
gear, wealth
gizz, wig
glaikit, foolish, giddy
gowd, gold
graith, furniture
gree, prize
guid-willie, full of goodwill

happer, hopper
hash, oaf
havins, good manners
hawkie, cow
heugh, pit

hoddin-grey, coarse grey woollen
howk, disinter

ingine, genius, ingenuity

jink, dodge, dart about
jo, sweetheart

kennin, a very little
kirn, churn
kirsen, christen
knappin-hammer, hammer for breaking stone

lag, slow
Lallan, Lowland
lave, the rest
lear, lore, learning
link, trip along, hurry
lough, lake
lowin, flaming
lowse, loose, untie
lug, ear

men', mend

nieve, fist
niffer, exchange

paitrick, partridge
pint-stowp, a two-quart drinking vessel
plack, four pennies
poussie, hare
pow, head
pownie, pony
propone, propose
pu', pull

rash-buss, clump of rushes
reekit, smoked, smoky
reestit, singed
rockin, party
roose, praise, flatter

sair, serve
scaur, timid
scawl, scold
shog, shake
shool, shovel
skelp, slap, strike
sklent, slant

slee, sly, ingenious
snakin, sneering
sough, moan
spier, ask
splore, row, disturbance
spunk, spark
spunkie, will-o'-the-wisp
steer, meddle with, molest
stirk, heifer
stoor, hoarse
syne, since, then, ago

tapsalteerie, topsy-turvy
tirl, knock for entrance at

unco, remarkably, uncommonly, very

wae, woeful, sorrowful
wark-lume, tool
warlock, wizard
warly, worldly
waught, deep draught
weel-gaun, well-going
whiddin, scurrying
whitter, draught

yell, dry (milkless)
yokin, yoking, set-to
yont, beyond

Selected Bibliographies

ABBREVIATIONS:
ELH: A Journal of English Literary History
JEGP: Journal of English and Germanic Philology
JHI: Journal of the History of Ideas
MLN: Modern Language Notes
MLQ: Modern Language Quarterly
MP: Modern Philology
N&Q: Notes and Queries
PMLA: Publications of the Modern Language Association
PQ: Philological Quarterly
RES: The Review of English Studies
SP: Studies in Philology
TLS: The Times Literary Supplement

GENERAL WORKS

The Age of Johnson: Essays Presented to Chauncey Brewster Tinker (New Haven: Yale University Press; 1949); B. S. Allen, *Tides in English Taste* (1619-1800): *A Background for the Study of Literature*, 2 vols. (Cambridge: Harvard University Press; 1937); W. J. Bate, *From Classic to Romantic: Premises of Taste in Eighteenth-Century England* (Cambridge: Harvard University Press; 1946); W. C. Brown, *The Triumph of Form: A Study of the Later Masters of the Heroic Couplet* (Chapel Hill: University of North Carolina Press; 1948); John Butt, *The Augustan Age* (Hutchinson's University Library. London: Hutchinson House; 1950); C. F. Chapin, *Personification in Eighteenth-Century English Poetry* (New York: King's Crown Press, Columbia University; 1955); C. V. Deane, *Aspects of Eighteenth Century Nature Poetry* (Oxford: Basil Blackwell; 1935); D.L. Durling, *Georgic Tradition in English Poetry* (New York: Columbia University Press; 1935); Oliver Elton, *A Survey of English Literature 1730-1780*, 2 vols. (London: E. Arnold & Co.; 1928), and *A Survey of English Literature 1780-1830*, 2 vols. (London: E. Arnold & Co.; 1912); Boris Ford, ed., *From Dryden to Johnson* (Pelican Guide to English Litera-

ture, vol. iv. Harmondsworth: Penguin Books Ltd.; 1957); Paul Fussell, Jr., *Theory of Prosody in Eighteenth-Century England, Connecticut College Monograph*, No. 5 (New London: Connecticut College; 1954); Francis Gallaway, *Reason, Rule, and Revolt in English Classicism* (New York: Charles Scribners' Sons; 1940); J. H. Hagstrum, *The Sister Arts: The Tradition of Literary Pictorialism and English Poetry from Dryden to Gray* (Chicago: University of Chicago Press; 1958); W. J. Hipple, Jr., *The Beautiful, The Sublime, & The Picturesque in Eighteenth-Century British Aesthetic Theory* (Carbondale: Southern Illinois University Press; 1957); F. R. Leavis, "English Poetry in the Eighteenth Century," *Scrutiny*, V (1937); Norman MacLean, "From Action to Image: Theories of the Lyric in the Eighteenth Century," in *Critics and Criticism: Ancient and Modern*, R. S. Crane, ed. (Chicago: University of Chicago Press; 1952); J. A. Mazzeo, ed., *Reason and Imagination: Studies in the History of Ideas 1600-1800* (New York: Columbia University Press; 1962); Josephine Miles, *Eras and Modes in English Poetry* (Berkeley and Los Angeles: University of California Press; 1957); George Sherburn, *The Restoration and Eighteenth Century* (1660-1789) (*A Literary History of England*, vol. iii. New York: Appleton-Century-Crofts, Inc.; 1948); J. R. Sutherland, *A Preface to Eighteenth Century Poetry* (Oxford: At the Clarendon Press; 1948); Wylie Sypher, *Rococo to Cubism in Art and Literature* (New York: Random House; 1960); E. L. Tuveson, *The Imagination as a Means of Grace: Locke and the Aesthetics of Romanticism* (Berkeley and Los Angeles: University of California Press; 1960). In connection with the scholars and critics mentioned in §5 of the Introduction, the following items should also be noted: John Arthos, *The Language of Natural Description in Eighteenth-Century Poetry* (Ann Arbor: The University of Michigan Press; 1949); B. H. Bronson, "Personification Reconsidered," *ELH*, XIV (1947); Marjorie H. Nicolson, *Newton Demands the Muse: Newton's "Optics" and the Eighteenth-Century Poets* (Princeton: Princeton University Press; 1946), and *Mountain Gloom and Mountain Glory: The Development of the Aesthetics of the Infinite* (Ithaca, N.Y.: Cornell University Press; 1959); Geoffrey Tillotson, *Augustan Studies* (London: University of London, Athlone Press; 1961); E. R. Wasserman, "The Inherent Values of Eighteenth-Century Personification," *PMLA*, LXV (1950).*

MARK AKENSIDE

I. A. Williams includes a bibliography in *Seven Eighteenth-Century Bibliographies* (London: Dulau & Company, Ltd.; 1924). The most complete edition is *The Poetical Works of M. A.* (ed. A. Dyce, "Aldine

---

* Mr. D. F. Foxon of the British Museum has in hand a *Bibliographical Catalogue of Separately Published English Poems (1701-1750)*.

Poets," 1835). The only modern, full-length study is by C. T. Houpt, M. A.: *A Biographical and Critical Study* (Philadelphia, 1944). Helpful articles are: W. L. Benwick, "A. and Others," *Durham Univ. Journal, New Series*, III (1942); A. O. Aldridge, "The Eclecticism of *The P. of I.*," *JHI*, V (1944), and "A. and Imagination," *SP*, XLII (1945); M. Kallich, "The Association of Ideas and A.'s *P. of I.*," *MLN*, LXII (1947); R. Marsh, "A and Addison: The Problem of Ideational Debt," *MP*, LIX (1961).

JAMES BEATTIE

Text (there is no modern edition): *The Poetical Works*, Alexander Dyce, ed. (Aldine Edition. London: William Pickering; 1831, etc.). Biographical, historical, and critical studies: E. A. Aldrich, "James Beattie's *Minstrel*: Its Sources and Influence . . . ," *Harvard . . . Summary of Theses* 1928 (Cambridge: Harvard University Press; 1931); Margaret Forbes, *Beattie and His Friends* (London: Archibald Constable & Co., Ltd.; 1904); William Forbes, *An Account of the Life and Writings of James Beattie*, 2 vols. (Edinburgh: Longman, 1806); E. C. Mossner, "Beattie's 'The Castle of Scepticism': An Unpublished Allegory against Hume, Voltaire and Hobbes," *Texas Studies in English*, XXVII (1948), and "Beattie on Voltaire: An Unpublished Parody," *Romanic Review*, XLI (1950); R. S. Walker, ed., *James Beattie's London Diary* 1773 (Aberdeen: Aberdeen University Press; 1946).

ROBERT BLAIR

Text (there is no modern edition): *The Political Works of Beattie, Blair, and Falconer*, George Gilfillan, ed. (Edinburgh: James Nichols; 1854). The famous Blake illustrations were published in 1808; there are several facsimile reproductions, e.g., *Twelve Designs for "The Grave"* . . . (New York: The Phoenix Press; 1926). Biography and criticism: Robert Anderson, ed., *The Poets of Great Britain*, 13 vols. (London: John and Arthur Arch; 1794-95); W. A. Drake, "A Note on Robert Blair," *The Freeman*, VIII (6 Feb. 1924).

WILLIAM BLAKE

G. L. Keynes, *A Bibliography of W. B.* (New York: The Grolier Club of New York; 1921). Definitive text: *Complete Writings of W. B. with All the Variant Readings*, G. L. Keynes, ed. (London: Nonesuch Press-New York: Random House; 1957). Standard life by Mona Wilson, *The Life of W. B.* (Rev. ed. London: R. Hart-Davis; 1948). Among the more recent studies are: S. Foster Damon, *W. B.: His*

Philosophy and Symbols (Boston and New York: Houghton Mifflin Co.; 1924. rptd. Gloucester, Mass.: Peter Smith; 1958); H. C. White, *The Mysticism of W. B.* (Univ. of Wisconsin Studies in Language and Literature, No. 23. Madison: The University of Wisconsin; 1927); J. Bronowski, *W. B., 1757-1827; A Man Without A Mask* (London: Secker & Warburg; 1944. rpt. Pelican Books. Harmondsworth, Middlesex: Penguin Books Ltd.; 1954); Mark Schorer, W. B.; *The Politics of Vision* (New York; Henry Holt and Company; 1946); Northrop Frye, *Fearful Symmetry* (Princeton: Princeton University Press; 1947); J. G. Davies, *The Theology of W. B.* (Oxford: Clarendon Press; 1948); B. Blackstone, *English Blake* (Cambridge: Cambridge University Press; 1949); Kathleen Raine, *W.B.* (London: The British Council and the National Book League, Longmans, Green & Co.; 1951); D. V. Erdman, B., *Prophet against Empire; A Poet's Interpretation of the History of His Own Times* (Princeton: Princeton University Press; 1954); G. F. Wingfield Digny, *Symbol and Image in W. B.* (Oxford: The Clarendon Press; 1957); R. F. Gleckner, *The Piper and the Bard* (Detroit: Wayne State University Press; 1959). A useful collection of critical essays will be found in *Discussions of W. B.*, ed. J. E. Grant (Discussions of Literature. Boston: D. C. Heath and Company; 1961). Commentary on *Songs of I. and E.* will be found in J. H. Wicksteed, *Blake's I. and E.* (London & Toronto: J. M. Dent & Sons, Ltd., New York: E. P. Dutton & Co.; 1928); F. W. Bateson, *Selected Poems of W. B.* (New York: The Macmillan Company; 1957); Kathleen Raine, "The Little Girl Lost and Found and The Lapsed Soul," in *The Divine Vision. Studies in the Poetry and Art of W. B.*, V. De S. Pinto, ed. (London: Victor Gollancz Ltd.; 1957); and R. F. Gleckner, *The Piper and the Bard* (1959). More recent items are: D. A. Dike, "The Difficult Innocence: Blake's Songs and Pastorals," *ELH*, XXVIII (1961); P. F. Fisher, Northrop Frye, ed., *The Valley of Vision. B. as Prophet and Revolutionary* (Toronto: The University of Toronto Press; 1961); E. D. Hirsch, Jr., "The Two Blakes," *RES*, new series, XII (1961). In *Blake's Apocalypse: A Study in Poetic Argument* (Garden City, N. Y.: Doubleday & Co., Inc.; 1963) Harold Bloom discusses the *Songs of I.*, particularly "The Little Black Boy," in chap. V; and the *Songs of E.*, particularly "The Tiger," in chap. VII.

ROBERT BURNS

Bibliography: *Catalogue of Robert Burns Collection in The Mitchell Library, Glasgow* (Glasgow: Glasgow Corporation Public Libraries; 1959). Texts: *The Poetry*, W. E. Henley and T. E. Henderson, eds., 4 vols. (London and Edinburgh: T. C. and E. C. Jack; 1896-97); *The Poetical Works*, J. L. Robertson, ed. (Oxford Standard Authors. London: Oxford University Press, Humphrey Milford; 1904, etc.); *The Songs*, J. C. Dick, ed. (London: Henry Frowde; 1903) contains the music as well as careful texts and notes; J. C. Dick, *Notes on Scottish Song* (London: Henry Frowde; 1908); *Poems and Songs*, James Barke, ed. (London: Collins; 1955); *The Merry Muses of Caledonia* (the bawdry), James Barke and S. G. Smith, eds. (Edinburgh: M. Macdonald; 1959). *The Letters*, J. D. Ferguson, ed., 2 vols. (Oxford: At the Clarendon Press; 1931). There are numerous selected editions of the poems and songs. Of the many biographical and critical studies the following are noteworthy: Thomas Crawford, *Burns: A Study of the Poems and Songs* (Edinburgh and London: Oliver & Boyd; 1960); David Daiches, *Robert Burns* (New York: Rinehart & Company; 1950); and *Robert Burns* (Writers and Their Work, No. 88. London: for the British Council and The National Book League, Longmans, Green & Co.; 1957); J. D. Ferguson, *Pride and Passion: Robert Burns, 1759-1796* (New York: Oxford University Press; 1939); Hans Hecht, *Robert Burns: The Man and His Work*, trans. Jane Lymburn, 2nd ed. (London, Edinburgh, Glasgow: William Hodge & Company, Ltd.; 1950); Hugh MacDiarmid, *Burns Today and Tomorrow* (Edinburgh: Castle Wynd Printers; 1959); A. D. McKillop, "The Living Burns," *The Rice Institute Pamphlet*, XLVII, No. 3 (1960); William Montgomerie, et al., *New Judgments: Robert Burns* . . . (Glasgow: William MacLellan; 1947); *Early Critical Reviews on Robert Burns*, J. D. Ross, ed. (Glasgow and Edinburgh: William Hodge & Company; 1900); F. B. Snyder, *The Life of Robert Burns* (New York: The Macmillan Company; 1932). Useful for background and reference are: W. B. Campbell, *A Burns' Companion* (Aberdeen: James Blair Printers Limited; 1953); *Scottish Poetry: A Critical Survey*, James Kinsley, ed. (London: Cassell & Co., Ltd.; 1955); J. M. Lindsay, *The Burns Encyclopaedia* (London: Hutchinson of London; 1959); James Wilson, *The Dialect of Robert Burns* . . . (London: Oxford University Press, Humphrey Milford; 1923); Kurt Wittig, *The Scottish Tradition in Literature* (Edinburgh and London: Oliver & Boyd; 1958). J. C. Dick's two valuable editions of the songs have been recently reissued, with additional material by Davidson Cook and H. G. Farmer (Hatbore, Pa.: Folklore Associates, 1962.)

THOMAS CHATTERTON

Bibliography: F. A. Hyett and William Bazeley, *The Bibliographer's Manual of Gloucestershire Literature*, 3 vols. (Gloucester: J. Bellows; 1895-97). Texts: *The Works*, Robert Southey and Joseph Cottle, eds., 3 vols. (London: Biggs and Cottle for T. N. Longman and V. Rees; 1803); *The Poems*, Sidney Lee, ed., 2 vols. (London: Methuen's Standard Library, 1906-09); *The Rowley Poems . . . Reprinted from Tyrwhitt's Third Edition*, M. E. Hare, ed. (Oxford: At the Clarendon Press; 1911). Modernized texts: *The Poetical Works*, W. W. Skeat, ed., 2 vols. (Aldine Edition. London: George Bell and Sons; 1871, etc.); *The Complete Poetical Works,* H. D. Roberts, ed., 2 vols. (Muses' Library. London: G. Routledge & Sons, Ltd.; 1906). All previous biographical and historical scholarship is subsumed in and replaced by E. H. W. Meyerstein, *A Life of Thomas Chatterton* (London: Ingpen & Grant; 1930). Other useful studies: B. H. Bronson, "Chattertoniana," *MLQ,* XI (1950), and "Thomas Chatterton," in *The Age of Johnson* (New Haven: Yale University Press; 1949); *Browning's Essay on Chatterton,* Donald Smalley, ed. (Cambridge: Harvard University Press; 1948); W. M. Dixon, "Chatterton," *Proceedings of the British Academy* 1930 (London: for The British Academy by Humphrey Milford, Oxford University Press; 1932); E. P. Ellinger, *Thomas Chatterton: The Marvellous Boy . . .* (Philadelphia: University of Pennsylvania Press; 1930); M. G. Lund, "The Sources of Chatterton's Genius," *University of Kansas City Review,* XXV (1959); E. H. W. Meyerstein, "Chatterton: His Significance Today," *Essays by Divers Hands: Transactions of the Royal Society of Literature,* n. s. XVI (London: Humphrey Milford, Oxford University Press; 1937); F. S. Miller, "The Historic Sense of Thomas Chatterton," *ELH,* XI (1944); L. F. Powell, "Thomas Tyrwhitt and the Rowley Poems," *RES,* VII (1931); Wylie Sypher, "Chatterton's African Eclogues and the Deluge," *PMLA,* LIV (1939); A. Watkin-Jones, "Bishop Percy, Thomas Warton, and Chatterton's Rowley Poems (1773-1790);" *PMLA,* L (1935); Theodore Watts-Dunton, "Thomas Chatterton," in *The English Poets,* T. H. Ward, ed., 4 vols. (London: Macmillan and Co., Ltd.; 1880-81).

WILLIAM COLLINS

There are two bibliographies, neither wholly satisfactory: in W. C. Bronson's edition of the *Poems of W. C.* (1898); and in I. A. Williams, *Seven XVIIIth Century Bibliographies* (London: Dulau & Company, Ltd.; 1924). Of modern editions, W. C. Bronson's *The Poems of W. C.* (1898) is still useful; Edmund Blunden's *The Poems of W. C.* (London: F. Etchells & H. Macdonald; 1929) is attractive; the most accurate is *Poems of W. C.,* C. Stone and A. L. Poole, eds., rev. F. Page in *The Poems of Gray and Collins* (London: Oxford University Press, Humphrey Milford; 1937). Of importance is W. C. *Drafts and Fragments of Verse* (Oxford: At the Clarendon Press; 1956), ed. J. S. Cunningham from the Warton papers in the library of Trinity College, Oxford. There are full-length studies of C.: H. W. Garrod, *The Poetry of C.* (Oxford: The Clarendon Press; 1928), an amplification of his Warton Lecture on C. in *Proceedings of the British Academy,* 1928; and E. G. Ainsworth, *Poor Collins; His Life, His Art, and His Influence* (Ithaca, N. Y.: Cornell University Press and London: H. Milford, Oxford University Press; 1937). The following essays and articles are helpful: J. M. Murry, "The Poetry of W. C.," in his

Countries of the Mind (N. Y.: E. P. Dutton & Co.; 1922); A. D. McKillop, "The Romanticism of W. C.," *SP*, XX (1923); A. S. P. Woodhouse, "Collins and the Creative Imagination; A Study in the Critical Background of His Odes (1746)," in *Studies in English, by Members of University College, Toronto* (Toronto: The University of Toronto Press; 1931); S. Musgrove, "The Theme of C's Odes," *N & Q*, Oct. 1943; N. Maclean, "From Action to Image: Theories of the Lyric in the Eighteenth Century," in *Critics and Criticism, Ancient and Modern* (Chicago: University of Chicago Press; 1952); C. F. Chapin, "The Values of Allegorical Personification: Collins and Gray," chap. IV, *Personification In Eighteenth-Century English Poetry* (New York: King's Crown Press, Columbia University; 1955); E. C. Brooks, "W. C.'s 'Ode on the Poetical Character'," *College English*, XVII (1956); J. H. Hagstrum, "William C.," chap. X, *The Sister Arts; the Tradition of Literary Pictorialism and English Poetry from Dryden to Gray* (Chicago: University of Chicago Press; 1958); A. D. McKillop, "Collins's *Ode to Evening*—Background and Structure," *Tennessee Studies in Literature*, V (1960); E. M. W. Tillyard, "William C.'s 'Ode on the Death of Thomson'," *Review of English Literature*, I (1960); (For material bearing on C.'s biography, see footnote 1 under Collins.) M. E. Brown, "On W. C.'s 'Ode to Evening,'" *Essays in Criticism*, XI (1961).

WILLIAM COWPER

Bibliography: L. C. Hartley, *William Cowper: The Continuing Revaluation* (Chapel Hill: University of North Carolina Press; 1960). Text: *Poetical Works*, H. S. Milford, ed., 4th ed. (Oxford Standard Authors. London: Oxford University Press, Humphrey Milford; 1959). *The Correspondence*, Thomas Wright, ed., 4 vols. (New York: Dodd, Mead and Company; 1904); there are various selected editions of the letters. Biography: "Memoir of William Cowper: An Autobiography," M. J. Quinlan, ed., *Proceedings of the American Philosophical Society*, XCVII (1935); M. J. Quinlan, *William Cowper: A Critical Life* (Minneapolis: University of Minnesota Press; 1953); Charles Ryskamp, *William Cowper of the Inner Temple, Esq.* (Cambridge: Cambridge University Press; 1959); Robert Southey, *Life of Cowper*, in the 1st 3 vols. of his ed. of *The Works*, 15 vols. (London: Baldwin & Craddock; 1836-37). Modern critical and historical studies: David Cecil, *The Stricken Deer* (London: Constable and Co., Ltd.; 1929); D. H. Craven, "Cowper's Use of 'Slight Connection' in *The Task*," *University of Colorado Studies*, gen. ser. XXIX, no. 3 (1954); Donald Davie, "The Critical Principles of William Cowper," *Cambridge Journal*, VII (1953); H. I'A. Fausset, *William Cowper* (London: Jonathan Cape; 1928); Morris Golden, *In Search of Stability: The Poetry of William Cowper* (New York: Bookman Associates;

1960); L. C. Hartley, *William Cowper Humanitarian* (Chapel Hill: University of North Carolina Press; 1938); Roderick Huang, *William Cowper: Nature Poet* (London: for the University of Malaya by Oxford University Press; 1957); H. P. Kroiter, "Cowper, Deism, and the Divinization of Nature," *JHI*, XXI (1960); Norman Nicholson, *William Cowper* (London: John Lehman; 1951), and *William Cowper* (Writers and Their Work, No. 121. London: for The British Council and The National Book League, Longman's, Green & Co.; 1960); Gilbert Thomas, *William Cowper and the Eighteenth Century*, 2nd ed. (London: George Allen and Unwin Ltd.; 1948).

GEORGE CRABBE

Text: *Poems*, A. W. Ward, ed., 3 vols. (Cambridge: Cambridge University Press; 1905-07); *The Poetical Works*, A. J. and R. M. Carlyle, eds. (Oxford Edition. London: Henry Frowde; 1908); *New Poems*, Arthur Pollard, ed. (Liverpool: Liverpool University Press; 1960). Biography: the classic *Life . . . by His Son* (vol. i of his ed. of *Collected Works* [1834]); Edmund Blunden, ed. (London: Cresset Press; 1947); E. M. Forster, ed. (Oxford World's Classics. London: Oxford University Press, Humphrey Milford; 1932); A. M. Broadley and Walter Jerrold, *Romance of an Elderly Poet . . .* (London: Stanley Paul & Co.; 1913). Valuable contemporary estimates: William Hazlitt, "Mr. Campbell and Mr. Crabbe," *London Magazine*, III (1821); rptd. in *The Spirit of the Age* (1825); Francis Jeffrey's four essay-reviews (1808-19); rptd. in *Contributions to the Edinburgh Review*, 4 vols. (London: Longman & Co.; 1844). Modern critical and historical studies: M. H. Abrams, *The Milk of Paradise* (Cambridge: Harvard University Press; 1934); R. L. Brett, *George Crabbe* (Writers and Their Work, No. 75. London: for The British Council and The National Book League, Longmans, Green & Co.; 1956); W. E. Broman, "Factors in Crabbe's Eminence in the Early Nineteenth Century," *MP*, L (1953); J. H. Evans, *The Poems of George Crabbe: A Literary and Historical Study* (London: The Sheldon Press; 1933); E. M. Forster, "George Crabbe and Peter Grimes," in *Two Cheers for Democracy* (New York: Harcourt Brace & Co.; 1951); Ian Gregor, "The Last Augustan: Some Observations on the Poetry of George Crabbe (1755-1832)," *Dublin Review*, CCXXIX (1955); Lilian Haddakin, *The Poetry of Crabbe* (London: Chatto & Windus; 1955); René Huchon, *George Crabbe and His Times*, trans. Frederick Clarke (London: John Murray; 1907); W. P. Ker, "George Crabbe," in *On Modern Literature*, Terence Spencer and James Sutherland, eds. (Oxford: At the Clarendon Press; 1955); Karl Kroeber, *Romantic Narrative Art* (Madison: University of Wisconsin Press; 1960); Varley Lang, "Crabbe and the Eighteenth Century," *ELH*, V (1938); Arthur Sale, "The Development of Crabbe's Narrative Art," *Cambridge Journal*,

V (1952); R. M. Thale, "Crabbe's *Village* and Topographical Poetry," *JEGP*, LV (1956); Rayner Unwin, "George Crabbe: The Real Picture of the Poor," in *The Rural Muse: Studies in the Peasant Poetry of England* (London: George Allen and Unwin Ltd.; 1954). On the modern opera: *Benjamin Britten: Peter Grimes* (Sadler's Wells Opera Books, No. 3. London: John Lane, The Bodley Head; 1940).

OLIVER GOLDSMITH

Bibliographies: T. Scott, *O. G. Bibliographically and Biographically Considered; Based On the Collection of Material in the Library of W. M. Elkins, esq.* (New York: The Bowling Green Press; 1928); R. S. Crane, *O. G.* bibliography in vol. II of *The Cambridge Bibliography of English Literature* (Cambridge: At the University Press; 1940) and in vol. V, Supplement to *Cambridge Bib.* (1957). Standard editions of the *Works* are by P. Cunningham (4 vols. London; 1884 and New York; 1881) and J. M. W. Gibbs (5 vols. 1884-6). The best modern editions of the poems are by A. Dobson: *The Poems and Plays of O. G.* (Everyman's Library. London and Toronto: J. M. Dent & Sons, New York: E. P. Dutton & Co.; 1910); and *The Poetical Works of O. G. Edited with Introduction and Notes* (London: Oxford University Press. Humphrey Milford; 1927). There is a bibliographical-textual study of *The Traveller* by W. B. Todd, "A Prospect of Society." *Reconstructed from the Earliest Version of "The Traveller"* (Charlottesville, Va.: University of Virginia Press; 1956). Of *The Deserted Village* there is a facsimile reprint (London: Noel Douglas; 1927). There are many biographies. Of the older ones the most helpful is *The Life and Times of O. G.*, by J. Forster (1854); the best modern biography is *Oliver Goldsmith*, by R. M. Wardle (Lawrence: University of Kansas Press and London: Constable and Company Ltd.; 1957). Articles bearing upon *The Traveller* and *Deserted Village* by H. G. Bell, Jr., E. Miner, E. D. Seeber, and R. W. Seitz are referred to in the course of the footnotes to the two poems in the present edition. There are helpful comments on G. as poet by Austin Dobson in his edition of the *Poems and Plays* (1910) and of *Poetical Works* (1927). The most extended recent analysis is by W. C. Brown in Chap. VI of *Triumph of Form* (Chapel Hill, N. C.: University of North Carolina Press; 1948); A. N. Jeffares has an interesting discussion of the poetry in his *Oliver Goldsmith* (Writers and Their Work No. 107. London: for the British Council and the National Book League, by Longmans, Green & Co.; 1959).

THOMAS GRAY

Bibliographies: C. S. Northrup, *A Bibliography of Thomas Gray* (New Haven: Yale University Press; 1917); H. W. Starr, *A Bibliography of Gray, 1917-1951* (Philadelphia: University of Pennsylvania Press for Temple University Publications; 1953). The standard edition is *Poems of Thomas Gray*, A. Lane Poole, ed., rev. by L. Whibley, in *The Poems of Gray and Collins* (London: Oxford University Press, Humphrey Milford; 1937. Other editions, helpful because of commentaries and notes, are: *The Poetical Works of Thomas G., English and Latin*, J. Bradshaw, ed. (1891); *Selections from the Poetry and Prose of Thomas G.*, W. L. Phelps, ed. (1894); *G.'s English Poems*, D. C. Tovey, ed. (1898). Invaluable for any study of G.'s career is *The Correspondence of Thomas G.*, P. Toynbee and L. Whibley, eds. (3 vols. Oxford: The Clarendon Press; 1935). The soundest general introduction to G.'s life and work is *Thomas G., A Biography*, by R. W. Ketton-Cremer (Cambridge: University Press; 1955); Lord David Cecil gives a delightful biographical commentary in "Thomas G.," in *Two Quiet Lives* (Indianapolis and New York: The Bobbs-Merrill Company, Publishers; 1948). Special studies are *Thomas G, Scholar*, by W. P. Jones (Cambridge: Harvard University Press 1937); and *G. As a Literary Critic*, by H. W. Starr (Philadelphia; 1941). The most extensive modern critical study is R. Martin's *Essai sur Thomas G.* (London: H. Milford, Oxford University Press and Paris: Les Presses Universitaires de France; 1934). Shorter critical studies and observations are: Lord D. Cecil, "The Poetry of Thomas G.," *Proceedings of the British Academy*, 1945, and rptd. in his *Poets and Story-Tellers* (London: Constable; 1949); S. C. Roberts, *Thomas G. of Pembroke* (Glasgow: Jackson, Son; 1952); G. Hough, "Gray," in his *Romantic Poets* (Hutchinson's University Library. London: Hutchinson House; 1953); "Thomas G., The Shaping of a Scholar-Poet," *TLS*, 24 June 1955; and G. Tillotson, *Augustan Studies* (London: University of London, the Athlone Press; 1961).

SAMUEL JOHNSON

Bibliographies: W. P. Courtney, rev. by D. N. Smith, *A Bibliography of S. J.* (Oxford: The Clarendon Press; 1915); R. W. Chapman and A. T. Hazen, "Johnsonian Bibliography: A Supplement to Courtney," *Proc. of the Oxford Bib. Society*, V (1939); J. L. Clifford, *Johnsonian Studies 1887-1950* (Minneapolis: University of Minnesota Press; 1951); *Samuel Johnson, L. L. D. (1709-1784). An Exhibition of First Editions, Manuscripts, Letters, and Portraits* (New York: Pierpont Morgan Library; 1959). The indispensable edition of the poems is *The Poems of Samuel Johnson*, D. N. Smith and E. L. McAdam, eds. (Oxford: The Clarendon Press; 1941). Recent critical commentary on

S. J. as poet includes the following: T. S. Eliot, "Johnson's 'London' and 'The Vanity of Human Wishes,'" Introduction to the Haslewood Books Edition (London: Frederick Etchells & Hugh Macdonald; 1930) and rptd. in *English Critical Essays (Twentieth Century)* (The World's Classics. London: Oxford University Press; 1933); F. R. Leavis, "The Augustan Tradition in the Eighteenth Century," in *Revaluation* (New York: George·W. Stewart, Publisher, Inc.; 1936); D. Nichol Smith, "Samuel Johnson's Poems," *RES*, XIX (1943) and rptd. in *New Light on Dr. Johnson* (New Haven: Yale University Press; 1959); T. S. Eliot, "Johnson as Critic and Poet," Ballard Matthews Lectures (1944), rptd. in *On Poetry and Poets* (London: Faber & Faber; 1957); Yvor Winters, "The Influence of Meter on Poetic Convention," in *In Defense of Reason* (New York: The Swallow Press & W. Morrow and Company; 1947); W. C. Brown, "Johnson: 'Pathos in Isolation,'" in *The Triumph of Form* (Chapel Hill: University of North Carolina Press; 1948); I. Jack, "Tragical Satire: The Vanity of Human Wishes," in *Augustan Satire* (Oxford: At the Clarendon Press; 1952); F. R. Leavis, "Johnson and Augustanism" and "Johnson as Poet," in *The Common Pursuit* (New York: George W. Stewart, Publisher, Inc.; 1952); M. Emslie, "Johnson's Satires and 'The Proper Wit of Poetry,'" *Cambridge Journal*, VII (1953-4); W. J. Bate, *The Achievement of Samuel Johnson* (New York: Oxford University Press; 1955); H. Gifford, "'The Vanity of Human Wishes,'" *RES*, VI (1955); J. Butt, "Johnson's Practice in the Poetical Imitation," and Mary Lascelles, "Johnson and Juvenal," both in *New Light on Dr. Johnson* (1959). A recent item is: J. L. Clifford and D. J. Greene, "Additions and Corrections to *Johnsonian Studies*, 1887-1950," and "A Bibliography of Johnsonian Studies, 1950-1960," in *Johnsonian Studies*, Magdi Wahba, ed. (Cairo: Société Orientale de Publicité, 1962).

JAMES MACPHERSON

Bibliography: G. F. Black, "Macpherson's Ossian and the Ossianic Controversy," *Bulletin of the New York Public Library*, XXX (1926). Text: *The Poems of Ossian*, William Sharp, ed. (Edinburgh: John Grant; 1926). The major contemporary appreciation of Ossian, often reprinted with the text: Hugh Blair, *A Critical Dissertation on the Poems of Ossian* (1763); for the many special studies of Macpherson's foreign vogue and influence, see Black's bibliography and *The Cambridge Bibliography of English Literature*. Valuable modern studies: J. F. Campbell, *Popular Tales of the West Highlands Orally Collected*, 4 vols. (London: Alexander Gardner; 1890-93); G. M. Fraser, "The Truth about Macpherson's 'Ossian,'" *Quarterly Review*, CCXLV (1925); J. R. Moore, "Wordsworth's Unacknowledged Debt to Macpherson's *Ossian*," *PMLA*, XL (1925); Bailey Saunders, *The*

Life and Letters of James Macpherson, 2nd ed. (London: Swan Sonnenschein & Co.; 1895); J. S. Smart, *James Macpherson: An Episode in Literature* (London: David Nutt; 1905); E. D. Snyder, *The Celtic Revival in English Literature 1760-1800* (Cambridge: Harvard University Press; 1923); D. S. Thomson, *The Gaelic Sources of Macpherson's "Ossian"* (Aberdeen: for the University of Aberdeen by Oliver and Boyd, Edinburgh; 1952).

WILLIAM SHENSTONE

Bibliography: I. A. Williams, *Seven XVIIIth Century Bibliographies* (London: Dulau & Company, Ltd.; 1924). Text (there is no modern edition): *Works in Verse and Prose*, 2 vols. (London: R. and J. Dodsley; 1764); *The Poetical Works*, George Gilfillan, ed. (Edinburgh: J. Nichol; 1854); *The Poetical Works*, C. C. Clarke, ed. (Edinburgh: William P. Nimmo; 1868); facsimile of the 1742 ed. of *The Schoolmistress* (Oxford: At the Clarendon Press; 1924). *Shenstone's Miscellany 1759-1763*, I. A. Gordon, ed. (Oxford: At The Clarendon Press; 1952). *Letters*, Duncan Mallam, ed. (Minneapolis: University of Minnesota Press; 1939); Marjorie Williams, ed. (Oxford: Basil Blackwell; 1939). Selected prose: *Men and Manners*, Havelock Ellis, ed. (London: The Golden Cockerell Press; 1927). Biographical, historical, and critical studies: R. P. Bond, "Shenstone's Heroi-Comical Poem," *SP*, XXVIII (1931); I. L. Churchill, "William Shenstone's Share in the Preparation of Percy's *Reliques*," *PMLA*, LI (1936); J. Fisher, "Shenstone, Gray, and the Moral Elegy," *MP*, XXXIV (1937); A. I. Hazeltine, *A Study of William Shenstone and of His Critics* . . . (Menasha, Wisc.: The Collegiate Press, George Banta Publishing Company; 1918); A. R. Humphreys, *William Shenstone: An Eighteenth-Century Portrait* (Cambridge: Cambridge University Press; 1937); Samuel Johnson, "William Shenstone," in *Lives of the English Poets* (1779-81); Duncan Mallam, "Some Inter-Relationships of Shenstone's Essays, Letters, and Poems," *PQ*, XXVIII (1949); V. F. Prettyman, "Shenstone's Reading of Spenser," in *The Age of Johnson* (New Haven: Yale University Press; 1949); E. M. Purkis, *William Shenstone: Poet and Landscape Gardener* (Wolverhampton: Whitehead Brothers Ltd.; 1931); Geoffrey Tillotson, "William Shenstone," in *Essays in Criticism and Research* (Cambridge: Cambridge University Press; 1942); Marjorie Williams, *William Shenstone: A Chapter in Eighteenth Century Taste* (Birmingham: Cornish Brothers Limited, Publishers to the University; 1935).

CHRISTOPHER SMART

G. J. Gray has a bibliography in *Transactions of the Bibliographical Society*, VI (1903). Most complete modern edition is *Collected Poems*, Norman Callan, ed. (Muses' Library. London: Routledge and Kegan Paul Ltd.; 1949); a selection with excellent commentary is *Poems by C. S.*, R. Brittain, ed. (Princeton: Princeton University Press; 1950). *Jubilate Agno* was first given by W. F. Stead in *Rejoice in the Lamb* (New York: Henry Holt and Company; 1939); most recent ed. is J. A., W. H. Bond, ed. (London: Rupert Hart-Davis; 1954). There are modern eds. of the *Song to David* by E. Blunden (London: Richard Cobden-Sanderson; 1924), R. Todd (Crown Classics. London: Grey Walls Press; 1947), and J. B. Broadbent (Cambridge: Rampant Lions Press-London: The Bodley Head; 1960). There are studies by K. A. McKenzie (*C. S.: sa vie et ces oeuvres*. Paris; 1925), E. G. Ainsworth and C. E. Noyes (*C. S., A Biog. and Critical Study*. Columbia: University of Missouri; 1943); Christopher Devlin (*Poor Kit Smart*. London: Rupert Hart-Davis; 1961); and R. Brittain (in his *Poems by C. S.*, 1950). Helpful studies of the *Song to David* are by R. D. Havens ("The Structure of Smart's *S. to D.*", RES, XIV [1938]) and R. Brittain (in his *Poems by C. S.*, 1950). Recent articles of importance are by D. J. Greene ("Smart, Berkeley, The Scientists and the Poets," JHI, XIV [1953]); A. Sherbo ("Christopher Smart, Reader of Obituaries," MLN, LXXI [1956]; and "The Probable Time of Composition of Christopher Smart's *Song to David, Psalms, and Hymns and Spiritual Songs*," JEGP, LV [1956]); and C. Price ("Six Letters By C. S." RES, n.s. VIII [1957]). An excellent short biog. and critical summary is by G. Grigson (Writers and Their Work No. 136. London: The British Council and the National Book League, by Longmans, Green & Co.; 1961). Other recent items are: Charles Parish, "C. S.'s Knowledge of Hebrew," SP, LVIII (1961), 516-532; K. M. Rogers, "The Pillars of the Lord; Some Sources of 'A Song to David,' " PQ, XL (1961).

JOSEPH WARTON

Eric Partridge gives a select bibliography in *The Three Wartons. A Choice of their Verse* (London: The Scholartis Press; 1927). The poems of J. W. are found in *Works of the British Poets* (ed. Peck, 1808); *Works of the English Poets* (ed. Chalmers, 1810); and *Works of the British Poets* (ed. Sanford, 1819); selections are given by Partridge in *The Three Wartons*. The older view of J. W., emphasizing his "pre-romantic" qualities, is given by Gosse, "Two Pioneers of Romanticism: J. and T. Warton," *Proceedings of the British Academy*, (1915-16); Edith J. Morley has an essay on J. W. as a critic of Pope in *Essays and Studies . . . English Association*, IX (1924); E. Partridge writes briefly of him as a poet in the Introduction to *The Three Wartons*; the best statement of J. W.'s theories of poetry is by Hoyt Trowbridge, "J. W. on the Imagination," *MP*, XXXV (1937-38).

EDWARD YOUNG

Bibliography: Francesco Cordasco, *Edward Young: A Handlist of Critical Notices and Studies* (New York: for Long Island University Press by Burt Franklin; 1950); Henry Pettit, *A Bibliography of Young's Night Thoughts, University of Colorado Studies: Series in Language and Literature*, No. 5 (1954). Text (there is no modern edition of the poetry): *The Poetical Works*, John Mitford, ed., 2 vols. (Aldine Edition. London: William Pickering; 1830, etc.); *The Complete Works*, John Doran, ed., 2 vols. (London: William Tegg and Co.; 1854); *Dramatic Works* (London: A. Mallard, J. Durfey; 1778); *Conjectures*, E. J. Morley, ed. (Manchester: Manchester University Press; 1918); M. W. Steinke, ed., with a valuable introduction (New York: F. C. Stechert Co., Inc.; 1917). Forty-three of Blake's illustrations of four of the *Nights* were published in 1797: reduced facsimile (Liverpool: The Liverpool Booksellers Co., Ltd.; 1911); an original series of 537 colored designs exists: selection ed. Geoffrey Keynes (Cambridge: Harvard University Press; 1927). Studies of historical interest: Samuel Johnson's essay in *Lives of the English Poets* (1779-81), although the biographical portion is not by Johnson; George Eliot, "Worldliness and Other-Worldliness: The Poet Young," *Westminster Review* (1857); rpt. in *Essays and Leaves from a Notebook* (Edinburgh: William Blackwood & Sons; 1884). Modern studies (excluding the many German dissertations and articles which are of little value): Margery Bailey, "Edward Young," in *The Age of Johnson* (New Haven: Yale University Press; 1949); Robert Birley, *Sunk without Trace* (London: Rupert Hart-Davis; 1962); I. St.-J. Bliss, "Young's *Night Thoughts* in relation to Contemporary Christian Apologetics," *PMLA*, XLIX (1934); Marjorie Bowen, "Edward Young," *Essays by Divers Hands: Transactions of the Royal Society of Literature*, n. s. VIII (London: Humphrey Milford, Oxford University Press; 1928); H. H. Clark, "The Romanticism of Edward Young," *Transactions of the Wisconsin Academy*, XXIV (1929); and "A Study of Melancholy in Edward Young," *MLN*, XXXIX (1924); C. E. Crawford, "What Was Pope's Debt to Edward Young?," *ELH*, XIII (1946); J. L. Kind, *Edward Young in Germany* (New York: Columbia University Press; 1906); Henry Pettit, introduction to his *Bibliography* (see above), and *The English Rejection of Young's Night-Thoughts, University of Colorado Studies: Series in Language and Literature*, No. 6 (1957); H. C. Shelley, *The Life and Letters of Edward Young* (London: Isaac Pitman & Sons; 1914); C. V. Wicker, *Edward Young and the Fear of Death: A Study in Romantic Melancholy, University of New Mexico Publications in Language and Literature*, No. 10 (1952).

Index of Authors

Akenside, Mark	112	Goldsmith, Oliver	184
Beattie, James	261	Gray, Thomas	79
Blair, Robert	36	Johnson, Samuel	42
Blake, William	307	Macpherson, James	273
Burns, Robert	322	Shenstone, William	66
Chatterton, Thomas	280	Smart, Christopher	145
Collins, William	121	Warton, Joseph	167
Cowper, William	223	Young, Edward	18
Crabbe, George	288		

Index of Titles and First Lines

❦

Titles of poems are printed in italics, and first lines of poems in roman. A first line is enclosed in parentheses when it is the first line of a passage or section which has in the present anthology been editorially selected from a longer work.

Address to the Deil, 329
Address to the Unco Guid, or The Rigidly Righteous, 343
Ah me! full sorely is my heart forlorn, 69
(Ah! who can tell how hard it is to climb, 264)
A little black thing among the snow, 319
A Man's a Man for A' That, 348
An Excelente Balade of Charitie, 284
An Ode on the Popular Superstitions of the Highlands of Scotland, 138
(As one who, long in thickets and in brakes, 232)
As once, if, not with light regard, 131
A Song to David, 148
Auld Lang Syne, 347
Awake, Æolian lyre, awake, 95
Burials (Part III from *The Parish Register*), 293
Carthon, 278
Earth raised up her head, 318
Earth's Answer (from *Songs of Experience*), 318
Elegy Written in a Country Church-yard, 89
Epistle to John Lapraik, An Old Scottish Bard, 334
God moves in a mysterious way, 230
Green Grow the Rashes, 345
Hear the voice of the Bard! 317
Holy Thursday (from *Songs of Experience*), 319
Holy Thursday (from *Songs of Innocence*), 314
Holy Willie's Prayer, 339
Home, thou return'st from Thames, whose Naiads long, 138
How sleep the brave, who sink to rest, 134
If ought of oaten stop, or pastoral song, 135

INDEX OF TITLES AND FIRST LINES

Introduction (from *Songs of Experience*), 317
Introduction (from *Songs of Innocence*), 311
In vain to me the smileing Mornings shine, 88
In Viriginè the sweltry sun 'gan sheene, 284
Is there, for honest poverty, 348
Is this a holy thing to see, 319
I wander thro' each chartered street, 321
John Anderson My Jo, 346
John Anderson my jo, John, 346
Let observation with extensive view, 54
Light Shining out of Darkness (from *Olney Hymns*), 230
Little Lamb, who made thee? 312
London (from *Songs of Experience*), 321
London: A Poem, 45
My mother bore me in the southern wild, 312
(Next died the Widow Goe, an active dame, 293)
Now the storm begins to lower, 109
Obscurest night involved the sky, 258
Ode on a Distant Prospect of Eton College, 84
Ode on the Poetical Character, 131
Ode to Evening, 135
Ode to Fancy, 180
Ode to Fear, 128
Ode to Pity, 126
Ode: Written in the Beginning of the Year 1746, 134
Oh! for a closer walk with God, 229
Oh that those lips had language! Life has passed, 254
(Old Peter Grimes made fishing his employ; 297)
Olney Hymns, 229
On the Receipt of My Mother's Picture, 254
O Parent of each lovely Muse, 180
O Thou, that sit'st upon a throne, 149
O Thou, the friend of man, assigned, 126
O Thou, wha in the Heavens dost dwell, 339
O thou! whatever title suit thee, 329
O, Wert thou in the Cauld Blast, 352
O, wert thou in the cauld blast, 352
O Ye wha are sae guid yoursel, 343
Peter Grimes (Letter XXII from *The Borough*), 296
Piping down the valleys wild, 311
Remote, unfriended, melancholy, slow, 194
'Ruin seize thee, ruthless King! 102
Scots Wha Hae, 350
Scots, wha hae wi' Wallace bled, 350
Should auld acquaintance be forgot, 347
Songs of Experience, 317
Songs of Innocence, 311

INDEX OF TITLES AND FIRST LINES

Sonnet: On the Death of Richard West, 88
Sweet Auburn! loveliest village of the plain, 210
The Bard, 101
The Borough, 296
The Castaway, 258
The Chimney Sweeper (from *Songs of Experience*), 319
The Chimney Sweeper (from *Songs of Innocence*), 313
The Complaint, or Night Thoughts on Life, Death and Immortality, 24
The Curfew tolls the knell of parting day, 89
The Deserted Village, 208
The Divine Image (from *Songs of Innocence*), 315
The Enthusiast or The Lover of Nature, 172
The Fatal Sisters, 108
The Garden (Book III from *The Task*), 231
The Grave, 38
The Lamb (from *Songs of Innocence*), 312
The Little Black Boy (from *Songs of Innocence*), 312
The Minstrel, or The Progress of Genius, 264
The Parish Register, 293
The Pleasures of Imagination, 115
The Progress of Poesy, 94
There's nought but care on ev'ry han', 345
The Schoolmistress, 69
The Task, 231
The Tiger (from *Songs of Experience*), 320
The Traveller, or A Prospect of Society, 191
The Vanity of Human Wishes, 54
The Village, 291
(The Village Life, and every care that reigns, 291)
Tiger! Tiger! burning bright, 320
(Tired Nature's sweet restorer, balmy Sleep! 24)
Though grief and fondness in my breast rebel, 45
Thou, to whom the world unknown, 128
To Mercy, Pity, Peace, and Love, 315
'Twas on a Holy Thursday, their innocent faces clean, 314
Walking with God (from *Olney Hymns*), 229
When my mother died I was very young, 313
While briars an' woodbines budding green, 334
(Whilst some affect the sun and some the shade, 38)
(With what attractive charms this goodly frame, 115)
Ye distant spires, ye antique towers, 84
Ye green-robed Dryads, oft at dusky eve, 172

A NOTE ABOUT THE EDITORS

RICARDO QUINTANA received his degrees from Harvard University and is Professor of English at the University of Wisconsin. As a visitor he has taught at California Institute of Technology, Cornell, Northwestern, Columbia, Harvard, and the University of Delaware; is the author of THE MIND AND ART OF JONATHAN SWIFT and SWIFT: AN INTRODUCTION; editor of TWO HUNDRED POEMS, EIGHTEENTH CENTURY PLAYS, GULLIVER'S TRAVELS AND OTHER WRITINGS; and co-editor of SEVENTEENTH CENTURY VERSE AND PROSE: 1600-1660 and SEVENTEENTH CENTURY VERSE AND PROSE: 1660-1700. He is also a frequent contributor of articles and reviews to scholarly journals.

ALVIN WHITLEY is Professor of English at the University of Wisconsin, where he has taught since receiving his Ph.D. degree at Harvard in 1950. He is co-editor of THE COMIC IN THEORY AND PRACTICE and the author of numerous articles in eighteenth- and nineteenth-century English literature.

A NOTE ON THE TYPE

THIS book is set in ELECTRA, a Linotype face designed by W. A. DWIGGINS. This face cannot be classified as either modern or old-style. It is not based on any historical model, nor does it echo any particular period or style. It avoids the extreme contrasts between thick and thin elements that mark most modern faces, and attempts to give a feeling of fluidity, power, and speed.

Composed, printed, and bound by
H. Wolff, Inc., New York.
Typography by Herbert H. Johnson